EATCS
Monographs on Theoretical Computer Science
Volume 7

EATCS Monographs on Theoretical Computer Science

Vol. 1: K. Mehlhorn: Data Structures and Algorithms 1: Sorting and Searching. XIV, 336 pages, 87 figs. 1984.

Vol. 2: K. Mehlhorn: Data Structures and Algorithms 2: Graph Algorithms and NP-Completeness. XII, 260 pages, 54 figs. 1984.

Vol. 3: K. Mehlhorn: Data Structures and Algorithms 3: Multidimensional Searching and Computational Geometry. XII, 284 pages, 134 figs. 1984.

Vol. 4: W. Reisig: Petri Nets. An Introduction. X, 161 pages, 111 figs. 1985.

Vol. 5: W. Kuich, A. Salomaa: Semirings, Automata, Languages. IX, 374 pages, 23 figs. 1986.

Vol. 6: H. Ehrig, B. Mahr: Fundamentals of Algebraic Specification 1. Equations and Initial Semantics. XI, 321 pages. 1985.

Vol. 7: F. Gécseg: Products of Automata. VIII, 107 pages, 18 figs. 1986.

Ferenc Gécseg

Products of Automata

With 18 Figures

Springer-Verlag
Berlin Heidelberg New York Tokyo

Editors
Prof. Dr. Wilfried Brauer
Institut für Informatik, Technische Universität München
Arcisstr. 21, 8000 München 2, Germany

Prof. Dr. Grzegorz Rozenberg
Institute of Applied Mathematics and Computer Science
University of Leiden, Wassenaarseweg 80, P.O. Box 9512
2300 RA Leiden, The Netherlands

Prof. Dr. Arto Salomaa
Department of Mathematics, University of Turku
20500 Turku 50, Finland

Author
Prof. Dr. Ferenc Gécseg
József Attila Tudományegyetem Bolyai Intézete
6720 Szeged/Hungary, Aradi v. tere 1

ISBN-13: 978-3-642-64884-7 e-ISBN-13:978-3-642-61611-2
DOI: 10.1007/ 978-3-642-61611-2

Library of Congress Cataloging in Publication Data.
Gécseg, F.
Products of automata.
(EATCS monographs on theoretical computer science ; v. 7)
Bibliography: p.
1. Sequential machine theory. I. Title. II. Series.
QA267.5.S4G38 1986 006.3 85-27900
ISBN-13: 978-3-642-64884-7

Softcover reprint of the hardcover 1st edition 1986
Bookbinding: Lüderitz & Bauer, Berlin
2145/3020-543210

Preface

Both theoretical and practical considerations motivate the representation of objects as certain compositions of simpler ones. In the theory of automata this observation has led to the concepts of products and complete systems of automata.

In the general form of the products of automata all the component automata are fed back to one another. With this very broad notion of products, the realization of automata with large numbers of states by means of compositions of basic components is a highly involved process; this increases the possibility of errors. In order to decrease the complexity of feedbacks, a hierarchy of products called α_i-products was introduced some 10 years ago, where i runs over the set of all non-negative integers. In an α_i-product the index set of the component automata is linearly ordered. The input of each automaton in the product may depend on the states of all automata preceding it, i.e., all component automata steer all those automata which follow them in the product. Furthermore, at most the next $i-1$ automata (including itself) may be fed back to the input of a given component automaton. Thus for α_i-products the lengths of feedbacks are at most i.

The aim of this monograph is to give a systematic account of α_i-products. It consists of five chapters, a reference section, and an index. The first chapter contains the necessary concepts and results from universal algebra, automata, and sequential machines. Chapters 2 and 3 deal with homomorphic and isomorphic representations, respectively. Chapter 4 is devoted to homomorphic and isomorphic simulations with respect to a generalization of α_i-products. The final chapter is concerned with infinite products and representations of automaton mappings in finite lengths.

I am grateful to the editors of the EATCS Monographs on Theoretical Computer Science for including this book in the series. I wish to thank my colleagues P. Dömösi, Z. Ésik, Gy. Horváth, B. Imreh, and J. Virágh who have read the book, and who have made several helpful suggestions and corrections. Z. Ésik and Gy. Horváth also helped in checking the final version of the manuscript. I am indebted to P. Folberth for the excellent typing of the manuscript. The difficult task of designing and drawing the figures was performed by I. Adamkovich and S. Koczkás; I am grateful to them as well. Finally, I have to express my deep gratitude to my wife for her loving support.

Szeged, May 1986 Ferenc Gécseg

Contents

1. Basic Concepts and Preliminaries

In this chapter we survey some basic concepts and results from the theories of automata and universal algebras. It is presumed that the reader has a certain routine in the structural theory of automata and universal algebras. Thus, the results of this chapter are stated without proofs. The only exceptions are certain special group theory results and two statements concerning products of automata, the constructive proofs of which will be needed in our later discussions.

1.1 Sets and Relations

We shall use the following concepts and notations from elementary set theory.

Sets will generally be denoted by upper-case Latin letters with or without indices and their elements by the corresponding lower case Latin letters.

If there is no danger of confusion, then we simply write a for the one-element set $\{a\}$.

$\emptyset$ denotes the empty set.

$|A|$ is the cardinality of the set A.

$a \in A$ means that a is an element of A. The opposite case is expressed by $a \notin A$.

$A \subseteq B$ means that A is a subset of B. Proper inclusion will be denoted by $A \subset B$.

$A - B$ denotes the complement of B with respect to A, i.e. $A - B$ consists of all elements of A which are not in B. We sometimes write $A \setminus B$ for $A - B$.

Let $(A_i \mid i \in I)$ be a family of subsets of a certain set indexed by the elements of I. Then $\cap (A_i \mid i \in I)$ stands for their intersection, and $\cup (A_i \mid i \in I)$ is their union. If I is finite, say $I = \{1, \dots, k\}$, then we frequently write $A_1 \cap \dots \cap A_k$ and $A_1 \cup \dots \cup A_k$ for $\cap (A_i \mid i \in I)$ and $\cup (A_i \mid i \in I)$, respectively.

We sometimes define a set A as the collection of all elements a satisfying certain properties $P_1, \dots, P_k$. For such A, we use the notation

$$A = \{a \mid a \text{ satisfies } P_1, \dots, a \text{ satisfies } P_k\} .$$

For two sets A and B, let $A \times B = \{(a, b) \mid a \in A, b \in B\}$. A subset $\varrho \subseteq A \times B$ is a (binary) *relation* from A to B. If $(a, b) \in \varrho$ for a pair $(a, b) \in A \times B$, then we also write $a \equiv b(\varrho)$. The opposite case will be expressed by $a \not\equiv b(\varrho)$, too.

If $\varrho \subseteq A \times B$ is a relation, then its *converse* is the relation ϱ^{-1} from B to A, defined by

$$\varrho^{-1} = \{(b, a) \mid (a, b) \in \varrho\} .$$

Take two relations $\varrho \subseteq A \times B$ and $\tau \subseteq B \times C$. The *product* of ϱ by τ is the relation $\varrho\tau$ from A to C for which $(a, c) \in \varrho\tau$ if and only if there is a $b \in B$ with $(a, b) \in \varrho$ and $(b, c) \in \tau$.

If $\varrho \subseteq A \times A$, then we say that ϱ is a relation on A. The following two special relations on a set A will frequently be used:

$$\iota_A = \{(a, a) \mid a \in A\} \ (\textit{diagonal relation} \text{ on } A) , \quad \text{and}$$

$$\omega_A = \{(a, b) \mid a, b \in A\} \ (\textit{total relation} \text{ on } A) .$$

For any relation ϱ on a set A and non-negative integer n, we define the *power* ϱ^n by

$$(1) \ \varrho^0 = \iota_A \quad \text{and} \quad \varrho^{n+1} = \varrho\varrho^n .$$

The relation $\varrho \subseteq A \times A$ is said to be

(i) *reflexive* if $\iota_A \subseteq \varrho$,
(ii) *symmetric* if $\varrho^{-1} \subseteq \varrho$,
(iii) *antisymmetric* if $\varrho \cap \varrho^{-1} \subseteq \iota_A$, and
(iv) *transitive* if $\varrho^2 \subseteq \varrho$.

A relation on A which is reflexive, symmetric and transitive is called an *equivalence relation* on A. If ϱ is an equivalence relation on A, then for every $a \in A$ we set

$$a/\varrho = \{b \mid b \in A, (a, b) \in \varrho\} .$$

This notation is extended to an arbitrary subset B of A by

$$B/\varrho = \{b/\varrho \mid b \in B\} .$$

The cardinality of A/ϱ is called the *index* of ϱ.

Let ϱ and τ be equivalence relations on a set A with $\tau \subseteq \varrho$. Then, for every $a \in A$, we set $a[\varrho/\tau] = \{b/\tau \mid b \in a/\varrho\}$.

A *partition* of a set A is a set π of pairwise disjoint nonvoid subsets A_i $(i \in I)$ such that $\cup (A_i \mid i \in I) = A$. Each A_i $(i \in I)$ is called a *block* of π. For every $a \in A$, $\pi(a)$ will denote the block of π containing a. It is well known that, if ϱ is an equivalence relation on A, then A/ϱ is a partition of A, and every partition of A can be given in this way.

A reflexive, antisymmetric and transitive relation ϱ on a set A is a *partial ordering* on A. It is easy to see that the converse of a partial ordering is also a partial ordering. For two partitions π_1 and π_2 of a set A, let us write $\pi_1 \leqq \pi_2$ if and only if each block of π_1 is contained by a block of π_2. Then $\leqq$ is a partial ordering on the set of all partitions of A.

A partial ordering ϱ on a set A is a *linear ordering* if $a \equiv b(\varrho)$ or $b \equiv a(\varrho)$ for arbitrary two elements a and b of A. We can easily prove

Theorem 1.1. *Let ϱ be a partial ordering on a finite set A. Then there exists a linear ordering τ on A such that $\varrho \subseteq \tau$.* □

A *mapping* or *function* from a set A to a set B is a relation $\varphi \subseteq A \times B$ such that, for every $a \in A$, there is exactly one $b \in B$ satisfying $a \equiv b(\varphi)$. If φ is a mapping from A to B, then we usually write $\varphi : A \to B$. The fact that $a \equiv b(\varphi)$ is also expressed by $\varphi(a) = b$ or $\varphi : a \to b$. If $\varphi(a) = b$, then b is the *image* of a, and a is an *inverse image* (or *counter image*) of b under φ. We extend the notation $\varphi(a)$ to an arbitrary subset $A' \subseteq A$ by $\varphi(A') = \{b \mid b = \varphi(a) \text{ for some } a \in A'\}$. If $B' \subseteq B$, then $\varphi^{-1}(B')$ denotes the subset of A consisting of all $a \in A$ for which $\varphi(a) \in B'$. A mapping $\varphi : A \to B$ is *onto* if $\varphi(A) = B$. It is *one-to-one* if different elements from A have different images.

The *composition* or *product* of two mappings $\varphi : A \to B$ and $\psi : B \to C$ is the product $\varphi\psi$ of φ and ψ as relations. Clearly, $\varphi\psi$ is a mapping from A to C.

The *restriction* of a mapping $\varphi : A \to B$ to a subset $A' \subseteq A$ is the mapping $\varphi \mid A' : A' \to B$ defined by $\varphi \mid A' = \varphi \cap (A' \times B)$. If a mapping ψ is obtained by a restriction of φ, then φ is an *extension* of ψ.

Let $(A_i \mid i \in I)$ be a family of sets. The *Cartesian product* A of A_i $(i \in I)$ is the set of all mappings $\varphi : I \to \cup (A_i \mid i \in I)$ such that, for every $i \in I$, $\varphi(i)$ is in A_i. For this Cartesian product we use the notation $A = \prod (A_i \mid i \in I)$. If I is finite, say $I = \{1, \dots, k\}$ $(k \geqq 0)$, then we also write $A = A_1 \times \dots \times A_k$. In this latter case it is convenient to think of the elements of A as k-tuples $\mathbf{a} = (a_1, \dots, a_k)$ with $a_i \in A_i$ $(i = 1, \dots, k)$. If $k = 1$, then we generally write a for (a) $(a \in A_1)$. Moreover, if $A_i = B$ for each $i (= 1, \dots, k)$, then A is also called the kth *Cartesian power* of B; in notation, $A = B^k$.

Take a Cartesian product $A = \prod (A_i \mid i \in I)$. For each $i \in I$, we define the ith *projection* $\mathrm{pr}_i : A \to A_i$ by $\mathrm{pr}_i(\varphi) = \varphi(i)$ $(\varphi \in A)$. If φ and ψ are two elements from A, and J is a subset of I, then the notation $\mathrm{pr}_J(\varphi) = \mathrm{pr}_J(\psi)$ means that $\mathrm{pr}_i(\varphi) = \mathrm{pr}_i(\psi)$ for every $i \in J$.

In the sequel the elements of a Cartesian product will generally be denoted by lower case Latin letters with or without indices. $\mathbf{N}$ will stand for the set of all nonnegative integers. Further, for every integer $k \geqq 0$, $[k]$ denotes the set $\{1, \dots, k\}$. If k and n are positive integers and $i \in \mathbf{N}$, then $n + i \pmod{k}$ is the least positive residue of $n + i$ modulo k. Finally, $\mathrm{lcm}\,[m_1, \dots, m_k]$ will denote the least common multiple of the integers $m_1, \dots, m_k$.

1.2 Algebraic Structures

We start with some general concepts and results of universal algebras needed in the later chapters.

Let A be a nonvoid set and $m \geqq 0$ an integer. A mapping $\sigma : A^m \to A$ is called an *m-ary operation* on A. The pair $\mathscr{A} = (A, \Sigma^{\mathscr{A}})$, where $\Sigma^{\mathscr{A}}$ is a set of operations on A, is termed a (universal) *algebra*.

We frequently deal with a class of algebras such that there is a natural correspondence between the operations of any two algebras from this class. To define such classes we introduce the concept of operational symbols.

Definition 2.1. A set of *operational symbols* is a set Σ together with a mapping

$$r : \Sigma \to \mathbf{N}$$

which assigns an arity to every $\sigma \in \Sigma$. For every $m \in \mathbf{N}$, Σ_m denotes the set of all m-ary operational symbols from Σ.

In the sequel the mapping r will not be mentioned explicitly in the definition of a set Σ of operational symbols.

Definition 2.2. Let Σ be a set of operational symbols. A *Σ-algebra* $\mathscr{A}$ is a pair consisting of a nonempty set A (of *elements* of $\mathscr{A}$) and a mapping that assigns to every operational symbol $\sigma \in \Sigma$ an m-ary operation

$$\sigma^{\mathscr{A}} : A^m \to A ,$$

where m is the arity of σ. The operation $\sigma^{\mathscr{A}}$ is called the *realization* of σ in $\mathscr{A}$.

The mapping $\sigma \to \sigma^{\mathscr{A}}$ will not be given explicitly, but we write $\mathscr{A} = (A, \Sigma)$ for the Σ-algebra $\mathscr{A}$ in Definition 2.2. If there is no danger of confusion, then we omit $\mathscr{A}$ in the realization $\sigma^{\mathscr{A}}$ of σ. The Σ-algebra $\mathscr{A}$ is *finite* if both A and Σ are finite. If Σ is not specified, then we speak of an algebra.

Definition 2.3. The Σ-algebra $\mathscr{B} = (B, \Sigma)$ is a *subalgebra* of the Σ-algebra $\mathscr{A} = (A, \Sigma)$ if $B \subseteq A$ and $\sigma^{\mathscr{B}} = \sigma^{\mathscr{A}} \mid B^m$ for arbitrary $m \in \mathbf{N}$ and $\sigma \in \Sigma_m$. We sometimes say that this "closed" subset B forms a subalgebra of $\mathscr{A}$. Moreover, $\mathscr{B}$ is a *proper subalgebra* of $\mathscr{A}$ if $\mathscr{B}$ is a subalgebra of $\mathscr{A}$ and $B \subset A$.

Take a Σ-algebra $\mathscr{A} = (A, \Sigma)$ and a subset $B \subseteq A$ such that $B \neq \emptyset$ if $\Sigma_0 = \emptyset$. The smallest subalgebra of $\mathscr{A}$ containing B is called the *subalgebra* of $\mathscr{A}$ *generated* by B, and B is a *generating set* of this subalgebra. If $\mathscr{A}$ can be generated by a singleton, then $\mathscr{A}$ is *cyclic*.

Definition 2.4. Let $\mathscr{A} = (A, \Sigma)$ and $\mathscr{B} = (B, \Sigma)$ be Σ-algebras. A mapping $\varphi : A \to B$ is a *homomorphism* from $\mathscr{A}$ to $\mathscr{B}$ if

$$\varphi(\sigma^{\mathscr{A}}(a_1, \dots, a_m)) = \sigma^{\mathscr{B}}(\varphi(a_1), \dots, \varphi(a_m))$$

holds for arbitrary $m \in \mathbf{N}$, $\sigma \in \Sigma_m$ and $a_1, \dots, a_m \in A$. We write $\varphi : \mathscr{A} \to \mathscr{B}$.

If there is a homomorphism $\varphi : \mathscr{A} \to \mathscr{B}$ such that φ maps A onto B, then $\mathscr{B}$ is called a *homomorphic image* of $\mathscr{A}$. A one-to-one homomorphism from $\mathscr{A}$ to $\mathscr{B}$ is an *embedding* of $\mathscr{A}$ into $\mathscr{B}$. If in addition it is a mapping onto B, then we speak of an *isomorphism*, and $\mathscr{A}$ and $\mathscr{B}$ are called *isomorphic*. The existence of an isomorphism between $\mathscr{A}$ and $\mathscr{B}$ is expressed by $\mathscr{A} \cong \mathscr{B}$.

Definition 2.5. Let $\mathscr{A} = (A, \Sigma)$ be a Σ-algebra. An equivalence relation ϱ on A is called a *congruence relation* of $\mathscr{A}$ if, for arbitrary $m \in \mathbf{N}$, $\sigma \in \Sigma_m$ and a_i, b_i $(\in A, i = 1, \dots, m)$, $a_i \equiv b_i(\varrho)$ $(i = 1, \dots, m)$ implies $\sigma(a_1, \dots, a_m) \equiv \sigma(b_1, \dots, b_m)$ (ϱ).

It is sometimes more convenient to deal with compatible partitions instead of congruence relations.

Definition 2.6. Take a Σ-algebra $\mathscr{A} = (A, \Sigma)$. A partition π of A is a *compatible partition of* $\mathscr{A}$ if, for arbitrary $m \in \mathbf{N}$, $\sigma \in \Sigma_m$ and a_i, b_i $(\in A, i = 1, \dots, m)$, $\pi(a_i) = \pi(b_i)$ $(i = 1, \dots, m)$ implies $\pi(\sigma(a_1, \dots, a_m)) = \pi(\sigma(b_1, \dots, b_m))$.

Clearly, if ϱ is a congruence relation of a Σ-algebra $\mathscr{A}$, then A/ϱ is a compatible partition of $\mathscr{A}$. Conversely, every congruence relation of $\mathscr{A}$ can be given in this way.

By means of congruence relations we can derive new Σ-algebras from a given Σ-algebra. Consider a Σ-algebra $\mathscr{A} = (A, \Sigma)$, and let ϱ be a congruence relation of $\mathscr{A}$. Take $\mathscr{A}/\varrho = (A/\varrho, \Sigma)$, where for arbitrary $m \in \mathbf{N}$, $\sigma \in \Sigma_m$ and $a_1, \dots, a_m \in A$, $\sigma^{\mathscr{A}/\varrho}(a_1/\varrho, \dots, a_m/\varrho) = \sigma^{\mathscr{A}}(a_1, \dots, a_m)/\varrho$. Obviously, $\mathscr{A}/\varrho$ is a Σ-algebra. This $\mathscr{A}/\varrho$ is the *quotient algebra* of $\mathscr{A}$ by the congruence relation ϱ.

Theorem 2.7. *Let $\mathscr{A}$ be a Σ-algebra and ϱ a congruence relation of $\mathscr{A}$. Then $\mathscr{A}/\varrho$ is a homomorphic image of $\mathscr{A}$. Conversely, if the Σ-algebra $\mathscr{B}$ is a homomorphic image of $\mathscr{A}$, then there exists a congruence relation ϱ of $\mathscr{A}$ such that $\mathscr{B} \cong \mathscr{A}/\varrho$.* □

By Theorem 2.7, up to isomorphism the quotient algebras of an algebra $\mathscr{A}$ are the same as its homomorphic images.

We present one more way to construct new algebras from given ones.

Definition 2.8. Let $\mathscr{A}_i = (A_i, \Sigma)$ $(i \in I)$ be Σ-algebras. Take the Σ-algebra $\mathscr{A} = (A, \Sigma)$ where $A = \prod (A_i \mid i \in I)$ and, for arbitrary $m \in \mathbf{N}$, $\sigma \in \Sigma_m$, $\mathbf{a}_1, \dots, \mathbf{a}_m \in A$ and $i \in I$,

$$\mathrm{pr}_i(\sigma^{\mathscr{A}}(\mathbf{a}_1, \dots, \mathbf{a}_m)) = \sigma^{\mathscr{A}_i}(\mathrm{pr}_i(\mathbf{a}_1), \dots, \mathrm{pr}_i(\mathbf{a}_m)) .$$

This algebra $\mathscr{A}$ is called the *direct product* of $\mathscr{A}_i$ $(i \in I)$, and we use the notation $\mathscr{A} = \prod (\mathscr{A}_i \mid i \in I)$. If $\mathscr{A}_i = \mathscr{B}$ for every $i \in I$, then $\mathscr{A}$ is a *direct power* of $\mathscr{B}$.

If in the above direct product $\mathscr{A}$ the index set I is finite, say $I = [k]$, then we also write

$$\mathscr{A} = \mathscr{A}_1 \times \dots \times \mathscr{A}_k .$$

We next extend operational symbols to symbols of "composed operations", to be called polynomial symbols. For this, we need a countable set $U = \{u_1, u_2, \dots\}$ of variables. For every $n \in \mathbf{N}$, the subset of U consisting of its first n elements will be denoted by U_n, i.e., $U_n = \{u_1, \dots, u_n\}$. Note that $U_0 = \emptyset$.

Definition 2.9. The set of *n-ary Σ-polynomial symbols* $(n \in \mathbf{N})$ is the smallest set $P(\Sigma, n)$ satisfying the following conditions:

(i) $\Sigma_0 \cup U_n \subseteq P(\Sigma, n)$.

(ii) For arbitrary $m > 0$, $\sigma \in \Sigma_m$ and $p_1, \dots, p_m \in P(\Sigma, n)$, $\sigma(p_1, \dots, p_m) \in P(\Sigma, n)$.

Here, and further on, we suppose that $\Sigma \cap U = \emptyset$.

By the following definition, we correspond polynomials of Σ-algebras to Σ-polynomial symbols:

Definition 2.10. Let $\mathscr{A} = (A, \Sigma)$ be a Σ-algebra and, for an $n \in \mathbf{N}$, take a $p \in P(\Sigma, n)$. The *realization* of p in $\mathscr{A}$ is the mapping $p^{\mathscr{A}} : A^n \to A$ that, for every $\mathbf{a} \in A^n$, fulfils the following conditions:

(i) If $p = \sigma(\in \Sigma_0)$ then $P^{\mathscr{A}}(\mathbf{a}) = \sigma^{\mathscr{A}}$.
(ii) If $p = u_i$ $(1 \leqq i \leqq n)$ then $p^{\mathscr{A}}(\mathbf{a}) = \mathrm{pr}_i(\mathbf{a})$.
(iii) If $p = \sigma(p_1, \dots, p_m)$ $(\sigma \in \Sigma_m,\ m > 0,\ p_1, \dots, p_m \in P(\Sigma, n))$, then $p^{\mathscr{A}}(\mathbf{a}) = \sigma^{\mathscr{A}}(p_1^{\mathscr{A}}(\mathbf{a}), \dots, p_m^{\mathscr{A}}(\mathbf{a}))$.

If there is no danger of confusion, then we generally write p for $p^{\mathscr{A}}$.

Using Σ-polynomial symbols, we define equations which are the simplest and most frequently used axioms in algebra.

Definition 2.11. Take a set Σ of operational symbols and an integer $n \in \mathbf{N}$. Let $p, q \in P(\Sigma, n)$. The *n-ary Σ-equation* $p = q$ is *satisfied* by the Σ-algebra $\mathscr{A} = (A, \Sigma)$ if

$$p(\mathbf{a}) = q(\mathbf{a})$$

holds for arbitrary $\mathbf{a} \in A^n$. We also say that $p = q$ *holds* in $\mathscr{A}$. If n is not specified, then we speak about Σ-equations (or simply about equations, when Σ is understood), i.e. a Σ-equation is an n-ary Σ-equation for some n. The Σ-algebra $\mathscr{A}$ *satisfies* a set E of Σ-equations if each equation in E is satisfied by $\mathscr{A}$.

For a set E of Σ-equations, let E^* be the class of all Σ-algebras which satisfy E.

Definition 2.12. A class $\mathscr{K}$ of Σ-algebras is *equational* if there exists a set E of Σ-equations such that $\mathscr{K} = E^*$.

It is said that $\mathbf{X}$ is an *operator*, if for an arbitrary class $\mathscr{K}$ of algebras, $\mathbf{X}(\mathscr{K})$ is also a class of algebras. If $\mathbf{X}$ and $\mathbf{Y}$ are operators, then we write $\mathbf{XY}(\mathscr{K})$ for $\mathbf{X}(\mathbf{Y}(\mathscr{K}))$. We shall need several operators; here we define only some of them.

$\mathbf{S}(\mathscr{K})$: subalgebras of algebras from $\mathscr{K}$;
$\mathbf{H}(\mathscr{K})$: homomorphic images of algebras from $\mathscr{K}$;
$\mathbf{I}(\mathscr{K})$: isomorphic images of algebras from $\mathscr{K}$;
$\mathbf{P}(\mathscr{K})$: direct products of algebras from $\mathscr{K}$;
$\mathbf{P}_f(\mathscr{K})$: direct products of algebras from $\mathscr{K}$ with finitely many factors.

For every class $\mathscr{K}$ of Σ-algebras, let $\mathscr{K}^*$ be the largest set of Σ-equations which are satisfied by each algebra in $\mathscr{K}$.

Theorem 2.13. *Let $\mathscr{K}$ be a class of Σ-algebras. Then* $\mathbf{HSP}(\mathscr{K}) = \mathscr{K}^{**}$, *and it is the smallest equational class containing $\mathscr{K}$.* □

This theorem implies that every equational class is closed under the formation of homomorphic images, subalgebras and direct products. Moreover, every algebra in the equational class "generated by $\mathscr{K}$" can be obtained as a homomorphic image of a subalgebra of a direct product of algebras from $\mathscr{K}$.

In the theory of equational classes of algebras, the free algebras play an important role.

Definition 2.14. Let $\mathscr{K}$ be a class of Σ-algebras, $\mathscr{A} = (A, \Sigma)$ an algebra in $\mathscr{K}$, and $\{a_i \mid i \in I\}$ a subset of A generating $\mathscr{A}$. It is said that $\mathscr{A}$ is a *free algebra* over $\mathscr{K}$ with the *free generating set* $\{a_i \mid i \in I\}$ if, for any $\mathscr{B} = (B, \Sigma)$ in $\mathscr{K}$, every mapping φ: $\{a_i \mid i \in I\} \to B$ can be extended to a homomorphism of $\mathscr{A}$ into $\mathscr{B}$.

For an arbitrary class $\mathscr{K}$ of Σ-algebras, the free algebras do not necessarily exist. However, if $\mathscr{K}$ is a nontrivial equational class, i.e., an equational class having an algebra with at least two elements, then for every cardinal there is an algebra $\mathscr{A} = (A, \Sigma)$ and a subset $B \subseteq A$ of the given cardinality such that $\mathscr{A}$ is free over $\mathscr{K}$ and B is a free generating set of $\mathscr{A}$. Moreover, all the free algebras in $\mathscr{K}$ having free generating sets of the same cardinality are isomorphic to each other. Finally, it should be noted that, if the equational class $\mathscr{K}$ is generated by finitely many finite algebras, then every finitely generated algebra in $\mathscr{K}$ is finite. This follows readily from Theorem 2.13 through the observation that every finitely generated subalgebra of a direct product of algebras from $\mathscr{K}$ is in $\mathbf{ISP}_f(\mathscr{K})$ if $\mathscr{K}$ consists of finitely many finite algebras.

We now turn to certain important special algebras needed in later chapters.

Let Σ be a nonvoid set of operational symbols such that $\Sigma_m = \emptyset$ if $m \neq 1$. Such a Σ-algebra is then called a *unoid*. Unoids are therefore algebras with unary operational symbols only.

Let $\Sigma = \Sigma_2 = \{\cdot\}$. A Σ-algebra $\mathscr{A} = (A, \Sigma)$ is a *semigroup* if $\cdot(a, \cdot(b, c)) = \cdot(\cdot(a, b), c)$ holds for arbitrary $a, b, c \in A$. In other words, a semigroup is an algebra with an associative binary operation. In the sequel we shall write ab instead of $\cdot(a, b)$. Moreover, a semigroup will be denoted by the set of its elements; the operation will not be mentioned explicitly.

Finite semigroups are frequently given by means of *multiplication tables*. If the semigroup S is of n elements then the table belonging to S has n columns and n rows. Each column and each row is labelled by an element from S. Different columns have different labels and, similarly, rows are also labelled in a one-to-one manner. If s is the label of the ith row and s' is the label of the jth column, then at the intersection of the ith row and j^{th} column we find the product of s by s':

	$\ldots s' \ldots$
$\vdots$	$\vdots$
s	$\ldots ss' \ldots$
$\vdots$	$\vdots$

A semigroup A is a *group* if it has an element e for which $ae = ea = a$ $(a \in A)$, and for every $a \in A$ there is an $a^{-1} \in A$ such that $aa^{-1} = a^{-1}a = e$. The element e is uniquely determined, and is called the *identity element* of A. Moreover, for every $a \in A$ there is exactly one a^{-1} satisfying the above equalities, and a^{-1} is the *inverse* of a.

Every group can be given as a Σ-algebra with a nullary, a unary, and a binary operation satisfying the equations determined by the equalities in the definition of the group. Thus, the class of all semigroups and that of all groups are examples of equational classes of algebras.

Considering groups as Σ-algebras, we can speak about subgroups of a given group. In other words, a subset H of a group G is a *subgroup* of G if H is a subsemigroup of G, H contains e, and $a^{-1} \in H$ whenever a is in H.

Let G be a group and H a subgroup of G. For every $g \in G$, we define $Hg = \{hg \mid h \in H\}$. This Hg is called the *right coset* of H by g. The *left coset* of H by g is defined similarly: $gH = \{gh \mid h \in H\}$. Both $\{Hg \mid g \in G\}$ and $\{gH \mid g \in G\}$ are partitions of G with the same cardinality. This common cardinality is the *index* of H in G, which is denoted by $G : H$.

Among the subgroups of a group G there are some distinguished ones. A subgroup H of G is *normal* if its right and left cosets coincide, i.e., $gH = Hg$ for every $g \in G$. If H is a normal subgroup, then the partition of G by H is compatible. On the other hand, every compatible partition of G can be given by a normal subgroup. Obviously, G and e are normal subgroups of G. If G has no other normal subgroups, then G is called *simple.* If G is simple, then, by Theorem 2.7, every homomorphic image of G is isomorphic to e or G.

In the sequel, if not stated otherwise, by a group we always mean a finite group.

As two general examples of semigroups and groups, we may mention the transformation semigroups and permutation groups of sets.

Let N be a finite nonvoid set. We may assume that $N = [n]$ for some $n \in \mathbf{N}$. A mapping $\varphi : N \to N$ is called a *transformation* of N. It can easily be shown that the transformations of N form a semigroup under the multiplication of mappings, which is called the *transformation semigroup of N*, or the *transformation semigroup of degree n.* Moreover, let $n > 1$ and take the following three transformations φ_1, φ_2, and φ_3 of N:

$\varphi_1(i) = i + 1 \pmod{n}$,
$\varphi_2(1) = 2$, $\varphi_2(2) = 1$ and $\varphi_2(i) = i$ if $i > 2$ $(i \in N)$, and
$\varphi_3(1) = \varphi_3(2) = 1$ and $\varphi_3(i) = i$ if $i > 2$ $(i \in N)$.

Then $\{\varphi_1, \varphi_2, \varphi_3\}$ is a generating set of the transformation semigroup of degree n.

Again, take the set $N\,(= [n])$. Every one-to-one mapping $\varphi : N \to N$ is a *permutation* of N. The set of all permutations of N forms a group which is called the *full permutation group of N* or the *full permutation group of degree n.* Each subgroup of this full permutation group is a *permutation group of N* or a *permutation group of degree n.* Obviously, if G is a permutation group of degree n, then it is (isomorphic to) a permutation group of degree m for every $m \geqq n$. Moreover, the set consisting of the permutations φ_1 and φ_2 defined above is a generating set of the full permutation group of N if $n > 1$.

The following group theory results will be used in our later discussions:

Theorem 2.15. *Let G be a subgroup of the transformation semigroup of* $[n]$ $(n \in \mathbf{N}$, $n > 0)$. *Then there exists a subset N of* $[n]$ *such that G is isomorphic to a permutation group H of N.*

Proof. Let e be the identity element of G, and set $N = \{e(i) \mid i \in [n]\}$. Moreover, let $H = \{g\,|N| \; g \in G\}$. Obviously, $g \mid N\; (g \in G)$ maps N into N since $g = ge$. Further, by $e = ee$, $e \mid N$ is the identity mapping of N. Finally, $(g \mid N)(g^{-1} \mid N) = e \mid N$ is also valid for every $g \in G$, showing that H is a permutation group of N. Moreover, the mapping $\varphi : g \to g \mid N$ $(g \in G)$ is a homomorphism of G onto H. It remains to be shown that φ is one-to-one. For this, we take two distinct elements, g_1 and g_2, of G. Using the equality $eg = g$ $(g \in G)$, we have that $g_1 \mid N$ and $g_2 \mid N$ are also different. □

Lemma 2.16. *Let G be a permutation group of degree n with $|G| > 1$. Then there is a proper subgroup H of G such that $G : H \leqq n$.*

Proof. Without loss of generality we may assume that n is least among all natural numbers m for which G is isomorphic to a permutation group of degree m. Obviously, $n > 1$. We may also suppose that G is a group of permutations of $[n]$. Denote by H the subset of G consisting of all h such that $h(1) = 1$, i.e., h keeps 1 fixed. Clearly, H is a proper subgroup of G. It is easy to show for arbitrary two elements $g_1, g_2 \in G$ that, if $g_1(1) = g_2(1)$, then $Hg_1 = Hg_2$. Therefore, $G:H \leqq n$. □

Using this lemma, we prove

Theorem 2.17. *Let G be a permutation group of degree n. Take a simple group G' which is a homomorphic image of G. Then G' is isomorphic to a permutation group of degree k with $k \leqq n$.*

Proof. If $|G'| = 1$, then our statement is obviously true. Thus suppose that $|G'| > 1$. Therefore, $n > 1$ also holds. We may further assume that n is least among all natural numbers m such that there exists a permutation group of degree m which can be mapped homomorphically onto G'. Let H be the subgroup of G given in the proof of Lemma 2.16. Then, $G:H \leqq n$. Denote by H' the image of H under the given homomorphism of G onto G'. Then H' is a proper subgroup of G', since in the opposite case G' could be given as a homomorphic image of a permutation group of degree less than n. Moreover, $G':H' \leqq n$ also holds.

Take the set $M = \{H'g' \mid g' \in G'\}$, and for each $g \in G'$ define the permutation h_g on M by $h_g(H'g') = H'g'g$ $(g' \in G')$. Denote by $\bar{G}$ the set of all such permutations h_g $(g \in G')$. Then $\bar{G}$ is a group, and the inequality $|\bar{G}| > 1$ obviously holds. Moreover, consider the mapping $\varphi: G' \to \bar{G}$ given by $\varphi(g) = h_g$ $(g \in G')$. Clearly, φ is a homomorphism of G' onto $\bar{G}$. As G' is simple and $|\bar{G}| > 1$, we have $G' \cong \bar{G}$. □

1.3 Automata and Sequential Machines

First of all we list some general concepts.

An *alphabet* X is a finite nonvoid set. The elements of X are called *letters*. A *word* over X is a finite string $p = x_1 \dots x_n$ $(x_i \in X, i = 1, \dots, n)$ of letters. The number of occurrences of letters in a word p is the *length* of p, which is denoted by $|p|$. For the *empty word*, i.e. for the word of length 0, we use the notation e. Denote by X^* the set of all words over X. For arbitrary $n \in \mathbf{N}$, the subset consisting of all words from X^* with length of at most n will be denoted by $X^{(n)}$. In X^* we introduce a multiplication which is the catenation of words, i.e., for arbitrary two words $p = x_1 \dots x_m$ and $q = x_{m+1} \dots x_n$ $(x_i \in X, i = 1, \dots, n)$,

$$pq = x_1 \dots x_m x_{m+1} \dots x_n .$$

Moreover, for arbitrary $p \in X^*$ and $n \in \mathbf{N}$, the power p^n is defined by $p^\circ = e$ and $p^n = pp^{n-1}$ if $n > 0$. Under the above multiplication X^* forms a *monoid*, i.e., a semigroup with identity element.

If X is an alphabet and $n > 0$ is an integer, then the elements of X^n are usually written as words over X with length n.

Definition 3.1. A system $\mathfrak{A} = (X, A, \delta)$ is an *automaton*, where
(i) X is an alphabet of *input signals* called the *input alphabet*,
(ii) A is a nonvoid set of *states*, and
(iii) δ is a mapping of $A \times X$ into A called the *transition function* (or *next-state function*).

Each element of X^* will be termed an *input word* of $\mathfrak{A}$. For the cardinality of the state set of $\mathfrak{A}$ we shall also use the notation $|\mathfrak{A}|$.

The automaton $\mathfrak{A}$ is *finite* if A is finite.

Finite automata are frequently given by means of *transition tables*. If $\mathfrak{A} = (X, A, \delta)$ is an automaton with m states and n input signals then the table of $\mathfrak{A}$ has n rows and m columns. Each row is labelled by an input signal such that different rows have different labels. Moreover, columns are also labelled by states in a one-to-one manner. If the label of the ith row is x and the label of the jth column is a, then the entry in the ith row and j^{th} column is $\delta(a, x)$:

δ	$\dots a \dots$
$\vdots$	$\vdots$
x	$\dots \delta(a, x) \dots$
$\vdots$	$\vdots$

Automata can be considered unoids, i.e. algebras with unary operations. Take the automaton $\mathfrak{A}$ from Definition 3.1 and, for every $x \in X$, let σ_x be a unary operational symbol. Set $\Sigma = \{\sigma_x \mid x \in X\}$, and define the Σ-algebra $\mathcal{A} = (A, \Sigma)$ by $\sigma_x^{\mathcal{A}}(a) = \delta(a, x)$ $(x \in X, a \in A)$. There is therefore a natural one-to-one correspondence between the class of all automata and that of all unoids with finitely many operational symbols. Using this correspondence, we can rephrase for automata the algebraic concepts subalgebra, homomorphisms, isomorphisms, congruence relations, compatible partitions, quotient algebras and direct products in an obvious way. Accordingly,

1. the automaton $\mathfrak{B} = (X, B, \delta')$ is a *subautomaton* of the automaton $\mathfrak{A} = (X, A, \delta)$ if $B \subseteq A$ and $\delta' = \delta \mid B \times X$;
2. the mapping $\varphi: A \to B$ is a *homomorphism* of the automaton $\mathfrak{A} = (X, A, \delta)$ into the automaton $\mathfrak{B} = (X, B, \delta')$ if $\varphi(\delta(a, x)) = \delta'(\varphi(a), x)$ $(a \in A, x \in X)$;
3. the equivalence relation ϱ on A is a *congruence relation* of the automaton $\mathfrak{A} = (X, A, \delta)$ if, for arbitrary states $a, b \in A$ and input signal $x \in X$, $a \equiv b\ (\varrho)$ implies $\delta(a, x) \equiv \delta(b, x)\ (\varrho)$;

4. the partition π of A is a *compatible partition* of the automaton $\mathfrak{A} = (X, A, \delta)$ if, for arbitrary $a, b \in A$ and $x \in X$, $\pi(\delta(a, x)) = \pi(\delta(b, x))$ if $\pi(a) = \pi(b)$;
5. if ϱ is a congruence relation of the automaton $\mathfrak{A} = (X, A, \delta)$, then the *quotient automaton* $\mathfrak{A}/\varrho = (X, A/\varrho, \delta_\varrho)$ of $\mathfrak{A}$ by ϱ is given by $\delta_\varrho(a/\varrho, x) = \delta(a, x)/\varrho$ $(a \in A, x \in X)$;
6. if $(\mathfrak{A}_i = (X, A_i, \delta_i) \mid i \in I)$ is a family of automata, then the *direct product* $\mathfrak{A} = (X, A, \delta)$ $(= \prod(\mathfrak{A}_i \mid i \in I))$ is determined by $A = \prod(A_i \mid i \in I)$ and $\mathrm{pr}_i(\delta(\mathbf{a}, x)) = \delta_i(\mathrm{pr}_i(\mathbf{a}), x)$ $(i \in I, \mathbf{a} \in A, x \in X)$.

We call an automaton $\mathfrak{A} = (X, A, \delta)$ *simple* if it has no other congruence relations but ι_A and ω_A.

For an automaton $\mathfrak{A} = (X, A, \delta)$, let us extend δ to the mapping $\delta^*: A \times X^* \to A$ given in the following way:

(i) $\delta^*(a, e) = a$ $(a \in A)$, and
(ii) $\delta^*(a, px) = \delta(\delta^*(a, p), x)$ $(a \in A, p \in X^*, x \in X)$.

In the sequel we shall simply write δ for δ^*.

An *X-equation* will have the form $up = uq$ or $up = vq$, where u, v are variables and $p, q \in X^*$. The automaton $\mathfrak{A} = (X, A, \delta)$ *satisfies* the X-equation $up = uq$ if $\delta(a, p) = \delta(a, q)$ holds for every $a \in A$. Similarly, $\mathfrak{A}$ *satisfies* the X-equation $up = vq$ if $\delta(a, p) = \delta(b, q)$ is valid under any $a, b \in A$. If $\mathfrak{A}$ satisfies an X-equation then we also say that the given X-equation *holds* in $\mathfrak{A}$. It should be noted that the above two types of X-equations correspond to the possible two forms of unoid equations. (Observe that for unoids we have only unary polynomial symbols.)

Other algebraic concepts can be reformulated for automata similarly. We shall use the operators **H**, **I**, **S**, **P** and $\mathbf{P}_f$ for automata in their obvious sense.

The above natural correspondence between automata and unoids implies that Theorems 2.7 and 2.13 are valid for automata, too, as is our remark that 'every finitely generated subalgebra of a direct product of algebras from $\mathscr{K}$ is isomorphic to a subalgebra of a direct product of algebras from $\mathscr{K}$ with finitely many factors if $\mathscr{K}$ consists of finitely many finite algebras' (see p. 7).

We recall three more concepts from the theory of automata.

An automaton $\mathfrak{B} = (Y, B, \delta')$ is an X-*subautomaton* of the automaton $\mathfrak{A} = (X, A, \delta)$ if $Y \subseteq X$, $B \subseteq A$ and $\delta' = \delta \mid B \times Y$.

Take two automata $\mathfrak{A} = (X, A, \delta)$ and $\mathfrak{B} = (Y, B, \delta')$. We say that $\mathfrak{A}$ and $\mathfrak{B}$ are X-*isomorphic* if there are two one-to-one and onto mappings $\varphi: X \to Y$ and $\psi: A \to B$ such that $\psi(\delta(a, x)) = \delta'(\psi(a), \varphi(x))$ $(a \in A, x \in X)$.

Consider an automaton $\mathfrak{A} = (X, A, \delta)$. Define a binary relation $\varrho_\mathfrak{A}$ on the monoid X^* in the following way: $p \equiv q$ $(\varrho_\mathfrak{A})$ $(p, q \in X^*)$ if and only if $\delta(a, p) = \delta(a, q)$ holds for every $a \in A$. In other words, two input words of $\mathfrak{A}$ are in the same $\varrho_\mathfrak{A}$-block if and only if they induce the same mapping on the state set of $\mathfrak{A}$. Obviously, $\varrho_\mathfrak{A}$ is a congruence relation of X^*. The quotient semigroup $X^*/\varrho_\mathfrak{A}$ is called the *characteristic semigroup* (or *input semigroup*) of $\mathfrak{A}$. For $X^*/\varrho_\mathfrak{A}$ we shall use the notation $\mathscr{S}(\mathfrak{A})$, too.

Observe that if $\mathfrak{B}$ is a homomorphic image of a subautomaton of $\mathfrak{A}$, then $\mathscr{S}(\mathfrak{A})$ can be mapped homomorphically onto $\mathscr{S}(\mathfrak{B})$.

In the sequel we shall deal mainly with finite automata. Thus, if not stated otherwise, by an automaton we mean a finite automaton.

We next definite certain special types of automata.

Let $\mathfrak{A} = (X, A, \delta)$ be an automaton.

1. $\mathfrak{A}$ is *discrete* if $\delta(a, x) = a$ for all $a \in A$ and $x \in X$.
2. $\mathfrak{A}$ is *trivial* if $|A| = 1$.
3. $\mathfrak{A}$ is *connected* if it can be generated by one of its states.
4. $\mathfrak{A}$ is *strongly connected* if, for an arbitrary pair $(a, b) \in A^2$, there is an input word $p \in X^*$ such that $\delta(a, p) = b$. In other words, $\mathfrak{A}$ is strongly connected if $\mathfrak{A}$ can be generated by any of its states.
5. A is *monotone* if there is a partial ordering $\leqq$ on A such that $a \leqq \delta(a, x)$ for all $a \in A$ and $x \in X$. (By Theorem 1.1, $\leqq$ can be taken linear.)
6. $\mathfrak{A}$ is a *nilpotent automaton* if there are a state $a_0 \in A$ and a natural number n such that, for arbitrary $a \in A$ and $p \in X^*$ with $|p| \geqq n$, the equality $\delta(a, p) = a_0$ holds. This a_0 is called the *absorbent state* of $\mathfrak{A}$.
7. $\mathfrak{A}$ is a *permutation automaton* if, for arbitrary $a, b \in A$ and $x \in X$, $\delta(a, x) = \delta(b, x)$ implies $a = b$. In other words, $\mathfrak{A}$ is a permutation automaton if every input signal of $\mathfrak{A}$ induces a permutation of the state set of $\mathfrak{A}$.
8. $\mathfrak{A}$ is a *counter* if X is a singleton, say $X = \{x\}$, $A = [n]$, for some natural number n, and $\delta(i, x) = i+1 \pmod{n}$ $(i \in [n])$.

We sometimes use the following generalization of a counter. $\mathfrak{A}$ is a *generalized counter* if $A = [n]$ for a natural number n and $\delta(i, x) = i+1 \pmod{n}$ $(i \in [n], x \in X)$. A generalized counter can be considered a counter with possibly more than one input signal.

9. $\mathfrak{A}$ is a *reset automaton* if, for an arbitrary $x \in X$,
a) $\delta(a, x) = a$ $(a \in A)$, or
b) there exists an $a_x \in A$ such that $\delta(a, x) = a_x$ $(a \in A)$.
$\mathfrak{A}$ is a *full reset automaton* if it is a reset automaton and
c) there exists an $x \in X$ for which $\delta(a, x) = a$ $(a \in A)$,
and
d) for every $a \in A$ there is an $x_a \in X$ such that $\delta(b, x_a) = a$ $(b \in A)$.
10. $\mathfrak{A}$ is a *shift register* if $A = X^m$ for some integer $m > 0$, and $\delta(x_1 x_2 \ldots x_m, x) = x_2 \ldots x_m x$, where $x_1, x_2, \ldots, x_m, x \in X$ are arbitrary. For this shift register, we use the notation $\mathfrak{R}_{m, X}$.

Let S be a finite semigroup. The automaton $\mathfrak{S} = (S, S, \delta)$ is then a *semigroup-like automaton* if $\delta(s_1, s_2) = s_1 s_2$ $(s_1, s_2 \in S)$, where $s_1 s_2$ is the product of s_1 by s_2 in the semigroup S. If S is a group, then we speak of a *group-like automaton* with group S. Moreover, if S is a simple group, then $\mathfrak{S}$ is called a *simple group-like automaton.* It should be noted that, if $\mathfrak{G} = (G, G, \delta)$ is a group-like automaton, then $\mathscr{S}(\mathfrak{G})$ is isomorphic to G.

In the next chapter we need

Theorem 3.2. *Assume that a finite group G is a homomorphic image of a permutation group H of $[m]$ for some $m > 0$. Then there exists a permutation automaton $\mathfrak{A}$ with m states such that the group-like automaton $\mathfrak{G} = (G, G, \delta_{\mathfrak{G}})$ is a homomorphic image of a subautomaton of a finite direct power of $\mathfrak{A}$.*

Proof. We may assume that $|G| > 1$. Let φ be a homomorphism of H onto G. For every $g \in G$, take a fixed $h_g \in \varphi^{-1}(g)$, and consider the automaton $\mathfrak{A} = (G, [m], \delta)$ given by $\delta(i, g) = h_g(i)$ $(i \in [m])$. We shall show that, whenever an equation $up = uq$ $(p, q \in G^*)$ holds in $\mathfrak{A}$, then it is valid in $\mathfrak{G}$. Through Theorem 2.13, this will imply that $\mathfrak{G} \in \mathbf{HSP}(\{\mathfrak{A}\})$. (Obviously, no equation of form $up = vq$ holds in $\mathfrak{A}$.) If it is considered that in an equational class generated by finitely many finite algebras every finitely generated algebra can be given as a homomorphic image of a subalgebra of a finite direct product of the generator algebras, the proof of Theorem 3.2 follows from the inclusion $\mathfrak{G} \in \mathbf{HSP}(\{\mathfrak{A}\})$.

Let $up = uq$ $(p = g_1 \dots g_k,\ q = g'_1 \dots g'_l;\ g_1, \dots, g_k, g'_1, \dots, g'_l \in G)$ hold in $\mathfrak{A}$. Then, for every $i \in [m]$, $(h_{g_1} \dots h_{g_k})(i) = (h_{g'_1} \dots h_{g'_l})(i)$, i.e., the equality $h_{g_1} \dots h_{g_k} = h_{g'_1} \dots h_{g'_l}$ is valid in H. Since φ is a homomorphism, $g_1 \dots g_k = g'_1 \dots g'_l$ holds in G. Thus, by the definition of $\mathfrak{G}$, $\delta_{\mathfrak{G}}(g, g_1 \dots g_k) = \delta_{\mathfrak{G}}(g, g'_1 \dots g'_l)$ is obviously valid for every $g \in G$. Therefore, $up = uq$ holds in $\mathfrak{G}$, too. □

Take an arbitrary automaton $\mathfrak{A} = (X, A, \delta)$. A sequence $a_1, a_2, \dots, a_n$ of pairwise distinct states of $\mathfrak{A}$ is a *cycle* in $\mathfrak{A}$ if there are input signals $x_1, x_2, \dots, x_n$ such that $\delta(a_i, x_i) = a_{i+1(\mathrm{mod}\ n)}$ for every $i \in [n]$. The integer n is the *length* of this cycle. It sometimes makes our discussion simpler if we write the above cycle in the form $a_0, a_1, \dots, a_n$ $(a_0 = a_n)$.

If we add outputs to automata, then we get the concept of sequential machines.

Definition 3.3. A system $\mathfrak{A} = (X, A, Y, \delta, \lambda)$ is a *sequential machine* (or a *Mealy machine*), where

(i) X is an alphabet of *input signals*, the *input alphabet*,
(ii) A is a nonvoid set of *states*,
(iii) Y is an alphabet of *output signals*, the *output alphabet*,
(iv) $\delta: A \times X \to A$ is the *transition function*, and
(v) $\lambda: A \times X \to Y$ is the *output function*.

The sequential machine $\mathfrak{A}$ is *finite* if A is finite. The system $\bar{\mathfrak{A}} = (X, A, \delta)$ is called the *underlying automaton* of the sequential machine $\mathfrak{A}$.

We need some more concepts concerning machines.

Definition 3.4. The machine $\mathfrak{B} = (X, B, Y, \delta', \lambda')$ is a *submachine* of the machine $\mathfrak{A} = (X, A, Y, \delta, \lambda)$ if

(1) $\bar{\mathfrak{B}} = (X, B, \delta')$ is a subautomaton of $\bar{\mathfrak{A}} = (X, A, \delta)$, and
(2) $\lambda' = \lambda \mid B \times X$.

Definition 3.5. Let $\mathfrak{A} = (X, A, Y, \delta, \lambda)$ and $\mathfrak{B} = (X, B, Y, \delta', \lambda')$ be sequential machines. The mapping $\varphi: A \to B$ is a *homomorphism* of $\mathfrak{A}$ into $\mathfrak{B}$ if

(i) φ is a homomorphism of $\bar{\mathfrak{A}} = (X, A, \delta)$ into $\bar{\mathfrak{B}} = (X, B, \delta')$, and
(ii) $\lambda'(\varphi(a), x) = \lambda(a, x)$ holds for arbitrary $a \in A$ and $x \in X$.

If there is a homomorphism of $\mathfrak{A}$ onto $\mathfrak{B}$, then $\mathfrak{B}$ is called a *homomorphic image* of $\mathfrak{A}$. A one-to-one homomorphism of $\mathfrak{A}$ onto $\mathfrak{B}$ is an *isomorphism* between $\mathfrak{A}$ and $\mathfrak{B}$. The existence of an isomorphism between $\mathfrak{A}$ and $\mathfrak{B}$ is denoted by $\mathfrak{A} \cong \mathfrak{B}$.

Consider a sequential machine $\mathfrak{A} = (X, A, Y, \delta, \lambda)$. We extend λ to a mapping $\lambda^*: A \times X^* \to Y^*$ in the following way:

(i) $\lambda^*(a, e) = e$ $(a \in A)$, and
(ii) $\lambda^*(a, px) = \lambda^*(a, p)\, \lambda(\delta(a, p), x)$ $(a \in A, p \in X^*, x \in X)$.
Thus, for a fixed $a \in A$, $\tau_{\mathfrak{A}, a}: p \to \lambda^*(a, p)$ $(p \in X^*)$ is a mapping of X^* into Y^*. In this case we say that $\tau_{\mathfrak{A}, a}$ is *induced by* $\mathfrak{A}$ *in the state* a. If a is not specified, then we speak of a mapping *induced by* A. A mapping is an *automaton mapping* if it can be induced by a finite sequential machine.

Further, we shall simply write λ for λ^*. Moreover, if not stated otherwise, by a sequential machine we shall mean a finite sequential machine.

1.4 Products and Complete Systems of Sequential Machines and Automata

Most of the earlier results concerning products are formulated for sequential machines. Products of sequential machines are obtained by compositions of certain machines in such a way that the resulting system is also a sequential machine. The most general form of such a composition of a finite system of sequential machines can be given by determining the actual input of each component machine, depending on the actual states of these machines and on the actual input signal of the system; otherwise, the work of the component machines is not affected. The output of the system also depends on the states of the component machines and on the input of the system.

Definition 4.1. Let $\mathfrak{A}_i = (X_i, A_i, Y_i, \delta_i, \lambda_i)$ $(i = 1, \dots, k;\ k > 0)$ be a system of sequential machines. Moreover, take two alphabets X, Y and two mappings

$$\varphi\colon A_1 \times \dots \times A_k \times X \to X_1 \times \dots \times X_k,$$
$$\psi\colon A_1 \times \dots \times A_k \times X \to Y.$$

Define the sequential machine $\mathfrak{A} = (X, A, Y, \delta, \lambda)$ by $A = A_1 \times \dots \times A_k$, $\delta((a_1, \dots, a_k), x) = (\delta_1(a_1, x_1), \dots, \delta_k(a_k, x_k))$ and $\lambda((a_1, \dots, a_k), x) = \psi(a_1, \dots, a_k, x)$, where $(a_1, \dots, a_k) \in A$, $x \in X$ and $(x_1, \dots, x_k) = \varphi(a_1, \dots, a_k, x)$. This machine $\mathfrak{A}$ is called the (general) *product* of $\mathfrak{A}_i$ $(i = 1, \dots, k)$ with respect to X, Y, φ and ψ. In notation,

$$\mathfrak{A} = \prod_{i=1}^{k} \mathfrak{A}_i[X, Y, \varphi, \psi] \quad \text{or} \quad \mathfrak{A} = (\mathfrak{A}_1 \times \dots \times \mathfrak{A}_k)\,[X, Y, \varphi, \psi]\,.$$

The mapping φ is called the *feedback function* of the product, while ψ is its *output function*.

It is clear from the definition of products of sequential machines that the output of a product is independent of the outputs of the component machines; it depends only on the underlying automata and on the input of the given product. Thus, in the sequel we confine ourselves to products of automata. For the sake of completeness, we give the formal definition of such products, too.

Definition 4.2. Let $\mathfrak{A}_i = (X_i, A_i, \delta_i)$ $(i = 1, \dots, k;\ k > 0)$ be a system of automata. Take two alphabets X, Y and two mappings

$$\varphi\colon A_1 \times \dots \times A_k \times X \to X_1 \times \dots \times X_k,$$
$$\psi\colon A_1 \times \dots \times A_k \times X \to Y.$$

Define the sequential machine $\mathfrak{A} = (X, A, Y, \delta, \lambda)$ by $A = A_1 \times \dots \times A_k$, $\delta((a_1, \dots, a_k), x) = (\delta_1(a_1, x_1), \dots, \delta_k(a_k, x_k))$ and $\lambda((a_1, \dots, a_k), x) = \psi(a_1, \dots, a_k, x)$, where $(a_1, \dots, a_k) \in A$, $x \in X$ and $(x_1, \dots, x_k) = \varphi(a_1, \dots, a_k, x)$. Then $\mathfrak{A}$ is the (general) *machine product* of the automata $\mathfrak{A}_i$ $(i = 1, \dots, k)$ with respect to X, Y, φ and ψ. We shall use the notations and notions of Definition 4.1 for machine products of automata, too.

Figure 1 shows a general machine product of the automata $\mathfrak{A}_1, \dots, \mathfrak{A}_k$.

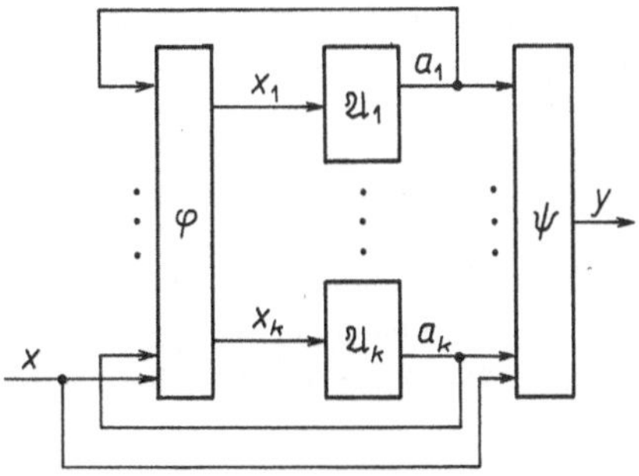

Fig. 1. Schematic diagram for the general machine product of automata $\mathfrak{A}_1, \dots, \mathfrak{A}_k$

Using a given system of automata, we want to simulate the work of sequential machines by machine products of automata from this system. Of course, the most important systems of automata are those which are complete in the sense that every automaton mapping can be induced by a machine product of automata from them.

Definition 4.3. A class $\mathscr{K}$ of automata is *complete* (with respect to the machine product) if every automaton mapping can be induced by a machine product of automata from $\mathscr{K}$.

Here and in the sequel, if we are dealing with a class $\mathscr{K}$ of automata, it is always assumed that $\mathscr{K}$ is nonvoid.

Another form of representation is given by

Definition 4.4. A class $\mathscr{K}$ of automata is *homomorphically complete* (with respect to the machine product) if every sequential machine is a homomorphic image of a submachine of a machine product of automata from $\mathscr{K}$.

It is clear that every homomorphically complete system of automata is complete. The converse statement is also true.

Theorem 4.5. *A class of automata is complete if and only if it is homomorphically complete.* □

The next result gives a characterization of homomorphically complete systems and thus, through Theorem 4.5, a characterization of complete systems.

Theorem 4.6. *A class $\mathcal{K}$ of automata is homomorphically complete if and only if $\mathcal{K}$ contains an automaton $\mathfrak{A} = (X, A, \delta)$ having a state $a_0 \in A$, two input signals $x_1, x_2 \in X$ and two input words $p_1, p_2 \in X^*$ such that $\delta(a_0, x_1) \neq \delta(a_0, x_2)$ and $\delta(a_0, x_1p_1) = \delta(a_0, x_2p_2) = a_0$.* □

We shall also refer to this theorem as *Letičevskiĭ's criterion.*

We next recall a stronger representation of automaton mappings by products.

Definition 4.7. A class $\mathcal{K}$ of automata is *isomorphically complete* (with respect to the machine product) if every sequential machine is isomorphic to a submachine of a macine product of automata from $\mathcal{K}$.

For isomorphic completeness we have

Theorem 4.8. *A class $\mathcal{K}$ of automata is isomorphically complete if and only if $\mathcal{K}$ contains an automaton $\mathfrak{A} = (X, A, \delta)$ with two distinct states $a_1, a_2 \in A$ and four (not necessarily different) input signals $x_1, x_2, x_3, x_4 \in X$ such that $\delta(a_1, x_1) = a_1$, $\delta(a_1, x_2) = a_2$, $\delta(a_2, x_3) = a_2$ and $\delta(a_2, x_4) = a_1$.* □

By Theorems 4.6 and 4.8, there are finite homomorphically and finite isomorphically complete systems of automata. Even more is true: if a class of automata is homomorphically complete, then it contains an automaton which itself forms a homomorphically complete system. A similar statement holds for isomorphic completeness.

Obviously, if the automaton $\mathfrak{B} = (X, B, \delta')$ is a homomorphic (isomorphic) image of the automaton $\mathfrak{A} = (X, A, \delta)$, then for every sequential machine $\bar{\mathfrak{B}} = (X, B, Y, \delta', \lambda')$ one can define a mapping $\lambda: A \times X \to Y$ in such a way that the sequential machine $\bar{\mathfrak{A}} = (X, A, Y, \delta, \lambda)$ can be mapped homomorphically (isomorphically) onto $\bar{\mathfrak{B}}$. Moreover, a machine product of automata can be given such that first, using the feedback function, we form its underlying automaton and then we add the output to this automaton. (These two facts explain why the conditions of homomorphic and isomorphic completeness can be expressed in terms of automata.)

The above observations demonstrate that it is reasonable to restrict the definition of the machine product in such a way that the resulting product is the underlying automaton. Such products have at least two advantages. First, they can be extended to sequential machines in an easy manner. Secondly, by choosing an initial state and a set of final states, they serve as finite state recognizers.

Definition 4.9. Let $\mathfrak{A}_i = (X_i, A_i, \delta_i)$ $(i = 1, \dots, k;\ k > 0)$ be a system of automata. Take an alphabet X and a mapping

$$\varphi: A_1 \times \dots \times A_k \times X \to X_1 \times \dots \times X_k .$$

Form the automaton $\mathfrak{A} = (X, A, \delta)$ with $A = A_1 \times \ldots \times A_k$ and $\delta((a_1, \ldots, a_k), x) = (\delta_1(a_1, x_1), \ldots, \delta_k(a_k, x_k))$, where $x \in X$, $(a_1, \ldots, a_k) \in A$ and $(x_1, \ldots, x_k) = \varphi(a_1, \ldots, a_k, x)$. The automaton $\mathfrak{A}$ is called the (general) *product* of $\mathfrak{A}_i$ $(i = 1, \ldots, k)$ with respect to X and φ, and is denoted by

$$\mathfrak{A} = \prod_{i=1}^{k} \mathfrak{A}_i[X, \varphi] \quad \text{or} \quad \mathfrak{A} = (\mathfrak{A}_1 \times \ldots \times \mathfrak{A}_k)[X, \varphi].$$

If $\mathfrak{A}_1 = \ldots = \mathfrak{A}_k = \mathfrak{B}$, then $\mathfrak{A}$ is a (general) *power of* $\mathfrak{B}$.

In the rest of this book the concept of the product will be used in the sense of Definition 4.9. Moreover, we frequently write the feedback function φ of the above product in the form

$$\varphi(\mathbf{a}, x) = (\varphi_1(\mathbf{a}, x), \ldots, \varphi_k(\mathbf{a}, x)),$$

where $\mathbf{a} \in A$ and $x \in X$. For every $i(= 1, \ldots, k)$, φ_i yielding the ith components of the vectors $\varphi(\mathbf{a}, x)$ is the ith *component feedback function* of the product.

We shall need an extension of φ_i $(1 \leqq i \leqq k)$ to words, which will also be denoted by φ_i. Let $\mathbf{a} \in A$ and $p \in X^*$ be arbitrary.

(1) If $p = e$, then $\varphi_i(\mathbf{a}, p) = e$, and
(2) $\varphi_i(\mathbf{a}, p) = \varphi_i(\mathbf{a}, q)\, \varphi_i(\delta(\mathbf{a}, q), x)$ for $p = qx$ $(q \in X^*, x \in X)$.

In other words, $\varphi_i(\mathbf{a}, p)$ is the word $\mathfrak{A}_i$ receives when we feed p to the product in state $\mathbf{a}$.

The general form of the products of automata $\mathfrak{A}_1, \ldots, \mathfrak{A}_k$ is illustrated in Fig. 2.

Let us introduce the operator $\mathbf{P}_g$: if $\mathcal{K}$ is a class of automata, then $\mathbf{P}_g(\mathcal{K})$ denotes the class of all products of automata from $\mathcal{K}$. It should be noted that every product has at least one, but only finitely many factors. In Chapter 5 we also shall consider the infinite case.

Let $\mathfrak{A}$ and $\mathfrak{B}$ be automata. We say that $\mathfrak{A}$ *homomorphically represents* $\mathfrak{B}$ if $\mathfrak{B} \in \mathbf{HS}(\{\mathfrak{A}\})$. Similarly, if $\mathfrak{B} \in \mathbf{IS}(\{\mathfrak{A}\})$, then we speak of *isomorphic representation.*

We next define homomorphic completeness.

Definition 4.10. A class $\mathcal{K}$ of automata is *homomorphically complete* with respect to the general product if $\mathbf{HSP}_g(\mathcal{K})$ is the class of all automata, i.e., if every automaton can be represented homomorphically by a product of automata from $\mathcal{K}$.

Isomorphic completeness is given by

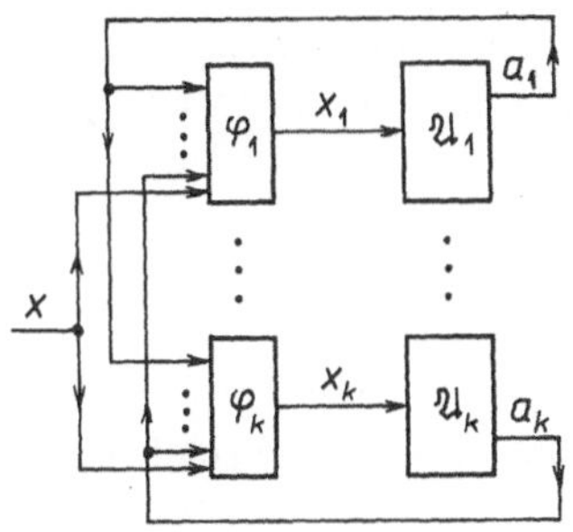

Fig. 2. Schematic diagram for the general product of automata $\mathfrak{A}_1, \ldots, \mathfrak{A}_k$

Definition 4.11. A class $\mathscr{K}$ of automata is *isomorphically complete* with respect to the general product if $\mathbf{ISP}_g(\mathscr{K})$ is the class of all automata.

It is clear that Theorems 4.6 and 4.8 are valid under Definitions 4.9, 4.10 and 4.11.

The above general form of products has many useful properties (e.g., the existence of simple finite homomorphically and isomorphically complete systems). On the other hand, it is quite complicated in the sense that all the component automata are fed back to one another. The loop-free product was the first important special case which decreased the complexity of the feedback. In a loop-free product there is a partial ordering between the components. A component automaton is steered by all automata preceding it under the given partial ordering, and there is no (other) feedback between the components.

Definition 4.12. Let $\mathfrak{A}_i$ $(i = 1, \dots, k;\ k > 0)$ be a system of automata, and $\leqq$ a partial ordering on $[k]$. A product

$$\prod_{i=1}^{k} \mathfrak{A}_i[X, \varphi]$$

is a *loop-free product* if, for every $i \in [k]$, φ_i is independent of its jth component ($j \in [k]$) whenever $j \nleqq i$ or $j = i$.

There have been many deep investigations concerning loop-free products. Here we mention only the following result, to which we shall also refer as the *Krohn-Rhodes theorem*:

Theorem 4.13. *Every automaton $\mathfrak{A}$ can be represented homomorphically by a loop-free product of two-state reset automata and group-like automata with simple groups which are homomorphic images of subgroups of $\mathscr{S}(\mathfrak{A})$.*

On the other hand, assume that an automaton $\mathfrak{A}$ is a homomorphic image of a sub-automaton of a loop-free product of automata $\mathfrak{A}_i$ $(i = 1, \dots, k)$. If G is a finite simple group which is a homomorphic image of a subgroup of $\mathscr{S}(\mathfrak{A})$, then for at least one $i (\in [k])$ a subgroup of $\mathscr{S}(\mathfrak{A}_i)$ can be mapped homomorphically onto G. Similarly, if H is a semi-group isomorphic to the characteristic semigroup of a full two-state reset automaton and H is a homomorphic image of a subsemigroup of $\mathscr{S}(\mathfrak{A})$, then for an $i (\in [k])$ a sub-semigroup of $\mathscr{S}(\mathfrak{A}_i)$ is isomorphic to H. □

A class $\mathscr{K}$ of automata is called *homomorphically complete* with respect to the loop-free product if every automaton can be represented homomorphically by a loop-free product of automata from $\mathscr{K}$. It follows directly from the second part of Theorem 4.13 that there is no finite class of automata which is homomorphically complete with respect to the loop-free product.

In order to obtain products with suitable representing power and with simple feed-backs, we introduce a hierarchy of products, at the bottom of which we shall find (an equivalent of) the loop-free product.

Definition 4.14. Let $\mathfrak{A}_t$ $(t = 1, \ldots, k; k > 0)$ be a system of automata and i a non-negative integer. A product

$$\mathfrak{A} = (X, A, \delta) = \prod_{t=1}^{k} \mathfrak{A}_t[X, \varphi]$$

is an α_i*-product* if each φ_t $(t = 1, \ldots, k)$ is independent of its jth component $(1 \leqq j \leqq k)$ whenever $j \geqq t + i$.

We sometimes speak of in α_i-product without specifying i. In such cases i is an arbitrary non-negative integer.

In the sequel, for α_i-products, in φ_t we shall generally indicate only those variables on which it may depend. For instance, if $i = 0$, then we frequently write $\varphi_1(x)$ for $\varphi_1(\mathbf{a}, x)$, where $\mathbf{a} \in A$ and $x \in X$.

Take the α_i-product $\mathfrak{A}$ above. If $\mathfrak{A}_t = \mathfrak{B}$ for every $t \in [k]$, then $\mathfrak{A}$ is an α_i*-power* of $\mathfrak{B}$. Moreover, if every φ_t $(1 \leqq t \leqq k)$ may depend only on the input signal, then we speak of a *quasi-direct product* of $\mathfrak{A}_1, \ldots, \mathfrak{A}_k$. If, in addition, $\mathfrak{A}_1 = \ldots = \mathfrak{A}_k = \mathfrak{B}$ also holds, then $\mathfrak{A}$ is a *quasi-direct power* of $\mathfrak{B}$. Obviously, the quasi-direct product is a special α_0-product, and each finite direct product having at least one factor is a quasi-direct product.

Figures 3 (3a, b and c) show, respectively, the general form of the α_2-, α_1- and α_0-products of $\mathfrak{A}_1$, $\mathfrak{A}_2$ and $\mathfrak{A}_3$.

In an α_i-product the set of indices of the component automata are ordered linearly. If we say that each automaton is steered by all those component automata which precede it, and speak of a feedback only in those cases when an automaton depends on a component automaton not preceding it, then i can be considered the length of feedbacks in an α_i-product.

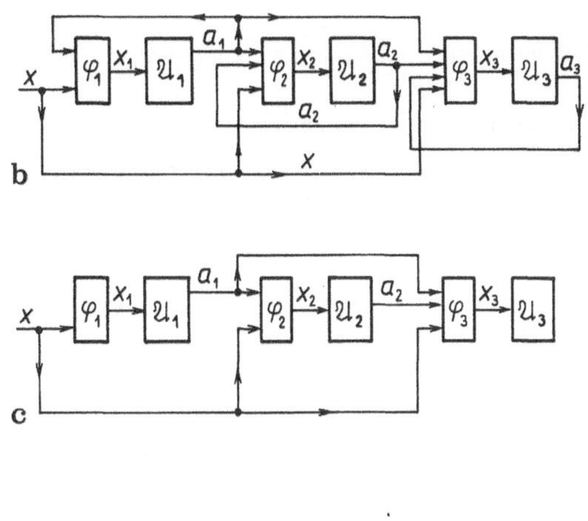

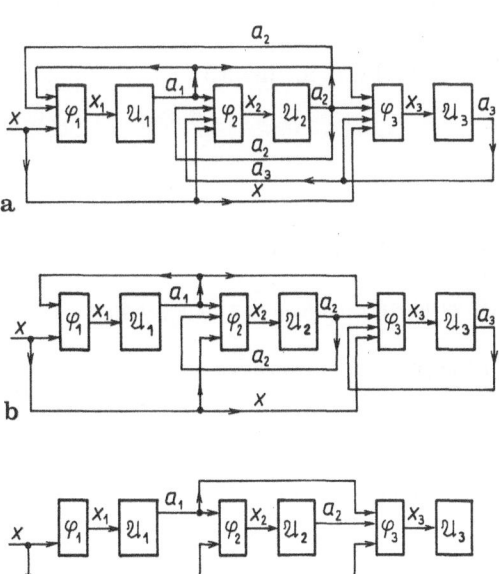

Fig. 3. **a** General form of the α_2-product of $\mathfrak{A}_1$, $\mathfrak{A}_2$ and $\mathfrak{A}_3$; **b** general form of the α_1-product of $\mathfrak{A}_1$, $\mathfrak{A}_2$ and $\mathfrak{A}_3$; **c** general form of the α_0-product of $\mathfrak{A}_1$, $\mathfrak{A}_2$ and $\mathfrak{A}_3$

In order to compare the representing powers of members of the above hierarchy with each other and with the representing power of the general product, we need some more terminology.

Let $\mathscr{K}$ be a class of automata and $i \geqq 0$ an integer. Then $\mathbf{P}_{\alpha_i}(\mathscr{K})$ will stand for the class of all α_i-products of automata from $\mathscr{K}$.

Definition 4.15. A class $\mathscr{K}$ of automata is *homomorphically complete* with respect to the α_i-product ($i \in \mathrm{N}$) if $\mathbf{HSP}_{\alpha_i}(\mathscr{K})$ is the class of all automata.

The concept of isomorphic completeness is similarly defined.

Definition 4.16. A class $\mathscr{K}$ of automata is *isomorphically complete* with respect to the α_i-product ($i \in \mathrm{N}$) if $\mathbf{ISP}_{\alpha_i}(\mathscr{K})$ is the class of all automata.

By Definitions 4.15 and 4.16, a class $\mathscr{K}$ of automata is homomorphically (isomorphically) complete with respect to the α_i-product if each automaton is a homomorphic (isomorphic) image of a subautomaton of an α_i-product of automata from $\mathscr{K}$.

Definition 4.17. The α_i-product is *homomorphically more general* than the α_j-product ($i > j$; $i, j \in \mathrm{N}$) if there exists a class $\mathscr{K}$ of automata for which $\mathbf{HSP}_{\alpha_j}(\mathscr{K}) \subset \mathbf{HSP}_{\alpha_i}(\mathscr{K})$. They are *homomorphically equivalent* if $\mathbf{HSP}_{\alpha_j}(\mathscr{K}) = \mathbf{HSP}_{\alpha_i}(\mathscr{K})$ holds for every class $\mathscr{K}$ of automata.

The corresponding concepts for isomorphic representation are given by

Definition 4.18. The α_i-product is *isomorphically more general* than the α_j-product ($i > j$; $i, j \in \mathrm{N}$) if there exists a class $\mathscr{K}$ of automata such that $\mathbf{ISP}_{\alpha_j}(\mathscr{K}) \subset \mathbf{ISP}_{\alpha_i}(\mathscr{K})$. Moreover, they are *isomorphically equivalent* if $\mathbf{ISP}_{\alpha_j}(\mathscr{K}) = \mathbf{ISP}_{\alpha_i}(\mathscr{K})$ holds for every class $\mathscr{K}$ of automata.

The above notions can be defined in a natural way for the pairs

(α_i-product, loop-free product),
(α_i-product, general product), and
(loop-free product, general product).

From Definitions 4.12 and 4.14, by Theorem 1.1, we have

Theorem 4.19. *The loop-free product is isomorphically equivalent to the α_0-product.* □

We next show that the formation of the product is transitive.

Theorem 4.20. *Let*

$$\mathfrak{A}_i = (X_i, A_i, \delta_i) = \prod_{j=1}^{l_i} \mathfrak{A}_{ij}(= (X_{ij}, A_{ij}, \delta_{ij}))\,[X_i, \varphi^{(i)}] \qquad (i = 1, \ldots, k)$$

and

$$\mathfrak{A} = (X, A, \delta) = \prod_{i=1}^{k} \mathfrak{A}_i[X, \varphi]$$

be products. Then there exists a product

$$\mathfrak{B} = (X, B, \delta') = (\mathfrak{A}_{11} \times \dots \times \mathfrak{A}_{1l_1} \times \dots \times \mathfrak{A}_{k1} \times \dots \times \mathfrak{A}_{kl_k})\,[X, \varphi']$$

such that $\mathfrak{A} \cong \mathfrak{B}$.

Proof. For arbitrary $i(= 1, \dots, k)$ and

$$\mathbf{b} = (a_{11}, \dots, a_{1l_1}, \dots, a_{i1}, \dots, a_{il_i}, \dots, a_{k1}, \dots, a_{kl_k})$$
$$(a_{ij} \in A_{ij}, i = 1, \dots, k, j = 1, \dots, l_i)$$

set $\mathbf{b}_i = (a_{i1}, \dots, a_{il_i})$. Moreover, for any $\mathbf{b} \in B$ and $x \in X$, let

$$\varphi'(\mathbf{b}, x) = (x_{11}, \dots, x_{1l_1}, \dots, x_{i1}, \dots, x_{il_i}, \dots, x_{k1}, \dots, x_{kl_k})$$
$$(x_{ij} \in X_{ij}, i = 1, \dots, k, j = 1, \dots, l_i)$$

where $(x_{i1}, \dots, x_{il_i}) = \varphi^{(i)}(\mathbf{b}_i, \varphi_i(\mathbf{b}_1, \dots, \mathbf{b}_k, x))$ $(i = 1, \dots, k)$. Obviously, φ' is well defined and the mapping $\mathbf{b} \to (\mathbf{b}_1, \dots, \mathbf{b}_k)$ $(\mathbf{b} \in B)$ determines an isomorphism between $\mathfrak{B}$ and $\mathfrak{A}$. □

From the constructive proof of Theorem 4.20, we directly obtain the following corollaries:

Corollary 4.21. *The formation of the α_0-product is transitive (up to isomorphism).* □

Corollary 4.22. *Let $\mathfrak{A}$ be an α_i-product of the automata $\mathfrak{B}_t$ $(t = 1, \dots, k)$ with $i > 0$, where each $\mathfrak{B}_t$ is an α_1-product of an automaton $\mathfrak{A}_t$ $(1 \leqq t \leqq k)$ with a single factor. Then there exists an α_i-product of $\mathfrak{A}_t$ $(t = 1, \dots, k)$ which is isomorphic to $\mathfrak{A}$.* □

We end this chapter with

Theorem 4.23. *Let $\mathfrak{A}_t = (X_t, A_t, \delta_t)$, $\mathfrak{B}_t = (X_t, B_t, \delta_t')$ and $\mathfrak{C}_t = (X_t, C_t, \delta_t'')$ $(t = 1, \dots, k)$ be automata such that*

(i) *$\mathfrak{B}_t$ is a subautomaton of $\mathfrak{C}_t$ $(t = 1, \dots, k)$, and*
(ii) *for every $t \in [k]$, $\mathfrak{A}_t$ is a homomorphic image of $\mathfrak{B}_t$ under a homomorphism ψ_t.*

Then, for every product [α_i-product $(i \in \mathbf{N})$] $\mathfrak{A} = (X, A, \delta) = \prod_{t=1}^{k} \mathfrak{A}_t[X, \varphi]$, there are a product [$\alpha_i$-product] $\mathfrak{C} = (X, C, \delta') = \prod_{t=1}^{k} \mathfrak{C}_t[X, \varphi']$ and a subautomaton $\mathfrak{B}$ of $\mathfrak{C}$ which can be mapped homomorphically onto $\mathfrak{A}$ under a mapping ψ. If each ψ_t $(t \in [k])$ is an isomorphism, then ψ can be chosen as an isomorphism, too.

Proof. Let us form the product [α_i-product] $\mathfrak{C}$ in the following way. Take an arbitrary $\mathbf{b} = (b_1, \dots, b_k)$ $(b_t \in B_t,\ t = 1, \dots, k)$ and an $x \in X$. Let $\mathbf{a} = (a_1, \dots, a_k)$ $(a_t \in A_t,\ t = 1, \dots, k)$ be the vector which satisfies the equalities $\psi_t(b_t) = a_t$ $(t = 1, \dots, k)$.

Then, $\varphi'(b_1, \ldots, b_k, x) = \varphi(a_1, \ldots, a_k, x)$. In all other cases φ' is given arbitrarily. Obviously, $\mathfrak{B} = (X, B, \delta'')$, determined by $B = \prod (B_t \mid t = 1, \ldots, k)$ and $\delta'' = \delta' \mid B \times X$, is a subautomaton of $\mathfrak{C}$. Define ψ by $\psi(\mathbf{b}) = \mathbf{a}$, where $\mathbf{b} = (b_1, \ldots, b_k)$, $\mathbf{a} = (a_1, \ldots, a_k)$, $b_t \in B_t$, $a_t \in A_t$ and $\psi_t(b_t) = a_t$ $(t = 1, \ldots, k)$. It is clear that the conclusions of Theorem 4.23 hold. □

These results, together with their constructive proofs, will be used frequently without any reference to them.

2. Homomorphic Representations

One of the most important tools of representations is homomorphism; while it is not too general, it is powerful enough. In this chapter, after studying certain special questions concerning homomorphic representations by α_0- and α_1-products, we show that from $i = 2$ the α_i-product is homomorphically equivalent to the general product, while for $i = 0, 1, 2$ the hierarchy is proper. Afterwards, we determine those automata which are simple in the sense that, whenever they can be represented homomorphically by a product, then a single-factor power of one of its components represents them homomorphically. The chapter ends with a proof of the existence of an algorithm to decide if a given automaton can be represented homomorphically by a product of automata from a fixed finite class.

2.1 A Homomorphically Complete System for the α_0-Product

In this section we present a class $\mathscr{K}$ of automata with three input signals such that every automaton of $n > 1$ states can be represented homomorphically by an α_0-product of automata from $\mathscr{K}$, the numbers of states of which do not exceed n. This class, beside its intrinsic interest, makes it possible to give simple proofs of certain results.

Definition 1.1. An automaton $\mathfrak{A} = (X, A, \delta)$ is *standard* if $X = \{x_0, x_1, x_2\}$, $A = [n]$ for some integer $n > 1$, and δ satisfies the three conditions below:

(i) $\delta(i, x_0) = i$,
(ii) $\delta(i, x_1) = i + 1 \pmod{n}$, and

$$\text{(iii)}\quad \delta(i, x_2) = \begin{cases} 2 \text{ if } i = 1, \\ 1 \text{ if } i = 2, \\ i \text{ if } i > 2, \end{cases}$$

where $i \in A$ is an arbitrary state.

Clearly, every standard automaton is a permutation automaton.

The following two lemmas are needed to prove that the class consisting of all standard automata and a suitably chosen two-state reset automaton (with three input signals) is homomorphically complete with respect to the α_0-product.

Lemma 1.2. *Let n and k be positive integers with $n > 1$. Then every counter with n^k states can be represented homomorphically by an α_0-power of an n-state standard automaton.*

Proof. Let $\mathfrak{A} = (\{x\}, [n^k], \delta)$ be an arbitrary counter with $n > 1$. If $k = 1$, then $\mathfrak{A}$ is isomorphic to an α_0-power of an n-state standard automaton with a single factor. Thus, assume that $k > 1$. By Corollary 1.4.21 and Theorem 1.4.23, it is enough to show that $\mathfrak{A}$ can be represented homomorphically by an α_0-product of an n^{k-1}-state counter and an n-state standard automaton.

Let $\mathfrak{B} = (\{x\}, [n^{k-1}], \delta')$ be a counter and $\mathfrak{C} = (\{x_0, x_1, x_2\}, [n], \delta'')$ a standard automaton. Take the α_0-product $\bar{\mathfrak{A}} = (\{x\}, \bar{A}, \bar{\delta}) = (\mathfrak{B} \times \mathfrak{C})[\{x\}, \varphi]$, where $\varphi_1(x) = x$, and for arbitrary $i \in [n^{k-1}]$,

$$\varphi_2(i, x) = \begin{cases} x_1 \text{ if } i = n^{k-1}, \\ x_0 \text{ otherwise.} \end{cases}$$

Clearly, $\bar{\mathfrak{A}}$ forms a cycle of length n^k. It is therefore isomorphic to $\mathfrak{A}$. □

Take two alphabets X and Y. For a fixed integer $n > 0$, consider a mapping $\tau : X^n \to Y^n$. Moreover, let $\mathfrak{R}_\tau = (X, R_\tau, \delta_\tau)$ be the automaton, where $R_\tau = \{(p, q) \in X^* \times Y^* \mid 1 \leqq |p|, |q| \leqq n, |p| + |q| = n + 1\}$ and, for arbitrary $(p, yq) \in R_\tau$ $(y \in Y)$ and $x \in X$,

$$\delta_\tau((p, yq), x) = \begin{cases} (px, q) \text{ if } |p| < n, \\ (x, \tau(p)) \text{ if } |p| = n. \end{cases}$$

Lemma 1.3. *For every $\tau : X^n \to Y^n$ $(n > 0)$, $\mathfrak{R}_\tau$ can be represented homomorphically by an α_0-product of an n-state counter and two-state reset automata.*

Proof. The characteristic semigroups of reset automata contain only the trivial (one-element) groups as their subgroups. Thus, by Theorem 1.4.13, every reset automaton can be represented homomorphically by an α_0-product of two-state reset automata. To prove Lemma 1.3, therefore; it is enough to show that $\mathfrak{R}_\tau$ can be represented homomorphically by an α_0-product of an n-state counter and certain reset automata.

Let $\mathfrak{A}_1 = (\{\bar{x}\}, [n], \delta_1)$ be a counter. Moreover, take the following automata $\mathfrak{A}_i = ([n] \times X, X \cup \{*\}, \delta_i)$ $(i = 2, \ldots, n + 1)$ and $\mathfrak{A}_{n+1+i} = ((X \cup \{*\})^n \times (Y \cup \{*\}), Y \cup \{*\}, \delta_{n+1+i})$ $(i = 1, \ldots, n)$, where, for arbitrary $a \in X \cup \{*\}$, $a', b \in Y \cup \{*\}$, $k \in [n]$, $x \in X$, $p \in (X \cup \{*\})^n$ and $i = 1, \ldots, n$,

$$\delta_{1+i}(a, (k, x)) = \begin{cases} x \text{ if } i \equiv k + 1 \pmod{n}, \\ * \text{ if } i > 1 \text{ and } k = n, \\ a \text{ otherwise,} \end{cases}$$

$$\delta_{n+1+i}(a', (p, b)) = \begin{cases} b \text{ if } p \notin X^n, \\ y \text{ if } p \in X^n \text{ and } y \text{ is the } (n - i + 1)^{\text{th}} \text{ letter of } \tau(p). \end{cases}$$

Clearly, all the $\mathfrak{A}_i$ $(i = 2, \dots, 2n + 1)$ are reset automata. Take the α_0-product

$$\mathfrak{B} = (X, B, \delta) = \prod_{i=1}^{2n+1} \mathfrak{A}_i[X, \varphi]$$

with $\varphi_1(x) = \bar{x}$, $(x \in X)$, $\varphi_i(k, a_2, \dots, a_{i-1}, x) = (k, x)$ $(i = 2, \dots, n + 1,\ a_j \in A_j,\ j = 2, \dots, i - 1)$, and

$$\varphi_{n+1+i}(k, a_2, \dots, a_{n+1}, \dots, a_{n+i}, x) = \begin{cases} (a_2 \dots a_{n+1}, *) & \text{if } i = 1\,, \\ (a_2 \dots a_{n+1}, a_{n+i}) & \text{otherwise,} \end{cases}$$

where $i = 1, \dots, n$, $k \in A_1$, $a_j \in A_j$ $(j = 2, \dots, n + i)$ and $x \in X$.

Take a pair $(p, yq) \in R_\tau$ $(y \in Y)$ and let $|p| = k$. We represent this (p, yq) by the following state $\mathbf{b}$ of $\mathfrak{B}$. The first component of $\mathbf{b}$ is k. Moreover, the $1^{\text{st}}, \dots, k^{\text{th}}$ letters of p are in the $2^{\text{nd}}, \dots, (k + 1)^{\text{th}}$ components of $\mathbf{b}$, in this order. Finally, the last $(n + 1) - k$ components of $\mathbf{b}$ contain the mirror image of yq. All other components of $\mathbf{b}$ have the value $*$. Let $\mathfrak{B}$ receive the input signal x in this state $\mathbf{b}$. The next state $\delta(\mathbf{b}, x)$ is obtained from $\mathbf{b}$ in the following way. Assume that $k < n$. The first component of $\mathbf{b}$ is then set to $k + 1$, the $(1 + k + 1)^{\text{th}}$ component is replaced by x, the contents of the $(n + 2)^{\text{th}}, \dots, (2n + 1)^{\text{th}}$ components are shifted one place to the right (the value of the rightmost component underflows) and the $(n + 2)^{\text{th}}$ component assumes the value $*$. All other components are unchanged. If $k = n$, then the first component of $\mathbf{b}$ is set to 1, the 2nd component gets the value x, the $3^{\text{rd}}, \dots, (1 + n)^{\text{th}}$ components are set to $*$, and the last n components contain the mirror image of $\tau(p)$. Therefore, $\delta(\mathbf{b}, x)$ represents (px, q) or $(x, \tau(p))$, depending on whether $|p| < n$ or not. On the bases of these properties, we give the formal definition of a subautomaton $\mathfrak{B}' = (X, B', \delta')$ of $\mathfrak{B}$ and that of a mapping $\psi : B' \to R_\tau$ under which $\mathfrak{R}_\tau$ is a homomorphic image of $\mathfrak{B}'$. Let B' consist of all $\mathbf{b} \in B$ for which there are words $p = x_1 \dots x_k$ $(x_1, \dots, x_k \in X)$ and $q = y_1 \dots y_{n+1-k}$ $(y_1, \dots, y_{n+1-k} \in Y)$ with $1 \leqq |p|, |q| \leqq n$ such that

$$\mathrm{pr}_i(\mathbf{b}) = \begin{cases} k \text{ if } i = 1, \\ x_{i-1} \text{ if } i = 2, \dots, k + 1, \\ y_{2n+2-i} \text{ if } i = n + k + 1, \dots, 2n + 1, \\ * \text{ otherwise.} \end{cases}$$

Moreover, let $\psi(\mathbf{b}) = (p, q)$. It is routine work to show that $\mathfrak{B}'$ is a subautomaton of $\mathfrak{B}$, and ψ is a homomorphism of $\mathfrak{B}'$ onto $\mathfrak{R}_\tau$. □

We need one more lemma to prove the main result of this section.

Lemma 1.4. *Let $\mathfrak{A} = (X, A, \delta)$ and $\mathfrak{B} = (Y, A, \delta')$ be automata. Assume that for an integer $n > 0$, there exists a mapping $\tau : X^n \to Y^n$ such that the following two conditions are satisfied:*

(i) $\delta(a, p) = \delta'(a, \tau(p))$ *for arbitrary* $a \in A$ *and* $p \in X^n$,
(ii) $\{\delta(\delta'(a, q), p) \mid a \in A,\ (p, q) \in R_\tau\} = A$.

Then an α_0-product of $\mathfrak{R}_\tau$ by $\mathfrak{B}$ homomorphically represents $\mathfrak{A}$.

Proof. Form the α_0-product $\mathfrak{C} = (X, C, \delta'') = (\mathfrak{R}_\tau \times \mathfrak{B})\,[X, \varphi]$, where, for arbitrary $(p, yq) \in R_\tau$ $(y \in Y)$, $a \in A$ and $x \in X$, $\varphi_1(x) = x$ and $\varphi_2((p, yq), x) = y$.

To an arbitrary state $\mathbf{c} = ((p, yq), a)$ of $\mathfrak{C}$ we correspond the state $\delta(\delta'(a, yq), p)$ of $\mathfrak{A}$. Assume that $\mathfrak{C}$ receives an input signal x in this state $\mathbf{c}$. If $|p| < n$, then $\delta''(\mathbf{c}, x) = ((px, q), \delta'(a, y))$, to which the state $\delta(\delta'(\delta'(a, y), q), px) = \delta(\delta(\delta'(a, yq), p), x)$ of $\mathfrak{A}$ is corresponded. In the opposite case, i.e., if $|p| = n$, then $\delta''(\mathbf{c}, x) = ((x, \tau(p)), \delta'(a, y))$. The state of $\mathfrak{A}$ corresponding to this $\delta''(\mathbf{c}, x)$ is $\delta(\delta'(\delta'(a, y), \tau(p)), x)$ which is equal to $\delta(\delta(\delta'(a, y), p), x)$ since, by (i), $\delta'(b, \tau(p)) = \delta(b, p)$ for arbitrary $b \in A$. (Observe that in the second case $q = e$.) In both cases we have that the mapping ψ given by $\psi(((p, q), a)) = \delta(\delta'(a, q), p)$ $(((p, q), a) \in C)$ is a homomorphism of $\mathfrak{C}$ into $\mathfrak{A}$. By (ii), ψ is a mapping onto A. □

Now we are ready to prove.

Theorem 1.5. *Every automaton with $n > 1$ states can be represented homomorphically by an α_0-product of two-state reset automata and n-state standard automata.*

Proof. Let $\mathfrak{A} = (X, A, \delta)$ be an arbitrary automaton with $n > 1$ states. From Theorems 1.4.13, 1.2.15 and 1.3.2, $\mathfrak{A}$ can be represented homomorphically by an α_0-product of two-state reset automata and n-state permutation automata. Thus, to prove Theorem 1.5 it is enough to show that every n-state permutation automaton is representable homomorphically by an α_0-product of two-state reset automata and n-state standard automata.

Take an arbitrary permutation automaton $\mathfrak{A} = (X, [n], \delta)$ with $n > 1$. For every $i (= 0, 1, 2)$, let t_i be the following permutation of $[n]$: $t_0(k) = k$, $t_1(k) = k + 1 \pmod n$ and

$$t_2(k) = \begin{cases} 2 \text{ if } k = 1, \\ 1 \text{ if } k = 2, \\ k \text{ otherwise,} \end{cases}$$

where $k \in [n]$ is arbitrary. Consider the automaton $\mathfrak{B} = (Y, [n], \delta')$ with $Y = \{y_0, y_1, y_2\}$ and $\delta'(k, y_i) = t_i(k)$ $(k \in [n], i = 0, 1, 2)$. Obviously, $\mathfrak{B}$ is an n-state standard automaton. Moreover, the set $\{t_1, t_2\}$ generates the group G of all permutations of $[n]$, and t_0 is the identity permutation of $[n]$. Let t be the least number such that every element of G can be given as a product of t_1 and t_2 with at most t factors.

For every $m \geqq t$, there exists a mapping $\tau : X^m \to Y^m$ such that $\delta(k, p) = \delta'(k, \tau(p))$ $(k \in [n], p \in X^m)$. Take $m = n^u \geqq t$ for some integer $u > 0$, and let τ be the mapping satisfying the previous equality under this m. Since both $\mathfrak{A}$ and $\mathfrak{B}$ are permutation automata, $\{\delta(\delta'(k, q), p) \mid k \in [n], (p, q) \in R_\tau\} = [n]$. Thus, from Lemma 1.4, $\mathfrak{A}$ can be represented homomorphically by an α_0-product of $\mathfrak{R}_\tau$ and $\mathfrak{B}$. Finally, by Lemmas 1.2 and 1.3, an α_0-product of n-state standard automata and two-state reset automata homomorphically represents $\mathfrak{R}_\tau$. □

2.2 A Minimal Homomorphically Complete System with Respect to the α_0-Product

It follows from Theorem 1.4.13 that there exists no finite system of automata which is homomorphically complete for the α_0-product. This implies the nonexistence of finite systems which are homomorphically complete with respect to the α_1-product. Thus, it is natural to raise the question of whether there are minimal homomorphically complete systems with respect to them. For $i = 1$ the problem is still unsolved. We show that for the α_0-product the answer is affirmative.

Definition 2.1. A class $\mathscr{K}$ of automata which is homomorphically complete with respect to the α_i-product ($i \in \mathbf{N}$) is *minimal* if, for each $\mathfrak{A} \in \mathscr{K}$, $\mathscr{K} - \mathfrak{A}$ is not homomorphically complete regarding the α_i-product.

Theorem 2.2. *There exists a class of automata which is homomorphically complete with respect to the α_0-product and minimal.*

Proof. Let $\mathscr{K} = \{\mathfrak{A}_i = (X_i, A_i, \delta_i) \mid i = 1, 2, \ldots\}$ be a (countable) system of automata such that for every automaton there exists an automaton in $\mathscr{K}$ which is X-isomorphic to it. Moreover, take an infinite sequence $p_0, p_1, \ldots$ of prime numbers with $p_1 > p_0$ and $p_j > p_{j-1} + p_0 \ldots p_{j-2} |A_{j-1}|$ $(j > 1)$.

Let us next form the system $\mathscr{K}' = \{\mathfrak{B}_i \mid i = 0, 1, \ldots\}$ of automata in the following way:

1. $\mathfrak{B}_0 = (X_0, D_0, \delta_0')$, where X_0 is an arbitrary alphabet, $D_0 = [p_0]$, and for arbitrary $d \in D_0$ and $x \in X_0$

$$\delta_0'(d, x) = d + 1 \pmod{p_0}.$$

In other words, $\mathfrak{B}_0$ is a generalized counter with p_0 states.

2. For every $i(= 1, 2, \ldots)$, $\mathfrak{B}_i = (C_i \times X_i, D_i \cup (C_i \times A_i), \delta_i')$, where $C_i = [p_0 \ldots p_{i-1}]$ and $D_i = [p_i]$. Moreover, for arbitrary $d \in D_i$, $(c, a) \in C_i \times A_i$ and $(c', x) \in C_i \times X_i$,

$$\delta_i'(d, (c', x)) = d + 1 \pmod{p_i}$$

and

$$\delta_i'((c, a), (c', x)) = \begin{cases} (c + 1, \delta_i(a, x)) \text{ if } c = c' \text{ and } c' < p_0 \ldots p_{i-1}, \\ (1, \delta_i(a, x)) \text{ if } c = c' = p_0 \ldots p_{i-1}, \\ 1 \ (\in D_i) \text{ if } c \neq c'. \end{cases}$$

Notice that D_i is a generalized counter subautomaton of $\mathfrak{B}_i$. Moreover, the $C_i \times A_i$ part is controlled by a $(p_0 \ldots p_{i-1})$-state generalized counter in such a way that, whenever the first component of a state and that of an input signal are equal, then in $\mathfrak{B}_i$ their second components behave in the same way as in the automaton $\mathfrak{A}_i$. Otherwise, $\mathfrak{B}_i$ passes into its generalized counter part D_i, and remains there. This latter remark implies that, if we apply an input word p having at least two consecutive occurrences of a letter to a state (c, a) of $\mathfrak{B}_i$, then $\delta_i'((c, a), p) \in D_i$.

We first show that $\mathscr{K}'$ is homomorphically complete with respect to the α_0-product. Take an arbitrary $\mathfrak{A}_i \in \mathscr{K}$. It is obvious that every generalized counter $\mathfrak{C} = (X, C, \delta')$ with $p_0 \dots p_{i-1}$ states can be represented homomorphically by an α_0-product (of the generalized counter subautomata) of $\mathfrak{B}_0, \dots, \mathfrak{B}_{i-1}$. Now form the α_0-product

$$\mathfrak{A} = (X_i, A, \delta) = (\mathfrak{C} \times \mathfrak{B}_i)\,[X_i, \varphi]$$

satisfying the following conditions. For every $x \in X_i$, $\varphi_1(x)$ is an arbitrarily fixed element in X. Moreover, $\varphi_2(c, x) = (c, x)$ $(c \in C, x \in X_i)$. It is easy to show that the set of all elements $(c, (c, a))$ forms a subautomaton of $\mathfrak{A}$ which can be mapped homomorphically onto $\mathfrak{A}_i$ under the mapping ψ given by $\psi((c, (c, a))) = a$. By the choice of $\mathscr{K}$, this implies that $\mathscr{K}'$ is homomorphically complete regarding the α_0-product.

To show the minimality of $\mathscr{K}'$, for every integer $i \geqq 0$, set $\mathscr{K}_i = \mathscr{K}' - \mathfrak{B}_i$. We shall prove that none of the counters with p_i states is in $\mathbf{HSP}_{\alpha_0}(\mathscr{K}_i)$. Let us first note that, if a counter $\mathfrak{C}$ is a homomorphic image of an automaton $\mathfrak{A}$, then $\mathfrak{A}$ has a subautomaton $\mathfrak{B}$ isomorphic to a counter which can be mapped homomorphically onto $\mathfrak{C}$. Moreover, $|\mathfrak{C}|$ always divides $|\mathfrak{B}|$. Therefore, it is enough to show that, whenever $\mathfrak{B} = (\{x\}, B, \delta')$ is a subautomaton of an α_0-product

$$\mathfrak{A} = (\{x\}, A, \delta) = \prod_{j=1}^{k} \mathfrak{C}_j[\{x\}, \varphi] \qquad (\mathfrak{C}_j = \mathfrak{B}_{i_j} \in \mathscr{K}_i,\ j = 1, \dots, k)$$

and $\mathfrak{B}$ is isomorphic to a counter, then $|B|$ is not divisible by p_i. For this, take a $\mathbf{b} = (b_{i_1}, \dots, b_{i_k}) \in B$ $(b_{i_j} \in B_{i_j},\ j = 1, \dots, k)$. For every j $(1 \leq j \leq k)$, denote by l_j the least positive integer such that $\delta'_{i_t}(b_{i_t}, \varphi_t(b_{i_1}, \dots, b_{i_{t-1}}, x^{l_j})) = b_{i_t}$ $(t = 1, \dots, j)$. We prove that $p_i \nmid l_j$ $(j = 1, \dots, k)$, which in the case $j = k$ means that $p_i \nmid |B|$. If $j = 1$, then $b_{i_1} \in D_{i_1}$, and thus $l_j = p_{i_1}$. For $i_1 = 0$ our claim is obviously true. Otherwise, by our remark following the definition of $\mathfrak{B}_{i_1}$, $\delta'_{i_1}(b_{i_1}, \varphi_1(x)\,\varphi_1(x)) \in D_{i_1}$. Therefore, b_{i_1} should also be in D_{i_1}.

Assume that $p_i \nmid l_t$ has been proved for every t less than a given j $(\leqq k)$, and let us distinguish the following two cases:

Case 1. $i_j < i$. For every t $(1 \leqq t \leqq k)$, define the relation ϱ_t on B in the following way: $\mathbf{c}_1 \equiv \mathbf{c}_2(\varrho_t)$ $(\mathbf{c}_1, \mathbf{c}_2 \in B)$ if and only if $\mathrm{pr}_s(\mathbf{c}_1) = \mathrm{pr}_s(\mathbf{c}_2)$ $(s = 1, \dots, t)$. Since $\mathfrak{A}$ is an α_0-product, each ϱ_t is a congruence relation of $\mathfrak{B}$. Therefore, as $\mathfrak{B}$ is isomorphic to a counter, for arbitrary $\mathbf{c}_1, \mathbf{c}_2 \in B$ and t $(1 \leqq t \leqq k)$ we have $|\mathbf{c}_1/\varrho_t| = |\mathbf{c}_2/\varrho_t|$. Moreover, $\varrho_1 \geqq \varrho_2 \geqq \dots \geqq \varrho_k$ and, for every t $(1 \leqq t < k)$ and arbitrary $\mathbf{c}_1, \mathbf{c}_2 \in B$, $\mathbf{c}_1[\varrho_t/\varrho_{t+1}]$ and $\mathbf{c}_2[\varrho_t/\varrho_{t+1}]$ are of the same cardinality. It should be observed that l_t is equal to the index of ϱ_t. Thus, $l_{t+1} = l_t\,|\mathbf{c}[\varrho_t/\varrho_{t+1}]|$ $(\mathbf{c} \in B,\ t = 1, \dots, k-1)$. It is also obvious that $|\mathbf{c}[\varrho_t/\varrho_{t+1}]| \leqq |D_{i_{t+1}} \cup (C_{i_{t+1}} \times A_{i_{t+1}})|$ if $i_{t+1} \neq 0$, and $|\mathbf{c}[\varrho_t/\varrho_{t+1}]| \leqq p_0$ for $i_{t+1} = 0$. But p_i is greater than the cardinality of $D_{i_j} \cup (C_{i_j} \times A_{i_j})$ in the case $i_j \neq 0$, and $p_i > p_0$ also holds. Therefore, $p_i \nmid l_j$.

Case 2. $i_j > i$. If $b_{i_j} \in D_{i_j}$, then $l_j = \mathrm{lcm}\,[l_{j-1}, p_{i_j}]$, implying $p_i \nmid l_j$. Thus, assume that $b_{i_j} = (c, a)$ $(c \in C_{i_j}, a \in A_{i_j})$. Let $\varphi_j(b_{i_1}, \dots, b_{i_{j-1}}, x^{l_{j-1}}) = p$ and $\delta'_{i_j}((c, a), p) = (c', a')$. If $c' = c$, then $p_0 \dots p_{i_j-1} \mid l_{j-1}$, implying $p_i \mid l_{j-1}$, which is a contradiction. Therefore, $c' \neq c$. But $\varphi_j(b_{i_1}, \dots, b_{i_{j-1}}, x)$ is equal to the last letter of $\varphi_j(b_{i_1}, \dots, b_{i_{j-1}},$

$x^{l_j-1}x)$. Consequently, from the definition of $\mathfrak{B}_{i_j}$, at least one of $\delta'_{i_j}((c, a), \varphi_j(b_{i_1}, \ldots, b_{i_{j-1}}, x))$ and $\delta'_{i_j}((c, a), \varphi_j(b_{i_1}, \ldots, b_{i_{j-1}}, x^{l_j-1}x))$ is in D_{i_j}. Thus, $b_{i_j} \in D_{i_j}$, which is again a contradiction. □

2.3 Homomorphic Representations of Automata by α_0- and α_1-Products of Smaller Automata

As mentioned in the previous section, there is no finite system of automata which is homomorphically complete with respect to the α_0- or α_1-product. Thus, it is reasonable to deal with the following problem: Is it possible to decide for an automaton $\mathfrak{A}$ and a finite class $\mathscr{K}$ of automata whether $\mathfrak{A} \in \mathbf{HSP}_{\alpha_0}(\mathscr{K})$ [$\mathfrak{A} \in \mathbf{HSP}_{\alpha_1}(\mathscr{K})$]? The answer to this question is unknown as yet. In this section we solve a weaker form of the above problem. It will be shown that there exists an algorithm to decide whether an automaton can be represented homomorphically by an α_0- or α_1-product of smaller automata.

Definition 3.1. Let $\mathfrak{A}$ and $\mathfrak{B}$ be automata. We say that $\mathfrak{A}$ is *smaller* than $\mathfrak{B}$ if $\mathfrak{A}$ has fewer states than $\mathfrak{B}$.

The next result gives an algorithm to decide whether an automaton can be represented homomorphically by an α_0-product of smaller automata.

Theorem 3.2. *An automaton $\mathfrak{A}$ with $n > 2$ states can be represented homomorphically by an α_0-product of smaller automata if and only if every simple group which is a homomorphic image of a subgroup of $\mathscr{S}(\mathfrak{A})$ is isomorphic to a permutation group of degree $n - 1$.*

Proof. The sufficiency follows from Theorem 1.4.13 through Theorem 1.3.2.

Using Theorems 1.2.15 and 1.2.17, from the second part of Theorem 1.4.13 we obtain the necessity of the conditions. □

For a class $\mathscr{K}$ of automata, let $\mathbf{P}_{1\alpha_1}(\mathscr{K})$ denote the class of all α_1-powers of automata from $\mathscr{K}$ with single factors.

The following lemma is obvious.

Lemma 3.3. *Let $\mathfrak{A} = (\mathfrak{A}_1 \times \ldots \times \mathfrak{A}_n)[X, \varphi]$ be an α_1-product. Then $\mathfrak{A}$ is isomorphic to an α_0-product $\mathfrak{B} = (\mathfrak{B}_1 \times \ldots \times \mathfrak{B}_n)[X, \varphi']$ where, for every $i \in [n]$, $\mathfrak{B}_i \in \mathbf{P}_{1\alpha_1}(\{\mathfrak{A}_i\})$.* □

From this lemma we immediately get

Theorem 3.4. *An automaton can be represented homomorphically by an α_1-product of smaller automata if and only if it can be represented homomorphically by an α_0-product of smaller automata.* □

Theorem 3.4. implies

Corollary 3.5. *There is an algorithm to decide whether an automaton can be represented homomorphically by an α_1-product of smaller automata.* □

We close this section with an example showing the existence of an automaton which can be represented homomorphically by an α_0-product of smaller automata with three factors, but none of the α_0-products of smaller automata with two factors represents it homomorphically. For this, we need a definition and a lemma.

Definition 3.6. Let $\mathfrak{A} = (X, A, \delta)$ be an automaton, and take a system $\Gamma = (A_i \subseteq A \mid i = 1, \ldots, k)$ of nonvoid subsets of A. Then Γ is a *cover* of $\mathfrak{A}$ if the following conditions are satisfied:

(i) $\cup (A_i \mid i = 1, \ldots, k) = A$, and
(ii) for arbitrary $i \in [k]$ and $x \in X$ there exists a $j \in [k]$ such that $\{\delta(a, x) \mid a \in A_i\} \subseteq A_j$.

The constructive proof of the next lemma presents a well-known method of homomorphic representations of automata by α_0-products.

Lemma 3.7. *Let $\mathfrak{A} = (X, A, \delta)$ be an automaton and $\Gamma = (A_i \mid i = 1, \ldots, k)$ one of its covers. Then there are two automata $\mathfrak{B} = (X, B, \delta')$ and $\mathfrak{C} = (B \times X, C, \delta'')$ such that $|B| = k$, $|C| = \max\{|A_i| \mid i = 1, \ldots, k\}$, and $\mathfrak{A}$ is a homomorphic image of a subautomaton of an α_0-product*

$$\bar{\mathfrak{A}} = (X, \bar{A}, \bar{\delta}) = (\mathfrak{B} \times \mathfrak{C})[X, \varphi].$$

Proof. Let $B = \{A_i \mid i = 1, \ldots, k\}$ and, for arbitrary i $(1 \leq i \leq k)$ and $x \in X$, denote by A_i^x a fixed A_j $(1 \leq j \leq k)$ with $\{\delta(a, x) \mid a \in A_i\} \subseteq A_j$. Define δ' by $\delta'(A_i, x) = A_i^x$ $(1 \leq i \leq k, x \in X)$.

To give C, set $l = \max\{|A_i| \mid i = 1, \ldots, k\}$, and let $C = [l]$. For arbitrary i $(1 \leq i \leq k)$, take a one-to-one mapping ψ_i of A_i into C. Then, for arbitrary $i \in C$ and $(A_j, x) \in B \times X$,

$$\delta''(i, (A_j, x)) = \begin{cases} \psi_t(\delta(a, x)) \text{ if } \psi_j^{-1}(i) \text{ exists, } \psi_j^{-1}(i) = a \text{ and } A_j^x = A_t, \\ \text{arbitrary } i' \in C \text{ otherwise.} \end{cases}$$

Obviously, $\mathfrak{C}$ is well defined.

Let φ_1 be the identity mapping on X, and $\varphi_2(b, x) = (b, x)$ for arbitrary $b \in B$ and $x \in X$. Take the subset $\bar{A}'$ of $\bar{A}$ consisting of all elements (A_j, i) for which there exists an $a \in A_j$ with $\psi_j(a) = i$. By the definitions of $\mathfrak{B}$ and $\mathfrak{C}$, $\bar{\mathfrak{A}}' = (X, \bar{A}', \bar{\delta}')$ is a subautomaton of $\bar{\mathfrak{A}}$, where $\bar{\delta}' = \bar{\delta} \mid \bar{A}' \times X$. Finally, the mapping $\psi : \bar{A}' \to A$ given by $\psi((A_j, i)) = a$ if and only if $a \in A_j$ and $\psi_j(a) = i$ is obviously a homomorphism of $\bar{\mathfrak{A}}'$ onto $\mathfrak{A}$. □

Example 3.8. Take the automaton $\mathfrak{A} = (X, A, \delta)$ where $X = \{x, y\}$, $A = \{a_1, a_2, a_3, a_4\}$ and δ is given by Table 1.

Assume that $\mathfrak{A}$ can be represented homomorphically by an α_0-product of smaller automata with two factors. In more detail, suppose that there is an α_0-product $\mathfrak{D}$

Table 1. Transition table of $\mathfrak{A}$

δ	a_1	a_2	a_3	a_4
x	a_2	a_3	a_4	a_1
y	a_2	a_3	a_1	a_4

Table 2. Transition table of $\mathfrak{B}$

δ'	$\{a_1, a_2\}$	$\{a_1, a_3\}$	$\{a_1, a_4\}$	$\{a_2, a_3\}$	$\{a_2, a_4\}$	$\{a_3, a_4\}$
x	$\{a_2, a_3\}$	$\{a_2, a_4\}$	$\{a_1, a_2\}$	$\{a_3, a_4\}$	$\{a_1, a_3\}$	$\{a_1, a_4\}$
y	$\{a_2, a_3\}$	$\{a_1, a_2\}$	$\{a_2, a_4\}$	$\{a_1, a_3\}$	$\{a_3, a_4\}$	$\{a_1, a_4\}$

$= (X, D, \delta_{\mathfrak{D}})$ of two automata $\mathfrak{B}$ and $\mathfrak{C}$ such that $|\mathfrak{B}|, |\mathfrak{C}| < 4$ and a subautomaton $\mathfrak{D}' = (X, D', \delta'_{\mathfrak{D}})$ of $\mathfrak{D}$ can be mapped homomorphically onto $\mathfrak{A}$ under a mapping $\psi : D' \to A$. We may suppose that $\mathfrak{D}'$ is strongly connected since $\mathfrak{A}$ is a strongly connected (permutation) automaton. For every $b \in \mathrm{pr}_1(D')$, take $\Gamma_b = \{d \mid d \in D', \mathrm{pr}_1(d) = b\}$, and let $\Gamma = \{\psi(\Gamma_b) \mid b \in \mathrm{pr}_1(D')\}$. Then Γ is a cover with the following properties:

(i) $|\Gamma| < 4$.
(ii) For arbitrary two $\psi(\Gamma_{b_1}), \psi(\Gamma_{b_2}) \in \Gamma$, $|\psi(\Gamma_{b_1})| = |\psi(\Gamma_{b_2})| < 4$.

It is therefore enough to show that, if a cover $\Gamma' = \{A_i \mid i = 1, \dots, k\}$ of $\mathfrak{A}$ satisfies $|A_i| = |A_j|$ and $1 \leqq |A_i| < 4$ for all $i, j \in [k]$, then $k \geqq 4$. But this can be proved by trivial computation. (In fact, it is sufficient to check the case $|A_i| = 2$ $(i = 1, \dots, k)$ since under the input signal x the automaton $\mathfrak{A}$ is isomorphic to a four-state counter.) Therefore, $\mathfrak{A}$ cannot be represented homomorphically by any of the α_0-products of smaller automata with two factors.

Take the system $\Gamma = \{\{a_1, a_2\}, \{a_1, a_3\}, \{a_1, a_4\}, \{a_2, a_3\}, \{a_2, a_4\}, \{a_3, a_4\}\}$ of subsets of A. Clearly, Γ is a cover of $\mathfrak{A}$. Using Lemma 3.7, we have two automata, $\mathfrak{B} = (X, B, \delta')$ and $\mathfrak{C} = (B \times X, C, \delta'')$, such that $|B| = 6$, $|C| = 2$, and an α_0-product $\mathfrak{D}$ of $\mathfrak{B}$ by $\mathfrak{C}$ can be mapped homomorphically onto $\mathfrak{A}$. (The transition function of $\mathfrak{B}$ is given by Table 2.)

Next, consider the system $\Gamma' = \{\{\{a_1, a_2\}, \{a_3, a_4\}\}, \{\{a_1, a_4\}, \{a_2, a_3\}\}, \{\{a_1, a_3\}, \{a_2, a_4\}\}\}$. It is routine work to show that Γ' is a cover of $\mathfrak{B}$. Therefore, by Lemma 3.7, there are automata $\mathfrak{B}_1$ and $\mathfrak{B}_2$ with $|\mathfrak{B}_1| = 3$ and $|\mathfrak{B}_2| = 2$ such that an α_0-product of $\mathfrak{B}_1$ by $\mathfrak{B}_2$ represents $\mathfrak{B}$ homomorphically. (In this case we can even take an isomorphic representation.) Thus, $\mathfrak{A}$ can be represented homomorphically by an α_0-product of $\mathfrak{B}_1$, $\mathfrak{B}_2$, and $\mathfrak{C}$. □

2.4 Homomorphically Complete Systems for α_i-Products with $i > 1$

In this section we show that every system of automata which is homomorphically complete with respect to the general product is also homomorphically complete regarding α_i-products with $i > 1$. We start with some preparations.

Let $\mathfrak{A} = (X, A, \delta)$ be an automaton satisfying Letičevskiĭ's criterion, i.e. there are a state $a_0 \in A$, two input signals $x_1, y_1 \in X$ and two input words $p = x_2 \dots x_{k_1}$, $q = y_2 \dots y_{k_2} \in X^*$ under which $\delta(a_0, x_1) \neq \delta(a_0, y_1)$ and $\delta(a_0, x_1 p) = \delta(a_0, y_1 q) = a_0$. Introduce the notations $a_i = \delta(a_0, x_1 \dots x_i)$ $(i = 1, \dots, k_1 - 1)$ and $a'_i = \delta(a_0, y_1 \dots y_i)$

($i = 1, \dots, k_2 - 1$). Clearly, we may suppose that $a_i \neq a_j$ if $i \neq j (0 \leqq i, j < k_1)$ and $a'_k \neq a'_l$ whenever $k \neq l$ $(0 \leqq k, l < k_2)$. Set $\bar{A} = \{a_1, \dots, a_{k_1-1}\}$ and $\bar{A}' = \{a'_1, \dots, a'_{k_2-1}\}$. (Note that at most one of $\bar{A}$ and $\bar{A}'$ may be empty.) It is also easy to see that we may put further restrictions on p and q according to the three cases below:

Case 1. $k_1, k_2 > 1$ and $\bar{A} \cap \bar{A}' = \emptyset$, as shown in Fig. 4.

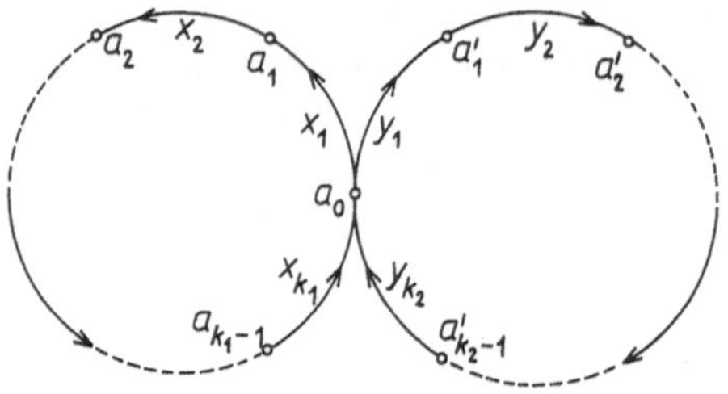

Fig. 4. Transitions under x_1p and y_1q in Case 1

Case 2. $k_1 > 1$ and $k_2 = 1$. This situation is illustrated in Fig. 5.

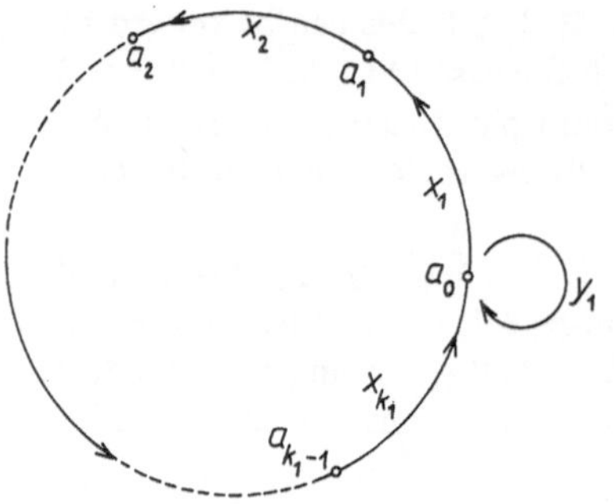

Fig. 5. Transitions under x_1p and y_1q in Case 2

Case 3. $k_1, k_2 > 1$ and for some i and j $(1 < i < k_1; 1 \leqq j < k_2)$, $\{a_1, \dots, a_{i-1}\} \cap \{a'_1, \dots, a'_{j-1}\} = \emptyset$, $a_i = a'_j$ and $q = y_2 \dots y_j x_{i+1} \dots x_{k_1}$, as visualized by Fig. 6.

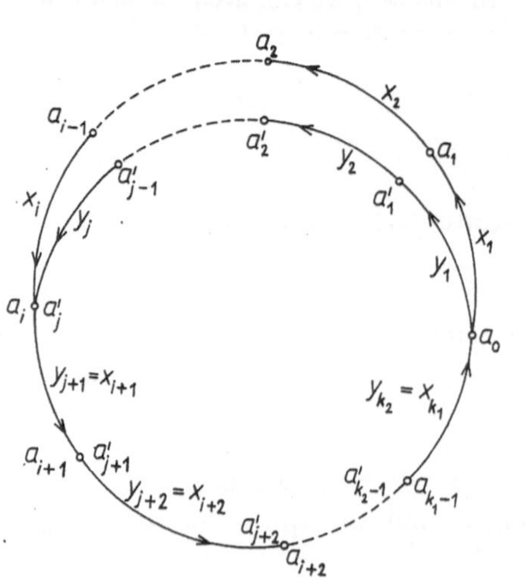

Fig. 6. Transitions under x_1p and y_1q in Case 3

Let us now form the α_1-product $\mathfrak{B} = (\{x_1, x_2\}, A, \delta') = (\mathfrak{A})\,[\{x_1, x_2\}, \varphi]$ with a single factor, where φ is given as follows.

(i) $\varphi(a_0, x_1) = x_1, \varphi(a_0, x_2) = y_1$.
(ii) $\varphi(a_i, x_j) = x_{i+1}$ $(i = 1, \dots, k_1 - 1; j = 1, 2)$.
(iii) $\varphi(a_i', x_j) = y_{i+1}$ $(i = 1, \dots, k_2 - 1; j = 1, 2)$.

In all other cases φ is given arbitrarily. Obviously, $\mathfrak{B}$ is well defined. Moreover, $\mathfrak{C} = (\{x_1, x_2\}, C, \delta'')$ with $C = \{a_0, \dots, a_{k_1-1}\} \cup \{a_1', \dots, a_{k_2-1}'\}$ and $\delta'' = \delta' \mid C \times \{x_1, x_2\}$ is a subautomaton of $\mathfrak{B}$. The subautomaton $\mathfrak{C}$ corresponding to Case 1 is shown in Fig. 7.

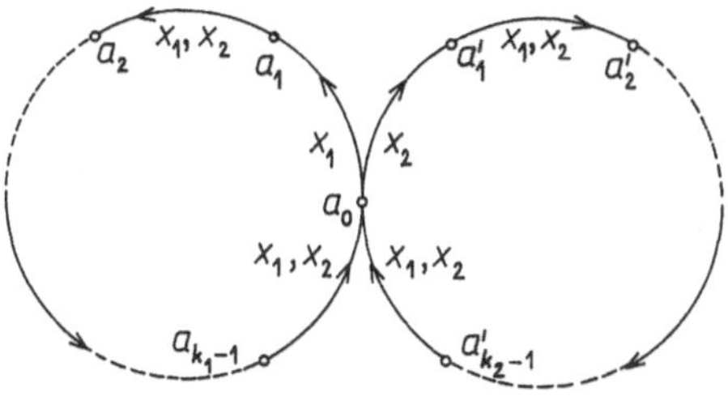

Fig. 7. Subautomaton $\mathfrak{C}$ of $\mathfrak{B}$ in Case 1

We can formulate the above result in the following way:

Lemma 4.1. *Let $\mathfrak{A}$ satisfy Letičevskii's criterion. Then an α_1-power of $\mathfrak{A}$ with a single factor has a subautomaton $\mathfrak{U} = (\{x_1, x_2\}, U, \delta_{\mathfrak{U}})$ such that the following conditions are satisfied:*

i) $U = \{u_0, \dots, u_{k_1-1}\} \cup \{u_0', \dots, u_{k_2-1}'\}$, *where* $k_1, k_2 \geqq 1$, $k_1 > 1$ *or* $k_2 > 1$, *and* $u_0 = u_0'$.

ii) $\delta_{\mathfrak{U}}(u_0, x_1) = u_1$, $\delta_{\mathfrak{U}}(u_0, x_2) = u_1'$ *and, for* $j \geqq 1$,

$$\delta_{\mathfrak{U}}(u_i, x_j) = \begin{cases} u_{i+1} & \textit{if } i < k_1 - 1\,, \\ u_0 & \textit{if } i = k_1 - 1\,, \end{cases}$$

$$\delta_{\mathfrak{U}}(u_i', x_j) = \begin{cases} u_{i+1}' & \textit{if } i < k_2 - 1\,, \\ u_0 & \textit{if } i = k_2 - 1\,, \end{cases}$$

where $j = 1, 2$.

iii) $u_1 \neq u_1'$. □

In Lemma 4.1 and further on, $u_1 = u_0$ if $k_1 = 1$. Similarly, u_1' stands for u_0 if $k_2 = 1$.

In Lemmas 4.3, 4.5, 4.6, and 4.8 and in Corollary 4.9, $\mathfrak{U} = (\{x_1, x_2\}, U, \delta_{\mathfrak{U}})$ will denote an arbitrary automaton satisfying the conditions (i)—(iii) of Lemma 4.1. To avoid technical difficulties, we shall suppose that $u_1' \notin \{u_0, \dots, u_{k_1-1}\}$. Moreover, for every integer t, u_t and u_t' will denote the states u_i and u_j' with $i \in \{0, \dots, k_1 - 1\}$

and $j \in \{0, \ldots, k_2 - 1\}$ such that $t \equiv i \pmod{k_1}$ and $t \equiv j \pmod{k_2}$. Finally, k will stand for lcm $[k_1, k_2]$.

For $i \geqq 1$, an α_i-product of α_1-powers of automata with single factors is obviously isomorphic to an α_i-product of the same automata, and thus we also have

Lemma 4.2. *Let $\mathfrak{A}$ and $\mathfrak{U}$ be the same as in Lemma 4.1. If, for some $i \geqq 1$, an automaton $\mathfrak{B}$ can be represented homomorphically by an α_i-power of $\mathfrak{U}$, then $\mathfrak{B}$ can be represented homomorphically by an α_i-power of $\mathfrak{A}$.* □

The following class of automata will play an important role in our investigations. Let m and n be natural numbers. Then $\mathfrak{S}_{m,n}$ will stand for the automaton $\mathfrak{S}_{m,n} = (\{x_1, x_2\}, [mn], \delta_{\mathfrak{S}_{m,n}})$ where for arbitrary $i\,(= 1, \ldots, mn)$,

$$\delta_{\mathfrak{S}_{m,n}}(i, x_1) = i + 1 \pmod{mn}$$

and

$$\delta_{\mathfrak{S}_{m,n}}(i, x_2) = \begin{cases} i + 1 \text{ if } i \not\equiv 0 \pmod{n}, \\ 1 \text{ otherwise}. \end{cases}$$

Therefore, $\mathfrak{S}_{m,n}$ is a counter under x_1. Moreover, in every state i, the input signal x_2 has the same effect as x_1 has if i is not a multiple of n; otherwise, x_2 sets $\mathfrak{S}_{m,n}$ to state 1.

We are now in a position to prove

Lemma 4.3. *Every automaton $\mathfrak{A} = (X, A, \delta)$ with m states can be represented homomorphically by an α_2-product*

$$\mathfrak{B} = (X, B, \delta') = (\mathfrak{R}_{mk,X} \times \mathfrak{S}_{m,k} \times \underbrace{\mathfrak{U} \times \ldots \times \mathfrak{U}}_{mk \text{ times}})\,[X, \varphi]$$

such that φ_1 depends only on the input.

Proof. Take the subset C of

$$B = X^{mk} \times [mk] \times \underbrace{U \times \ldots \times U}_{mk \text{ times}}$$

consisting of all vectors $\mathbf{b} = (x_1 \ldots x_{mk}, i, v_1, \ldots, v_{mk})$ $(x_1, \ldots, x_{mk} \in X)$, for which there are an $r \in [k]$ and $t \in [m]$ such that $i \not\equiv r \pmod{k}$, $tk + i - r \leqq mk$ and

(1) $$v_{tk-r+1} \ldots v_{mk} v_1 \ldots v_{tk-r} = u'_1 \ldots u'_k u_{k+1} \ldots u_{mk}$$

if $i \geqq k$, and

(2) $$v_{tk-r+1} \ldots v_{tk} v_1 \ldots v_{tk-r} v_{tk+1} \ldots v_{mk} = u'_1 \ldots u'_k u_{k+1} \ldots u_{tk} u_{r+1} \ldots u_{mk-tk+r}$$

if $i < k$.

Figures 8a and b visualize vector **b** corresponding to cases (1) and (2), respectively.

It should be observed that i determines a distinguished position of u_1': there is exactly one j ($2 < j \leq mk$) such that $j + i \equiv 3 \pmod{k}$ and the jth component of **b** is u_1'. (It is clear from the definition of **b** that, for every l ($2 < l \leq mk$) with $l \neq tk - r + 3$ and $l + i \equiv 3 \pmod{k}$, the lth component of **b** is u_1, and $u_1 \neq u_1'$.)

Assume that $A = \{a_1, \dots, a_m\}$. We shall construct the α_2-product

$$\mathfrak{B} = (X, B, \delta') = (\mathfrak{R}_{mk,X} \times \mathfrak{S}_{m,k} \times \underbrace{\mathfrak{U} \times \dots \times \mathfrak{U}}_{mk \text{ times}})[X, \varphi]$$

such that, for the above C, we have a subautomaton $\mathfrak{C} = (X, C, \delta'')$ of $\mathfrak{B}$ with the following properties.

For every $t \in [m]$, take a state

$$\mathbf{b}_t = (x_1 \dots x_{mk}, 1, u_2', \dots, u_k', u_{k+1}, u_{k+2}, \dots, u_{tk}, u_1', u_2, u_3, \dots, u_{mk-tk+1}),$$

where the distinguished position of u_1' in $\mathbf{b}_t$ is at the $(2 + tk)^{\text{th}}$ component. Let us correspond a_t to $\mathbf{b}_t$. Under an input signal $x_1' \in X$, the shift register part works independently of all other components, the second component counts the number of input signals fed into $\mathfrak{B}$, i.e., it is set to two, and the distinguished position of u_1' is moved one place to the left. This latter step will be carried out in such a way that the $3^{\text{rd}}, \dots, (2 + tk)^{\text{th}}$ components of $\mathbf{b}_t$ are shifted circularly one place to the left; and so are the $(2 + tk + 1)^{\text{th}}, \dots, (2 + mk)^{\text{th}}$ components. At this moment we have

$$\delta''(\mathbf{b}_t, x_1') = (x_2 \dots x_{mk}x_1', 2, u_3', \dots, u_k', u_{k+1}, u_{k+2}, \dots$$
$$\dots, u_{tk}, u_1', u_2', u_3, \dots, u_{mk-tk+2}).$$

We correspond $\delta(a_t, x_1')$ to $\delta''(\mathbf{b}_t, x_1')$. We repeat the above process until the length of the applied input word is less than tk. Thus, for an input word $x_1' \dots x_{tk-1}' \in X^{tk-1}$, we have

$$\delta''(\mathbf{b}_t, x_1' \dots x_{tk-1}') = (x_{tk} \dots x_{mk}x_1' \dots x_{tk-1}',$$
$$tk, u_1', u_2', \dots, u_k', u_{k+1}, u_{k+2}, \dots, u_{mk}),$$

to which $\delta(a_t, x_1' \dots x_{tk-1}')$ is assigned.

Next, take an arbitrary input signal $x_{tk}' \in X$ under which $\delta(a_t, x_1' \dots x_{tk-1}'x_{tk}') = a_s$. We shall then have

$$\delta''(\mathbf{b}_t, x_1' \dots x_{tk-1}'x_{tk}') = (x_{tk+1} \dots x_{mk}x_1' \dots x_{tk-1}'x_{tk}', 1, u_2', \dots$$
$$\dots, u_k', u_{k+1}, u_{k+2}, \dots, u_{sk}, u_1', u_2, u_3, \dots, u_{mk-sk+1}),$$

to which a_s is corresponded.

components	1	2	2+ 1	2+ 2	…	2+ $tk-r$	2+ $tk-r+1$	2+ $tk-r+2$	…	2+ tk	2+ $tk+1$	…	2+ $(t+1)k-r$	2+ $(t+1)k-r+1$	2+ $(t+1)k-r+2$	…	2+ mk
state	$y_1 \cdots y_{mk}$	i	$u_{mk-tk+r+1}$	$u_{mk-tk+r+2}$	…	u_{mk}	u'_1	u'_2	…	u'_r	u'_{r+1}	…	u'_k	u_{k+1}	u_{k+2}	…	$u_{mk-tk+r}$

a

components	1	2	2+ 1	2+ 2	…	2+ $k-r$	2+ $k-r+1$	2+ $k-r+2$	…	2+ $tk-r$	2+ $tk-r+1$	2+ $tk-r+2$	…	2+ tk	2+ $tk+1$	2+ $tk+2$	…	2+ mk
state	$y_1 \cdots y_{mk}$	i	u'_{r+1}	u'_{r+2}	…	u'_k	u_{k+1}	u_{k+2}	…	u_{tk}	u'_1	u'_2	…	u'_r	u_{r+1}	u_{r+2}	…	$u_{mk-tk+r}$

b

Fig. 8. a) Vector **b** in case (1); **b)** Vector **b** in case (2).

Denote the above correspondence by ψ. Then ψ is a homomorphism. To prove it, for arbitrary t $(1 \leqq t \leqq m)$ and $x_1, \dots, x_{mk} \in X$, set

$$B_t(x_1 \dots x_{mk}) = \{\delta''(\mathbf{b}_t(x_1 \dots x_{mk}), p) \mid p \in X^*, |p| < tk\},$$

where

$$\mathbf{b}_t(x_1 \dots x_{mk}) = (x_1 \dots x_{mk}, 1, u_2', \dots, u_k', u_{k+1}, \dots, u_{tk}, u_1', u_2, \dots, u_{mk-tk+1}).$$

We first show that $B_{t_1}(x_1 \dots x_{mk}) \cap B_{t_2}(x_1' \dots x_{mk}') = \emptyset$ $(x_1, \dots, x_{mk}, x_1', \dots, x_{mk}' \in X$, $1 \leqq t_1, t_2 \leqq m)$ if $t_1 \neq t_2$. Take two words $p_1, p_2 \in X^*$ with $|p_1| < t_1k$ and $|p_2| < t_2k$. Let $\delta''(\mathbf{b}_{t_1}(x_1 \dots x_{mk}), p_1) = \mathbf{c}_1$ and $\delta''(\mathbf{b}_{t_2}(x_1' \dots x_{mk}'), p_2) = \mathbf{c}_2$. If $|p_1| = |p_2| = l$, then $\mathbf{c}_1$ and $\mathbf{c}_2$ differ at least in their $(2 + t_1k - l)^{\text{th}}$ components. (The $(2 + t_1k - l)^{\text{th}}$ component of $\mathbf{c}_1$ is u_1' and the $(2 + t_1k - l)^{\text{th}}$ component of $\mathbf{c}_2$ is u_1.) If $|p_1| \neq |p_2|$, then at least the second components of $\mathbf{c}_1$ and $\mathbf{c}_2$ are different. Moreover, if $t_1 = t_2 = t$ and $p_1 \neq p_2$, then $\delta''(\mathbf{b}_t(x_1 \dots x_{mk}), p_1) \neq \delta''(\mathbf{b}_t(x_1' \dots x_{mk}'), p_2)$, since they differ at least in their first or second components, depending on whether or not $|p_1| = |p_2|$. Thus the correspondence ψ is a mapping. It is therefore a homomorphism.

We give next the formal definition of the α_2-product $\mathfrak{B}$.

For arbitrary $x_1, \dots, x_{mk} \in X$, $i \in [mk]$, $v_1, \dots, v_{mk} \in U$, $x \in X$ and t $(1 \leqq t < mk)$,

$$\varphi_1(x_1 \dots x_{mk}, i, x) = x,$$

$$\varphi_2(x_1 \dots x_{mk}, i, v_1, x) = \begin{cases} x_2 & \text{if } v_1 = u_1' \text{ and } i \equiv 0 \pmod{k}, \\ x_1 & \text{otherwise,} \end{cases}$$

$$\varphi_{2+t}(x_1 \dots x_{mk}, i, v_1, \dots, v_t, v_{t+1}, x) = \begin{cases} x_2 & \text{if } v_{t+1} = u_1', \\ & \text{or } t \equiv 0 \pmod{k}, i < k \\ & \text{and } v_{t-i+1} = u_1', \\ & \text{or } v_1 = u_1', \ i \equiv t \equiv 0 \pmod{k} \\ & \text{and } \delta(a_{i/k}, x_{mk-i+2} \dots \\ & \dots x_{mk}x) = a_{t/k}, \\ x_1 & \text{otherwise,} \end{cases}$$

and similarly,

$$\varphi_{2+mk}(x_1 \dots x_{mk}, i, v_1, \dots, v_{mk}, x) = \begin{cases} x_2 & \text{if } i < k \text{ and } v_{mk-i+1} = u_1', \\ & \text{or } v_1 = u_1', \ i \equiv 0 \pmod{k} \text{ and} \\ & \delta(a_{i/k}, x_{mk-i+2} \dots x_{mk}x) = a_m, \\ x_1 & \text{otherwise.} \end{cases}$$

Clearly, φ_1 depends only on the input.

It is easy to show that $\mathfrak{C}$ is a subautomaton of $\mathfrak{B}$. For this, take a $\mathbf{b} = (x_1 \dots x_{mk}, i, v_1, \dots, v_{mk}) \in C$ $(x_1, \dots, x_{mk} \in X)$ which, under an $r \in [k]$ and a $t \in [m]$ with $i \equiv r \pmod{k}$ and $tk + i - r \leqq mk$, satisfies the conditions (1) and (2) given at the beginning of the proof. Moreover, let $x \in X$ be an arbitrary input signal. Then, $\delta''(\mathbf{b}, x)$

$= (x_2 \dots x_{mk}x, i', v'_1, \dots, v'_{mk})$, where i' and $v'_1, \dots, v'_{mk}$ are determined according to the three cases below:

Case 1. If $r \neq k$ and $i > k$; or $r = k$ and $t \neq 1$, then $i' = i + 1$ and $v'_1 = v_2, \dots, v'_{mk-1} = v_{mk}, v'_{mk} = v_1$. (Observe that now $k \leqq i < mk$.)

Case 2. If $r \neq k$ and $i < k$, then $i' = i + 1$, $v'_1 = v_2, \dots, v'_{tk-1} = v_{tk}$, $v'_{tk} = v_1$, $v'_{tk+1} = v_{tk+2}, \dots, v'_{mk} = v_{tk+1}$.

Case 3. If $r = k$ and $t = 1$, then $i' = 1$, $v'_1 = v_2, \dots, v'_{sk-1} = v_{sk}$, $v'_{sk} = v_1$, $v'_{sk+1} = v_{sk+2}, \dots, v'_{mk-1} = v_{mk}, v'_{mk} = v_{sk+1}$, where $s \in [m]$ is given by $\delta(a_{i/k}, x_{mk-i+2} \dots x_{mk}x) = a_s$.

It is easy to see that in each of these three cases $\delta''(\mathbf{b}, x) \in C$.

In Case 1 $v'_1, \dots, v'_{mk}$ is obtained by a right-to-left circulation of $v_1, \dots, v_{mk}$. We obtain the same sequence by taking, for an arbitrary integer l with $lk \geqq (t + 1)k - r$, a right-to-left circulation of $v_1, \dots, v_{lk}$ together with a right-to-left circulation of $v_{lk+1}, \dots, v_{mk}$, since $v_1 = v_{lk+1}$. Therefore, $\mathfrak{C}$ has the properties stated at the beginning of the proof.

Finally, we give the formal definition of the homomorphism ψ of $\mathfrak{C}$ onto $\mathfrak{A}$. Let $\mathbf{b} = (x_1 \dots x_{mk}, i, v_1, \dots, v_{mk}) \in C$ $(x_1, \dots, x_{mk} \in X)$ be arbitrary. Then there are uniquely determined integers $r \in [k]$ and $t \in [m]$ fulfilling $i \equiv r \pmod k$ and $tk + i - r \leqq mk$, such that exactly one of the conditions (1) and (2) holds, depending on whether $i \geqq k$ or $i < k$. Put $\psi(\mathbf{b}) = \delta(a_{(tk+i-r)/k}, x_{mk-i+2} \dots x_{mk})$. Corresponding to the above three cases, one can easily verify that ψ is a homomorphism. On the other hand, ψ is obviously onto. □

Example 4.4. Let $\mathfrak{A} = (\{x, y\}, \{a_1, a_2, a_3\}, \delta)$ be an automaton, where δ is given by the transition table below:

δ	a_1	a_2	a_3
x	a_1	a_3	a_2
y	a_2	a_1	a_1

Moreover, let $k_1 = 3$ and $k_2 = 2$. The transition in $\mathfrak{C}$ from the state $(q, 1, u'_0, u'_1, u'_0, u'_1, u'_0, u_1, u_2, u_0, u_1, u_2, u_0, u'_1, u_2, u_0, u_1, u_2, u_0, u_1)$ $(q \in \{x, y\}^{18})$ under the input word $p = xxyxyxrx$ is shown by Fig. 9, where $r = yyyxy$. In this figure, q_i $(1 \leqq i \leqq 12)$ is the suffix of q with length $18 - i$. Each state is followed by its image under ψ. The distinguished occurrence of u'_1 is denoted by a boldface $\mathbf{u}'_1$. □

We shall also show that both $\mathfrak{S}_{m,k}$ and $\mathfrak{R}_{mk,X}$ can be represented homomorphically by an α_2-power of $\mathfrak{U}$. For this, we need the following simple result:

Lemma 4.5. *The counter* $\mathfrak{C} = (\{x\}, [k], \delta)$ *can be represented isomorphically by a quasi-direct power of* $\mathfrak{U}$.

Proof. Take the quasi-direct power

$$\mathfrak{B} = (\{x\}, U \times U, \delta') = (\mathfrak{U} \times \mathfrak{U})\,[\{x\}, \varphi]$$

with $\varphi_1(x) = x_1$ and $\varphi_2(x) = x_2$. Obviously, the subautomaton of $\mathfrak{B}$ generated by the state (u_0, u_0) is isomorphic to a counter of state k. □

$\mathfrak{R}_{mk,X}$	$\mathfrak{S}_{m,k}$	$\mathfrak{U}$ . . . . $\mathfrak{U}$	image
q	1	$u'_0\ u'_1\ u'_0\ u'_1\ u'_0\ u_1\ u_2\ u_0\ u_1\ u_2\ u_0\ \mathbf{u}'_1\ u_2\ u_0\ u_1\ u_2\ u_0\ u_1$	a_2
		$x \downarrow$	
q_1x	2	$u'_1\ u'_0\ u'_1\ u'_0\ u_1\ u_2\ u_0\ u_1\ u_2\ u_0\ \mathbf{u}'_1\ u'_0\ u_0\ u_1\ u_2\ u_0\ u_1\ u_2$	a_3
		$x \downarrow$	
q_2xx	3	$u'_0\ u'_1\ u'_0\ u_1\ u_2\ u_0\ u_1\ u_2\ u_0\ \mathbf{u}'_1\ u'_0\ u'_1\ u_1\ u_2\ u_0\ u_1\ u_2\ u_0$	a_2
		$y \downarrow$	
q_3xxy	4	$u'_1\ u'_0\ u_1\ u_2\ u_0\ u_1\ u_2\ u_0\ \mathbf{u}'_1\ u'_0\ u'_1\ u'_0\ u_2\ u_0\ u_1\ u_2\ u_0\ u_1$	a_1
		$x \downarrow$	
q_4xxyx	5	$u'_0\ u_1\ u_2\ u_0\ u_1\ u_2\ u_0\ \mathbf{u}'_1\ u'_0\ u'_1\ u'_0\ u'_1\ u_0\ u_1\ u_2\ u_0\ u_1\ u_2$	a_1
		$y \downarrow$	
q_5xxyxy	6	$u_1\ u_2\ u_0\ u_1\ u_2\ u_0\ \mathbf{u}'_1\ u'_0\ u'_1\ u'_0\ u'_1\ u'_0\ u_1\ u_2\ u_0\ u_1\ u_2\ u_0$	a_2
		$x \downarrow$	
$q_6xxyxyx$	7	$u_2\ u_0\ u_1\ u_2\ u_0\ \mathbf{u}'_1\ u'_\sigma\ u'_1\ u'_0\ u'_1\ u'_0\ u_1\ u_2\ u_0\ u_1\ u_2\ u_0\ u_1$	a_3
		$r = yyyxy \downarrow$	...
$q_{11}xxyxyxr$	12	$\mathbf{u}'_1\ u'_0\ u'_1\ u'_0\ u'_1\ u'_0\ u_1\ u_2\ u_0\ u_1\ u_2\ u_0\ u_1\ u_2\ u_0\ u_1\ u_2\ u_0$	a_2
		$x \downarrow$	
$q_{12}xxyxyxrx$	1	$u'_0\ u'_1\ u'_0\ u'_1\ u'_0\ u_1\ u_2\ u_0\ u_1\ u_2\ u_0\ u_1\ u_2\ u_0\ u_1\ u_2\ u_0\ \mathbf{u}'_1$	a_3

Fig. 9. A transition in $\mathfrak{C}$

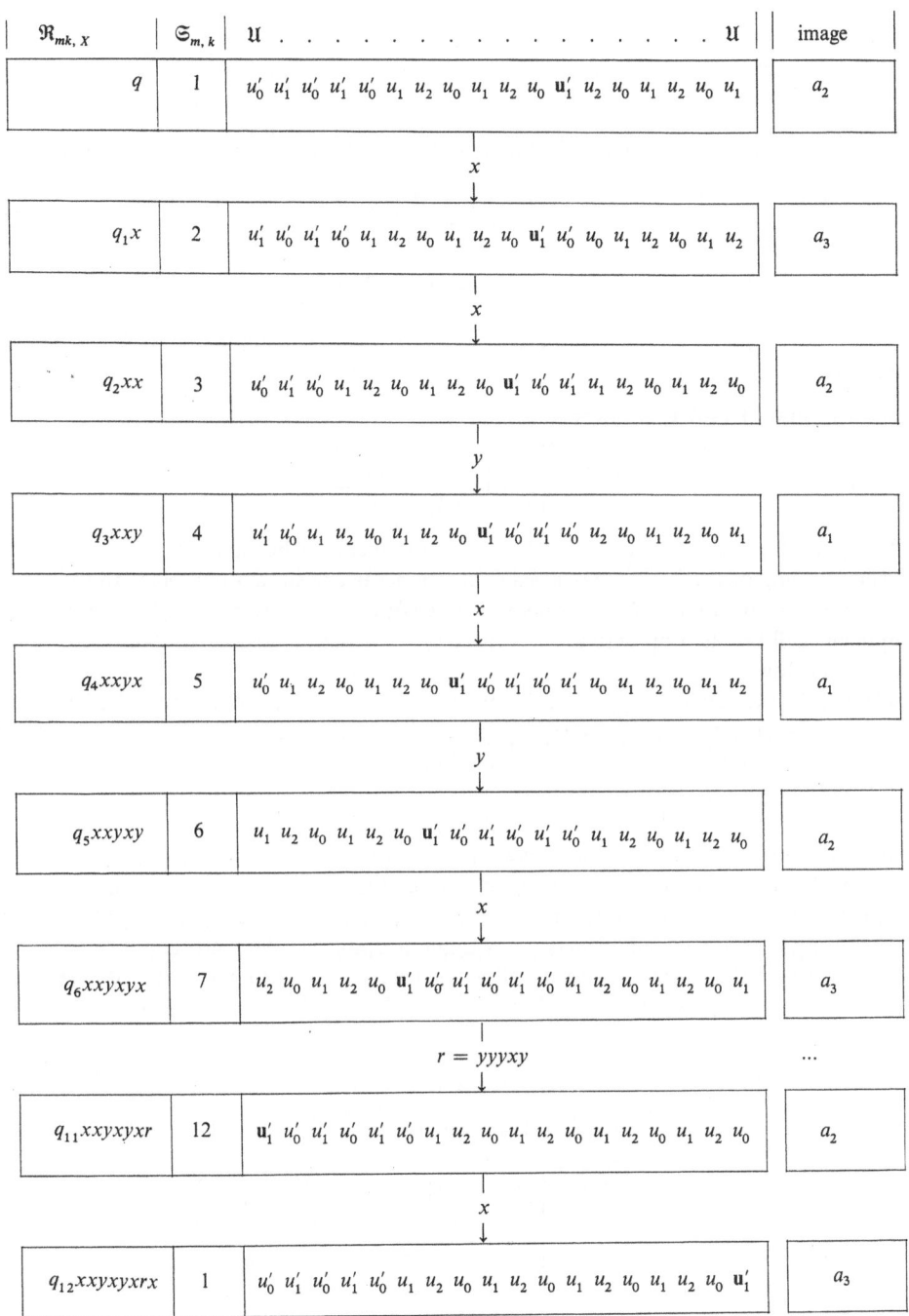

Lemma 4.6. *For arbitrary natural number m, $\mathfrak{S}_{m,k}$ can be represented homomorphically by an α_2-power of $\mathfrak{U}$ such that all but last component feedback functions are independent of the input.*

Proof. Let $\mathfrak{C}_k = (\{x\}, [k], \delta_{\mathfrak{C}_k})$ be a k-state counter. We first construct an α_2-product

$$\mathfrak{A} = (\{x_1, x_2\}, A, \delta) = (\mathfrak{C}_k \times \underbrace{\mathfrak{U} \times \dots \times \mathfrak{U}}_{mk\,\text{times}})[\{x_1, x_2\}, \varphi]$$

such that the subautomaton $\mathfrak{A}' = (\{x_1, x_2\}, A', \delta')$ of $\mathfrak{A}$ given below can be mapped homomorphically onto $\mathfrak{S}_{m,k}$. The state set of $\mathfrak{A}'$ consists of those elements $\mathbf{a} = (i, v_1, \dots, v_{mk}) \in A$ for which there exists a $j \in [mk]$ satisfying the following conditions:

(i) $i \equiv j \pmod k$ and $v_{mk-j+1} = u_1'$,
(iia) $(v_1, \dots, v_{k-i}) \in \{(u_{i+1}, \dots, u_k), (u_{i+1}', \dots, u_k')\}$ if $i \neq k$,
(iib) $(v_{tk-i+1}, \dots, v_{tk-i+k}) \in \{(u_1, \dots, u_k), (u_1', \dots, u_k')\}$ $(1 \leqq t < m)$, and
(iic) $(v_{mk-i+1}, \dots, v_{mk}) \in \{(u_1, \dots, u_i), (u_1', \dots, u_i')\}$.

Under any input signal x_l $(l = 1, 2)$, the first component will be set to $i + 1 \pmod k$, and the contents of the 2nd, ..., $(1 + mk)$th components are shifted one place to the left, and the value of the 2nd component underflows. Moreover, the $(1 + mk)$th component will be filled up with v_{mk+1}, where v_{mk+1} is determined according to the three cases below:

Case 1. $i \neq k$. Then, $v_{mk+1} = u_{i+1}$ or $v_{mk+1} = u_{i+1}'$, depending on whether $(v_{mk-i+1}, \dots, v_{mk}) = (u_1, \dots, u_i)$ or $(v_{mk-i+1}, \dots, v_{mk}) = (u_1', \dots, u_i')$.

Case 2. $i = k$ and $l = 2$, or $i = k$, $l = 1$ and $(v_1, \dots, v_{mk}) = (u_1', \dots, u_k', u_1, \dots, u_{(m-1)k})$. In this case, $v_{mk+1} = u_1'$.

Case 3. $i = k$, $l = 1$ and $(v_1, \dots, v_{mk}) \neq (u_1', \dots, u_k', u_1, \dots, u_{(m-1)k})$. Then, $v_{mk+1} = u_1$.

It is obvious that in all three cases $\delta(\mathbf{a}, x_l) \in A'$. Moreover, u_1' has a distinguished occurrence in $\mathbf{a}$ determined by $\min\{j \mid j \equiv i \pmod k,\ v_{mk-j+1} = u_1'\}$. Taking the mapping $\psi: A' \to [mk]$ given by $\psi((i, v_1, \dots, v_{mk})) = \min\{j \mid j \equiv i \pmod k, v_{mk-j+1} = u_1'\}$ $((i, v_1, \dots, v_{mk}) \in A')$, we shall clearly get a homomorphism of $\mathfrak{A}'$ onto $\mathfrak{S}_{m,k}$.

We next give the formal definition of φ ensuring the subautomaton $\mathfrak{A}'$ with the above properties. For arbitrary $i \in [k]$, $v_1, \dots, v_{mk} \in U$, j $(1 \leqq j < mk)$ and $t (= 1, 2)$, let

$$\varphi_1(i, v_1, x_t) = x,$$

$$\varphi_{1+j}(i, v_1, \dots, v_j, v_{j+1}, x_t) = \begin{cases} x_2 & \text{if } v_{j+1} = u_1', \\ x_1 & \text{otherwise,} \end{cases}$$

$$\varphi_{1+mk}(i, v_1, \dots, v_{mk}, x_1) = \begin{cases} x_2 & \text{if } i \in [k-1] \text{ and } v_{mk-i+1} = u_1', \\ & \text{or } i = k \text{ and } (v_1, \dots, v_{mk}) = (u_1', \dots, u_k', u_1, \dots, u_{(m-1)k}), \\ x_1 & \text{otherwise,} \end{cases}$$

$$\varphi_{1+mk}(i, v_1, \dots, v_{mk}, x_2) = \begin{cases} x_2 & \text{if } i = k, \\ & \text{or } i \in [k-1] \text{ and } v_{mk-i+1} = u_1', \\ x_1 & \text{otherwise.} \end{cases}$$

Since φ_1 is a constant mapping, by Lemma 4.5, $\mathfrak{S}_{m,k}$ can be represented homomorphically by an α_2-power of $\mathfrak{U}$ with $2 + mk$ factors such that all but the last component feed-back functions are independent of the input. □

Example 4.7. For $m = 3$, $k_1 = 2$ and $k_2 = 3$, Fig. 10 shows a transition in $\mathfrak{A}'$ under the input word $x_1x_2x_1x_1$. The distinguished occurrence of u_1' is denoted by a boldface $\mathbf{u}_1'$. Moreover, each state is followed by its image under ψ. □

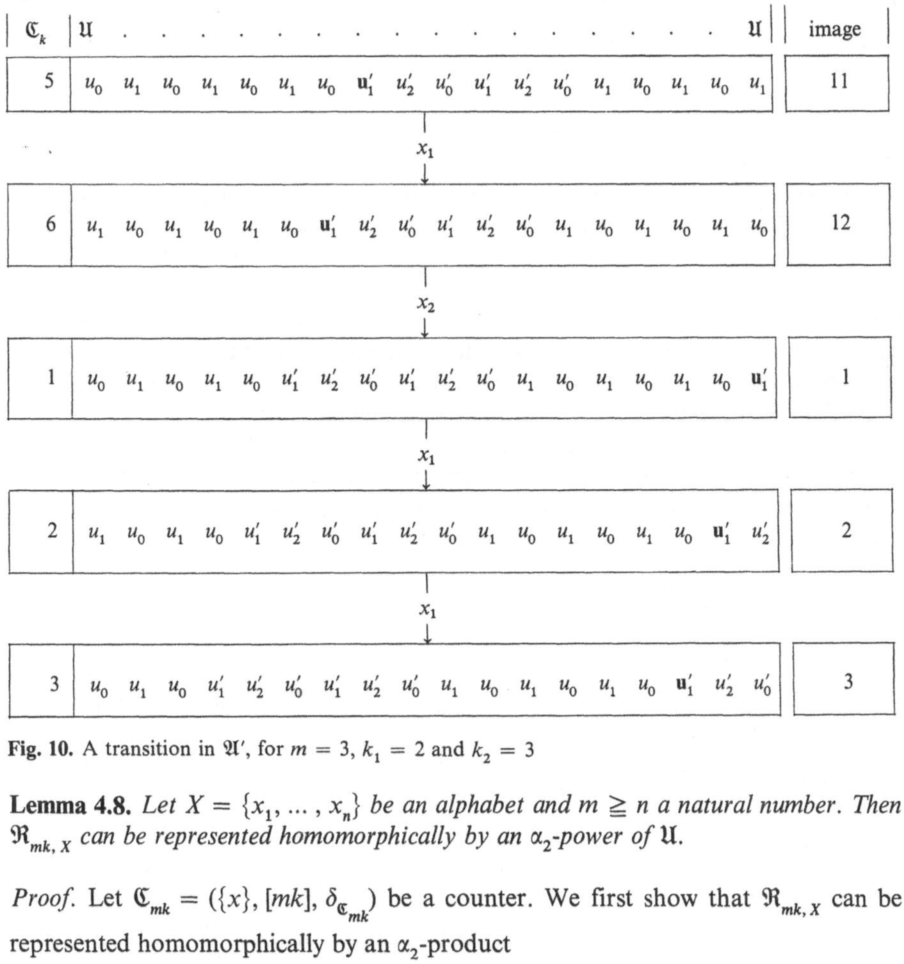

Fig. 10. A transition in $\mathfrak{A}'$, for $m = 3$, $k_1 = 2$ and $k_2 = 3$

Lemma 4.8. *Let $X = \{x_1, \ldots, x_n\}$ be an alphabet and $m \geqq n$ a natural number. Then $\mathfrak{R}_{mk,X}$ can be represented homomorphically by an α_2-power of $\mathfrak{U}$.*

Proof. Let $\mathfrak{C}_{mk} = (\{x\}, [mk], \delta_{\mathfrak{C}_{mk}})$ be a counter. We first show that $\mathfrak{R}_{mk,X}$ can be represented homomorphically by an α_2-product

$$\mathfrak{A} = (X, A, \delta) = (\mathfrak{C}_{mk} \times \underbrace{\mathfrak{U} \times \ldots \times \mathfrak{U}}_{(m+n)\,mk^2 \text{ times}})\,[X, \varphi].$$

The α_2-product $\mathfrak{A}$ will be formed in such a way that the last $(m + n)\,mk^2$ components will be treated as mk buffers $b_1, \ldots, b_{mk}$ of length $(m + n)\,k$. The counter points to the buffer used last. If $i \in [mk]$ is the content of the first component, then b_i contains the input signal that arrived last. Buffers are used in a circular way: if $i < mk$, then b_{i+1}, otherwise, b_1 is the next available buffer. Thus, the mk input signals that arrived last are contained by the buffers $b_{i+1}, \ldots, b_{mk}, b_1, \ldots, b_i$ in this order. The states u_1

and u_1' of $\mathfrak{U}$ are used to encode an input signal via the mapping $\tau: X \to \{u_1, u_1'\}^n$ given by $\tau(x_j) = u_1^{j-1} u_1' u_1^{n-j}$ $(j = 1, \ldots, n)$. In order to store an input signal x_j into the next available buffer, the $(m+j)k^{\text{th}}$ component of this buffer is set to u_1', and all the $(m+j')k^{\text{th}}$ components for $j' = 1, \ldots, j-1, j+1, \ldots, n$ are set to u_1. During this transition, all already stored input signals are shifted one place to the left, and the values of the first components of the buffers underflow.

More precisely, input signals are stored in such a way that, if the value of the counter is $i-1$ (or mk if $i = 1$), then the content $(v_1, \ldots, v_{(m+n)k})$ of the ith buffer b_i satisfies the following conditions:

$$v_{(t-1)k+1} \ldots v_{tk} \in \{u_1 \ldots u_k, u_1' \ldots u_k'\} \; (1 \leqq t \leqq m+1), \quad \text{and}$$
$$v_l = u_l \; ((m+1)k \leqq l \leqq (m+n)k) .$$

If this moment x_j is fed to $\mathfrak{A}$, then the contents of the $((m+j)k+1)^{\text{th}}, \ldots, (m+n)k^{\text{th}}$ components of the ith buffer are circulated one place from right to left, and the contents of its $1^{\text{st}}, \ldots, (m+j)k^{\text{th}}$ components are shifted one place to the left (the value of the first component underflows), and the $(m+j)k^{\text{th}}$ component becomes u_{t+1}' if its value was u_t' before the shifting. (Now $u_{t+1}' = u_1'$ since $u_t' = u_0'$ $(= u_0)$.) This process is repeated during the next $k-1$ tacts, independently of the input signals which arrive at $\mathfrak{A}$. From the $(k+1)^{\text{th}}$ tact up to the $(mk+1)^{\text{th}}$ one, the full contents of b_i are shifted one place to the left, the values of the first component underflow, and after each shifting the last component is filled up with u_{t+1} if its previous value was u_t.

We next give a formal definition of vectors occurring as those contents of buffers obtained by the previous process. For this, we need mk funktions $\varrho_j : A \to U^n$ which will select the code of an input signal stored in b_j.

For arbitrary $i, j \in [mk]$, introduce the notation

$$d(i, j) = \begin{cases} i - j \text{ if } j \leqq i, \\ mk - j + i \text{ if } j > i. \end{cases}$$

Let $\mathbf{a} = (i, v_1^1, \ldots, v_{(m+n)k}^1, \ldots, v_1^{mk}, \ldots, v_{(m+n)k}^{mk}) \in A$ and $j \in [mk]$ be arbitrary. Define $\varrho_j : A \to U^n$ by

$$\varrho_j(\mathbf{a}) = v_{mk-d(i,j)+k}^j \ldots v_{mk-d(i,j)+nk}^j .$$

Using these ϱ_j, we give one more function $\varrho : A \to U^{mnk}$, defined by

$$\varrho(\mathbf{a}) = \varrho_{i+1}(\mathbf{a}) \ldots \varrho_{mk}(\mathbf{a}) \, \varrho_1(\mathbf{a}) \ldots \varrho_i(\mathbf{a}) .$$

Therefore, ϱ will read off the buffers the word formed by the input signals that arrived during the last mk tacts.

Denote by B the set of all elements $\mathbf{a} = (i, v_1^1, \ldots, v_{(m+n)k}^1, \ldots, v_1^{mk}, \ldots, v_{(m+n)k}^{mk}) \in A$ which satisfy the conditions below:

(i) There exists a word $y_1 \ldots y_{mk}$ $(y_1, \ldots, y_{mk} \in X)$ with $\varrho(\mathbf{a}) = \tau(y_1) \ldots \tau(y_{mk})$.

(iia) For every $j \in [mk]$, if $d(i, j) \geqq k - 1$, then

$$v_1^j \ldots v_{k-(r+1)}^j \in \{u_{r+2} \ldots u_k, u_{r+2}' \ldots u_k'\},$$
$$v_{tk-r}^j \ldots v_{(t+1)k-(r+1)}^j \in \{u_1 \ldots u_k, u_1' \ldots u_k'\} \; (1 \leqq t < m+n),$$
$$v_{(m+n)k-r}^j \ldots v_{(m+n)k}^j \in \{u_1 \ldots u_{r+1}, u_1' \ldots u_{r+1}'\} ,$$

where $r \in \{0, 1, \dots, k-1\}$ is an integer with $j + r \equiv i \pmod{k}$.
(iib) For every $j \in [mk]$, if $d(i,j) < k-1$, then

$$v_1^j \dots v_{k-(d(i,j)+1)}^j \in \{u_{d(i,j)+2} \dots u_k, u'_{d(i,j)+2} \dots u'_k\},$$

$$v_{tk-d(i,j)}^j \dots v_{(t+1)k-(d(i,j)+1)}^j \in \{u_1 \dots u_k, u'_1 \dots u'_k\} \qquad (1 \leqq t \leqq m),$$

$$v_{tk-d(i,j)}^j \dots v_{(t+1)k-(d(i,j)+1)}^j \in \{u_1 \dots u_k, u'_1 \dots u'_{d(i,j)+1} u_{d(i,j)+2} \dots u_k\}$$

$$(m < t < m+n),$$

$$v_{(m+n)k-d(i,j)}^j \dots v_{(m+n)k}^j \in \{u_1 \dots u_{d(i,j)+1}, u'_1 \dots u'_{d(i,j)+1}\}.$$

(iii) For every $j \in [mk]$, $\{v_t^j, \dots, v_{(m+n)k}^j\} \subseteq \{u_0, \dots, u_{k_1-1}\}$, where $t = (m+n)k - d(i,j) + k$.

It should be observed that, by (i), for every j with $d(i,j) < k-1$, either $v_{(m+n)k-d(i,j)}^j \dots v_{(m+n)k}^j = u'_1 \dots u'_{d(i,j)+1}$ or there is exactly one t $(m+1 \leqq t < m+n)$ such that

$$v_{tk-d(i,j)}^j \dots v_{(t+1)k-(d(i,j)+1)}^j = u'_1 \dots u'_{d(i,j)+1} u_{d(i,j)+2} \dots u_k.$$

We next define the feedback function φ of the product $\mathfrak{A}$ under which B forms a subautomaton $\mathfrak{B} = (X, B, \delta')$, and every input signal effects the shifting of the components of a vector from B as described at the beginning of the proof. Then the mapping $\psi : B \to X^{mk}$ given by

$$\psi(\mathbf{b}) = y_1 \dots y_{mk} \Leftrightarrow \varrho(\mathbf{b}) = \tau(y_1) \dots \tau(y_{mk}) \ (\mathbf{b} \in B, y_1, \dots, y_{mk} \in X)$$

will be a homomorphism of $\mathfrak{B}$ onto $\mathfrak{R}_{mk,X}$.

For arbitrary $i \in [mk]$, $v_1, \dots, v_{(m+n)mk^2} \in U$, $j \in [n]$ and t $(1 \leqq t < (m+n)mk^2)$, let

$$\varphi_1(i, v_1, x_j) = x,$$

$$\varphi_{1+t}(i, v_1, \dots, v_t, v_{t+1}, x_j)$$

$$= \begin{cases} x_2 \text{ if } v_{t+1} = u'_1 \text{ and } t \not\equiv 0 \pmod{(m+n)k}, \text{ or} \\ \quad t = i'(m+n)k - (n-j)k, \text{ where } i' \in [mk] \text{ is determined} \\ \quad \text{by } i + 1 \equiv i' \pmod{mk}, \text{ or } t \equiv 0 \pmod{k} \text{ and there exist} \\ \quad \text{an } i' \in [mk] \text{ and an } r \in \{0, \dots, k-2\} \text{ such that} \\ \quad i' + r \equiv i \pmod{mk},\ v_{t-r} = u'_1 \text{ and} \\ \quad (i'-1)(m+n)k < t \leqq i'(m+n)k, \\ x_1 \text{ otherwise,} \end{cases}$$

and similarly,

$$\varphi_{1+(m+n)mk^2}(i, v_1, \dots, v_{(m+n)mk^2}, x_j)$$

$$= \begin{cases} x_2 \text{ if } i = mk-1 \text{ and } j = n, \text{ or} \\ \quad \text{there exists an } r \in \{0, \dots, k-2\} \text{ with} \\ \quad mk + r \equiv i \pmod{mk} \text{ and } v_{(m+n)mk^2-r} = u'_1, \\ x_1 \text{ otherwise.} \end{cases}$$

We now prove that B forms a subautomaton of $\mathfrak{A}$. Take a state $\mathbf{a} = (i, v_1^1, \ldots, v_{(m+n)k}^1, \ldots, v_1^{mk}, \ldots, v_{(m+n)k}^{mk})$ satisfying the conditions (iia), (iib) and (iii), and let $y_1 \ldots y_{mk}$ $(y_1, \ldots, y_{mk} \in X)$ be a word under which $\mathbf{a}$ satisfies (i). Moreover, let $y \in X$ be an arbitrary input signal, and denote by $\mathbf{b} = (i', \bar{v}_1^1, \ldots, \bar{v}_{(m+n)k}^1, \ldots, \bar{v}_1^{mk}, \ldots, \bar{v}_{(m+n)k}^{mk})$ the state $\delta(\mathbf{a}, y)$, where $i' = i + 1$ if $i < mk$, and $i' = 1$ for $i = mk$. Let $j \in [mk]$ be arbitrary, and distinguish the following three cases:

Case 1. $d(i, j) \geqq k - 1$ and $j \not\equiv i + 1 \pmod{mk}$. Then $\bar{v}_1^j \ldots \bar{v}_{(m+n)k}^j = v_2^j \ldots v_{(m+n)k}^j v_{(m+n)k+1}^j$, where $v_{(m+n)k+1}^j = u_{l+1}$ if $v_{(m+n)k}^j = u_l$. (Observe that $v_{(m+n)k}^j \in \{u_0, \ldots, u_{k_1-1}\}$ since $d(i, j) \geqq k - 1$.) Therefore, $\bar{v}_{mk-d(i',j)+k}^j \ldots \bar{v}_{mk-d(i',j)+nk}^j = v_{mk-d(i,j)+k}^j \ldots v_{mk-d(i,j)+nk}^j$, i.e. $\varrho_j(\mathbf{b}) = \varrho_j(\mathbf{a})$.

Case 2. $j \equiv i + 1 \pmod{mk}$. Let $y = x_l$ $(1 \leqq l \leqq n)$. Then, by (iia), $\{v_1^j \ldots v_k^j, \ldots, v_{mk+1}^j \ldots v_{(m+1)k}^j\} \subseteq \{u_1 \ldots u_k, u_1' \ldots u_k'\}$ and, by (iii), $v_{(m+1)k+1}^j \ldots v_{(m+2)k}^j = \ldots = v_{(m+n)k-(k-1)}^j \ldots v_{(m+n)k}^j = u_1 \ldots u_k$. Thus, $\bar{v}_1^j \ldots \bar{v}_{mk}^j = v_2^j \ldots v_{mk+1}^j$ and, for every $t \in [n]$, $\bar{v}_{(m+t)k-(k-1)}^j \ldots \bar{v}_{(m+t)k}^j$ equals $v_{(m+t)k-(k-2)}^j \ldots v_{(m+t)k}^j u_1'$ or $v_{(m+t)k-(k-2)}^j \ldots v_{(m+t)k}^j u_1$, depending on whether or not $t = l$. Therefore, $\varrho_j(\mathbf{b}) = \tau(y)$.

Case 3. $d(i, j) < k - 1$. Assume that $v_{(m+t)k-d(i,j)}^j = u_1'$ $(t \in [n])$. In this case, $\bar{v}_1^j \ldots \bar{v}_{(m+t)k}^j = v_2^j \ldots v_{(m+t)k}^j u_{d(i,j)+2}'$ and $\bar{v}_{(m+t)k+1}^j \ldots \bar{v}_{(m+n)k}^j = v_{(m+t)k+2}^j \ldots v_{(m+n)k}^j v_{(m+t)k+1}^j$. Therefore, $\varrho_j(\mathbf{b}) = \varrho_j(\mathbf{a})$.

We have that

$$\begin{aligned}\varrho(\mathbf{b}) &= \varrho_{i+2}(\mathbf{b}) \ldots \varrho_{mk}(\mathbf{b})\, \varrho_1(\mathbf{b}) \ldots \varrho_i(\mathbf{b})\, \varrho_{i+1}(\mathbf{b}) \\ &= \varrho_{i+2}(\mathbf{a}) \ldots \varrho_{mk}(\mathbf{a})\, \varrho_1(\mathbf{a}) \ldots \varrho_i(\mathbf{a})\, \tau(y) \\ &= \tau(y_2) \ldots \tau(y_{mk})\, \tau(y)\,.\end{aligned}$$

(The indices of ϱ are taken as their least positive residues modulo mk). Therefore, $\mathbf{b}$ satisfies (i). It is clear from our discussions above that $\mathbf{b}$ satisfies (iia), (iib), and (iii). It is also obvious that ψ is a homomorphism of $\mathfrak{B}$ onto $\mathfrak{R}_{mk, X}$.

Finally, since $\mathfrak{C}_{mk}$ is a homomorphic image of a quasi-direct power of $\mathfrak{S}_{m,k}$ (with a single factor) and φ_1 is a constant mapping, by Lemma 4.6, $\mathfrak{R}_{mk, X}$ can be represented homomorphically by an α_2-power of $\mathfrak{U}$. □

If $m \geqq n$, then $\mathfrak{R}_{n,X}$ is obviously a homomorphic image of $\mathfrak{R}_{m,X}$. Therefore, from Lemma 4.8 we have

Corollary 4.9. *For arbitrary natural number n and alphabet X, the shift register $\mathfrak{R}_{n,X}$ can be represented homomorphically by an α_2-power of $\mathfrak{U}$.* □

Figure 11 illustrates the change in the contents of the first buffer for $m = n = 2$, $k_1 = 2$, and $k_2 = 3$.

Moreover, Fig. 12 shows under the input word $x_1 x_1 x_2 x_2$ a transition in $\mathfrak{B}$ for $m = n = k_1 = k_2 = 2$.

In both figures the codes of input signals are indicated by boldface **u**'s.

We have performed all the preparations to prove

counter	1st buffer																							
3	u_0	u_1	u_0	u_1'	u_2'	u_0'	u_1'	u_2'	u_0'	u_1	u_0	u_1	u_0	u_1	u_0	$\mathbf{u}_1'$	u_2'	u_0'	u_0	u_1	u_0	$\mathbf{u}_1$	u_0	u_1
4	u_1	u_0	u_1'	u_2'	u_0'	u_1'	u_2'	u_0'	u_1	u_0	u_1	u_0	u_1	u_0	$\mathbf{u}_1'$	u_2'	u_0'	u_1'	u_1	u_0	$\mathbf{u}_1$	u_0	u_1	u_0
5	u_0	u_1'	u_2'	u_0'	u_1'	u_2'	u_0'	u_1	u_0	u_1	u_0	u_1	u_0	$\mathbf{u}_1'$	u_2'	u_0'	u_1'	u_2'	u_0	$\mathbf{u}_1$	u_0	u_1	u_0	u_1
6	u_1'	u_2'	u_0'	u_1'	u_2'	u_0'	u_1	u_0	u_1	u_0	u_1	u_0	$\mathbf{u}_1'$	u_2'	u_0'	u_1'	u_2'	u_0'	$\mathbf{u}_1$	u_0	u_1	u_0	u_1	u_0
7	u_2'	u_0'	u_1'	u_2'	u_0'	u_1	u_0	u_1	u_0	u_1	u_0	$\mathbf{u}_1'$	u_2'	u_0'	u_1'	u_2'	u_0'	$\mathbf{u}_1$	u_0	u_1	u_0	u_1	u_0	u_1
8	u_0'	u_1'	u_2'	u_0'	u_1	u_0	u_1	u_0	u_1	u_0	$\mathbf{u}_1'$	u_2'	u_0'	u_1'	u_2'	u_0'	$\mathbf{u}_1$	u_0	u_1	u_0	u_1	u_0	u_1	u_0

Fig. 11. Change in the contents of the first buffer, for $m = n = 2$ and $k_2 = 3$

counter	1st buffer	2nd buffer	3rd buffer	4th buffer	word represented
3	$u_0'\ u_1\ u_0\ \mathbf{u}_1'\ u_0'\ \mathbf{u}_1\ u_0\ u_1$	$u_1'\ u_0'\ u_1'\ u_0'\ \mathbf{u}_1'\ u_0'\ \mathbf{u}_1\ u_0$	$u_0'\ u_1'\ u_0\ u_1\ u_0\ \mathbf{u}_1\ u_0\ \mathbf{u}_1'$	$u_1\ u_0\ \mathbf{u}_1\ u_0\ \mathbf{u}_1'\ u_0'\ u_1\ u_0$	$x_2x_1x_1x_2$
				x_1 ↓	
4	$u_1\ u_0\ \mathbf{u}_1'\ u_0'\ \mathbf{u}_1\ u_0\ u_1\ u_0$	$u_0'\ u_1'\ u_0'\ \mathbf{u}_1'\ u_0'\ \mathbf{u}_1\ u_0\ u_1$	$u_1'\ u_0\ u_1\ u_0\ \mathbf{u}_1\ u_0\ \mathbf{u}_1'\ u_0'$	$u_0\ u_1\ u_0\ u_1'\ u_0'\ \mathbf{u}_1'\ u_0\ \mathbf{u}_1$	$x_1x_1x_2x_1$
	x_1 ↓				
1	$u_0\ u_1'\ u_0'\ u_1\ u_0\ \mathbf{u}_1'\ u_0\ \mathbf{u}_1$	$u_1'\ u_0'\ \mathbf{u}_1'\ u_0'\ \mathbf{u}_1\ u_0\ u_1\ u_0$	$u_0\ u_1\ u_0\ \mathbf{u}_1\ u_0\ \mathbf{u}_1'\ u_0'\ u_1$	$u_1\ u_0\ u_1'\ u_0'\ \mathbf{u}_1'\ u_0'\ \mathbf{u}_1\ u_0$	$x_1x_2x_1x_1$
		x_2 ↓			
2	$u_1'\ u_0'\ u_1\ u_0\ \mathbf{u}_1'\ u_0'\ \mathbf{u}_1\ u_0$	$u_0'\ u_1'\ u_0'\ u_1\ u_0\ \mathbf{u}_1\ u_0\ \mathbf{u}_1'$	$u_1\ u_0\ \mathbf{u}_1\ u_0\ \mathbf{u}_1'\ u_0'\ u_1\ u_0$	$u_0\ u_1'\ u_0'\ \mathbf{u}_1'\ u_0'\ \mathbf{u}_1\ u_0\ u_1$	$x_2x_1x_1x_2$
			x_2 ↓		
3	$u_0'\ u_1\ u_0\ \mathbf{u}_1'\ u_0'\ \mathbf{u}_1\ u_0\ u_1$	$u_1'\ u_0'\ u_1\ u_0\ \mathbf{u}_1\ u_0\ \mathbf{u}_1'\ u_0'$	$u_0\ u_1\ u_0\ u_1'\ u_0'\ \mathbf{u}_1\ u_0\ \mathbf{u}_1'$	$u_1'\ u_0'\ \mathbf{u}_1'\ u_0'\ \mathbf{u}_1\ u_0\ u_1\ u_0$	$x_1x_1x_2x_2$

Fig. 12. A transition in $\mathfrak{B}$, for $m = n = k_1 = k_2 = 2$

Theorem 4.10. *A class $\mathcal{K}$ of automata is homomorphically complete with respect to the α_2-product if and only if $\mathcal{K}$ contains an automaton satisfying Letičevskiĭ's criterion.*

Proof. If $\mathcal{K}$ is homomorphically complete with respect to the α_2-product, then it is obviously homomorphically complete with respect to the product. Therefore, by Theorem 1.4.6, $\mathcal{K}$ contains an automaton satisfying Letičevskiĭ's criterion.

Conversely, assume that $\mathcal{K}$ contains an automaton $\mathfrak{A}$ which satisfies Letičevskiĭ's criterion. Denote by $\mathfrak{U}$ an automaton obtained from $\mathfrak{A}$ by Lemma 4.1. As a consequence of Lemma 4.2, it is enough to show that $\mathfrak{U}$ is homomorphically complete with respect to the α_2-product.

In Lemma 4.3 it was shown that every automaton $\mathfrak{B} = (X, B, \delta)$ with m states can be represented homomorphically by an α_2-product

$$(\mathfrak{R}_{mk, X} \times \mathfrak{S}_{m, k} \times \underbrace{\mathfrak{U} \times \dots \times \mathfrak{U}}_{mk \text{ times}})[X, \varphi]$$

such that φ_1 depends only on the input. Moreover, by Corollary 4.9, $\mathfrak{R}_{mk, X}$ is a homomorphic image of a subautomaton of an α_2-power of $\mathfrak{U}$. Finally, by virtue of Lemma 4.6, $\mathfrak{S}_{m, k}$ can be represented homomorphically by an α_2-power of $\mathfrak{U}$ whose component feedback functions, except the last one, are independent of the input. From these results, taking into consideration Theorems 1.4.20 and 1.4.23 as well as their proofs, we have that $\mathfrak{B}$ can be represented homomorphically by an α_2-power of $\mathfrak{U}$. Since $\mathfrak{B}$ is an arbitrary automaton, this means that $\mathcal{K}$ is homomorphically complete with respect to the α_2-product. □

2.5 Comparison of the Homomorphic Representation Powers of α_i-Products

In the previous section it was shown that the α_2-product is equivalent to the general product from the point of view of homomorphic completeness. We now show that even more is true: as regards homomorphic representations from $i = 2$, the α_i-products are as powerful as the general product, while for $i = 0, 1, 2$ the hierarchy is proper.

We start with two definitions.

Definition 5.1. A state a of an automaton $\mathfrak{A} = (X, A, \delta)$ is *ambiguous* if there are two input signals $x_1, x_2 \in X$ under which $\delta(a, x_1) \neq \delta(a, x_2)$.

Definition 5.2. Take an automaton $\mathfrak{A} = (X, A, \delta)$, an integer $n > 0$ and a vector $\mathbf{a} = (a^{(1)}, \dots, a^{(n)}) \in A^n$ with $a^{(i)} \neq a^{(j)}$ if $i \neq j$ $(1 \leqq i, j \leqq n)$. The system $(\mathfrak{A}, \mathbf{a})$ is *k-free*, where k is a non-negative integer, if for arbitrary two input words $p, q \in X^{(k)}$, $\delta(a^{(i)}, p) \neq \delta(a^{(j)}, q)$ $(1 \leqq i, j \leqq n)$ whenever $i \neq j$ or $p \neq q$.

The following lemma will be used in the proof of the main result of this section:

Lemma 5.3. *Let $\mathscr{K}$ be a class of automata. Assume that, for a $k \geqq 0$, there exists an automaton $\mathfrak{A} = (X, A, \delta) \in \mathscr{K}$ having a state $a \in A$ and an input word p with $|p| = k$ such that $\delta(a, p)$ is ambiguous. Then, for arbitrary alphabet Y and integer $n > 0$, $\mathbf{P}_{\alpha_0}(\mathscr{K})$ contains an automaton $\mathfrak{B} = (Y, B, \delta_{\mathfrak{B}})$ such that $(\mathfrak{B}, \mathbf{b})$ is k-free under a $\mathbf{b} \in B^n$.*

Proof. We first show that, if $n = 1$, then for every $l \leqq k + 1$ in $\mathbf{P}_{\alpha_0}(\mathscr{K})$ there is a $\mathfrak{C}' = (Z, C', \delta')$ with $|Z| \geqq 2$ such that, for a $\mathbf{c}' \in C'$, the system $(\mathfrak{C}', \mathbf{c}')$ is l-free. We proceed by induction on l. If $l = 0$, then our statement is obviously true.

Suppose that the above statement has been proved for an $l \leqq k$. Let $(\mathfrak{C}_l, \mathbf{c}_l)$ be an l-free system where $\mathfrak{C}_l = (Z, C_l, \delta_l) \in \mathbf{P}_{\alpha_0}(\mathscr{K})$ and $\mathbf{c}_l \in C_l$. Take two different words p and q from $Z^{(l+1)}$ with $|p| = l + 1$ or $|q| = l + 1$. Moreover, let $a' \in A$ be a state and $r = x_1 \dots x_l$ $(x_1, \dots, x_l \in X)$ a word such that $\delta(a', r)$ is ambiguous, i.e. for some $x_1', x_2' \in X$, $\delta(\delta(a', r), x_1') \neq \delta(\delta(a', r), x_2')$. By our assumptions, such a' and r exist. Take the α_0-product

$$\bar{\mathfrak{C}} = (Z, \bar{C}, \bar{\delta}) = (\mathfrak{C}_l \times \mathfrak{A})\,[Z, \varphi]\,,$$

where φ_1 is the identity mapping on Z. Moreover, let $p = z_1 \dots z_u$ and $q = z_1' \dots z_v'$ $(z_i, z_j' \in Z,\ i = 1, \dots, u,\ j = 1, \dots, v)$, and distinguish the following two cases.

(i) $u < v\ (= l + 1)$. Then let

$$\varphi_2(\delta_l(\mathbf{c}_l, z_1 \dots z_{i-1}), z_i) = x_i\ (i = 1, \dots, u)\,,$$

$$\varphi_2(\delta_l(\mathbf{c}_l, z_1' \dots z_{j-1}'), z_j') = x_j\ (j = 1, \dots, v-1), \quad \text{and}$$

$$\varphi_2(\delta_l(\mathbf{c}_l, z_1' \dots z_{v-1}'), z_v') = \begin{cases} x_1' & \text{if } \delta(a', rx_1') \neq \delta(a', x_1 \dots x_u), \\ x_2' & \text{otherwise,} \end{cases}$$

(ii) $u = v\ (= l + 1)$. In this case let

$$\varphi_2(\delta_l(\mathbf{c}_l, z_1 \dots z_{i-1}), z_i) = \varphi_2(\delta_l(\mathbf{c}_l, z_1' \dots z_{i-1}'), z_i') = x_i\ (i = 1, \dots, u-1)\,,$$

$$\varphi_2(\delta_l(\mathbf{c}_l, z_1 \dots z_{u-1}), z_u) = x_1',\ \varphi_2(\delta_l(\mathbf{c}_l, z_1' \dots z_{u-1}'), z_u') = x_2'\,.$$

Since $(\mathfrak{C}_l, \mathbf{c}_l)$ is l-free, $\bar{\mathfrak{C}}$ is well defined. We show that $\bar{\delta}((\mathbf{c}_l, a'), p) \neq \bar{\delta}((\mathbf{c}_l, a'), q)$. In case (i), $\bar{\delta}((\mathbf{c}_l, a'), p) = (\delta_l(\mathbf{c}_l, p), \delta(a', x_1 \dots x_u))$ and $\bar{\delta}((\mathbf{c}_l, a'), q)$ equals $(\delta_l(\mathbf{c}_l, q), \delta(a', rx_2'))$ or $(\delta_l(\mathbf{c}_l, q), \delta(a', rx_1'))$, depending on whether $\delta(a', x_1 \dots x_u)$ is equal to $\delta(a', rx_1')$ or not. In case (ii), $\bar{\delta}((\mathbf{c}_l, a'), p) = (\delta_l(\mathbf{c}_l, p), \delta(a', rx_1'))$ and $\bar{\delta}((\mathbf{c}_l, a'), q) = (\delta_l(\mathbf{c}_l, q), \delta(a', rx_2'))$.

We next show that for two arbitrary different words $p, q \in Z^{(l+1)}$ there are a $\mathfrak{C}_{(p,q)} = (Z, C_{(p,q)}, \delta_{(p,q)}) \in \mathbf{P}_{\alpha_0}(\mathscr{K})$ and a $\mathbf{c}_{(p,q)} \in C_{(p,q)}$ such that $\delta_{(p,q)}(\mathbf{c}_{(p,q)}, p) \neq \delta_{(p,q)}(\mathbf{c}_{(p,q)}, q)$. If $|p|, |q| < l + 1$, then let $\mathfrak{C}_{(p,q)} = \mathfrak{C}_l$ and $\mathbf{c}_{(p,q)} = \mathbf{c}_l$, while in the opposite case we take $\mathfrak{C}_{(p,q)} = \bar{\mathfrak{C}}$ and $\mathbf{c}_{(p,q)} = (c_l, a')$, where $\bar{\mathfrak{C}}$ is the automaton constructed to these p and q above.

Now, set $I = \{(p, q) \mid p, q \in Z^{(l+1)}, p \neq q)\}$. Take the direct product $\mathfrak{C}' = (Z, C', \delta') = \prod (\mathfrak{C}_{(p,q)} \mid (p, q) \in I)$ and the state $\mathbf{c}' \in C'$ given by $\mathrm{pr}_{(p,q)}(\mathbf{c}') = \mathbf{c}_{(p,q)}$ $((p, q) \in I)$. Obviously, the system $(\mathfrak{C}', \mathbf{c}')$ is $(l + 1)$-free and $\mathfrak{C}' \in \mathbf{P}_{\alpha_0}(\mathscr{K})$. Thus, there exist a $\mathfrak{C} = (Z, C, \delta_{\mathfrak{C}})$ in $\mathbf{P}_{\alpha_0}(\mathscr{K})$ and a $\mathbf{c} \in C$ such that $(\mathfrak{C}, \mathbf{c})$ is $(k + 1)$-free.

Next, take two different input signals z_1 and z_2 from Z, and set $\mathbf{c}_i = \delta_{\mathfrak{C}}(\mathbf{c}, z_i)$ $(i = 1, 2)$. Clearly, $(\mathfrak{C}, (\mathbf{c}_1, \mathbf{c}_2))$ is a k-free system. Let $m' \geqq \log n$ and form the quasi-direct power

$$\mathfrak{B}' = (\underbrace{\mathfrak{C} \times \ldots \times \mathfrak{C}}_{m' \text{ times}})\,[\{z_1, z_2\}, \varphi'],$$

where $\varphi_i'(z_j) = z_j$ $(i = 1, \ldots, m',\ j = 1, 2)$. Moreover, let $\mathbf{b}' = (\mathbf{b}_1, \ldots, \mathbf{b}_n) \in (B')^n$ be a vector with $\mathrm{pr}_i(\mathbf{b}_j) \in \{\mathbf{c}_1, \mathbf{c}_2\}$ $(i = 1, \ldots, m', j = 1, \ldots, n)$ such that $\mathbf{b}_{j_1} \neq \mathbf{b}_{j_2}$ if $j_1 \neq j_2$ $(1 \leqq j_1, j_2 \leqq n)$. Clearly, $\mathfrak{B}' \in \mathbf{P}_{\alpha_0}(\mathscr{K})$ and $(\mathfrak{B}', \mathbf{b}')$ is k-free.

Finally, let $m \geqq \log |Y|$, and consider the quasi-direct power

$$\mathfrak{B} = (Y, B, \delta_{\mathfrak{B}}) = (\underbrace{\mathfrak{B}' \times \ldots \times \mathfrak{B}'}_{m \text{ times}})\,[Y, \varphi''],$$

where φ'' is a one-to-one mapping of Y into $\{z_1, z_2\}^m$. Moreover, take the vector $\mathbf{b} = (\mathbf{b}^{(1)}, \ldots, \mathbf{b}^{(n)}) \in B^n$ given by $\mathrm{pr}_j(\mathbf{b}^{(i)}) = \mathbf{b}_i$ $(j = 1, \ldots, m, i = 1, \ldots, n)$. Obviously, $\mathfrak{B} \in \mathbf{P}_{\alpha_0}(\mathscr{K})$. It is also easy to show that $(\mathfrak{B}, \mathbf{b})$ is k-free. For this, take two words $p, q \in Y^{(k)}$. If $j_1 \neq j_2$ $(1 \leqq j_1, j_2 \leqq n)$, then $\delta_{\mathfrak{B}}(\mathbf{b}^{(j_1)}, p)$ and $\delta_{\mathfrak{B}}(\mathbf{b}^{(j_2)}, q)$ are different in all of their components. Assume that $j_1 = j_2 = j$ and $p \neq q$. Then there is an i $(1 \leqq i \leqq m)$ for which $\varphi_i''(p) \neq \varphi_i''(q)$. Thus, $\delta_{\mathfrak{B}}(\mathbf{b}^{(j)}, p)$ and $\delta_{\mathfrak{B}}(\mathbf{b}^{(j)}, q)$ differ at least in their i^{th} components. □

We next prove

Theorem 5.4. *The α_2-product is homomorphically equivalent to the general product.*

Proof. Let $\mathscr{K}$ be an arbitrary class of automata. We show that $\mathbf{HSP}_{\alpha_2}(\mathscr{K}) = \mathbf{HSP}_g(\mathscr{K})$. For this, we distinguish the following three cases:
Case 1. $\mathscr{K}$ satisfies Letičevskiĭ's criterion. Then, by Theorem 4.10, both $\mathbf{HSP}_{\alpha_2}(\mathscr{K})$ and $\mathbf{HSP}_g(\mathscr{K})$ are the class of all finite automata.
Case 2. $\mathscr{K}$ does not satisfy Letičevskiĭ's criterion and there is an $\mathfrak{A} = (X, A, \delta) \in \mathscr{K}$ such that $\delta(a_0, x_1) \neq \delta(a_0, y_1)$ and $\delta(a_0, y_1 p) = a_0$ for some $a_0 \in A$, $x_1, y_1 \in X$ and $p \in X^*$. We shall show that $\mathbf{HSP}_g(\mathscr{K}) = \mathbf{HSP}_{\alpha_1}(\mathscr{K})$. Such an $\mathfrak{A}$ is illustrated in Fig. 13.
Clearly, $A' = \{\delta(a_0, x_1 q) \mid q \in X^*\}$ is disjoint with $\{a_0, a_1, \ldots, a_n\}$.

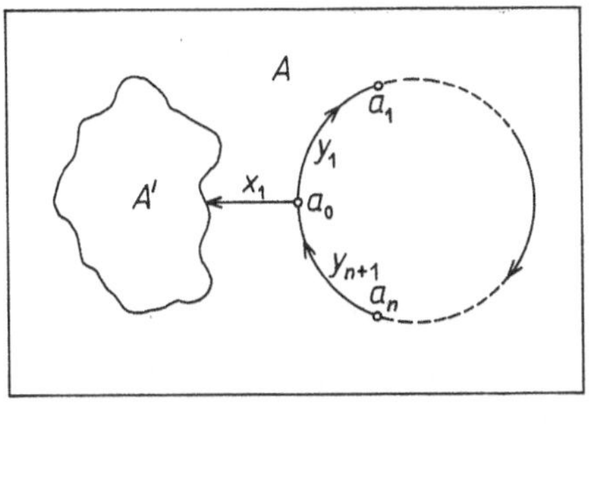

Fig. 13. A schematic illustration of $\mathfrak{A}$

Let M be the set of lengths of all cycles in automata from $\mathscr{K}$. Moreover, N will stand for the set of all positive integers which are divisors of least common multiples of integers from M:

$$N = \{n \mid (\exists t \geqq 1, m_1, \dots, m_t \in M)\ (n \mid \operatorname{lcm}[m_1, \dots, m_t])\} .$$

Define $\mathscr{K}'$ as the largest set of automata such that

(i) $\mathscr{K}'$ does not satisfy Letičevskiĭ's criterion, and
(ii) whenever n is the length of a cycle in an automaton from $\mathscr{K}'$, then $n \in N$.

We shall prove that $\mathbf{HSP}_g(\mathscr{K}) \subseteq \mathscr{K}' \subseteq \mathbf{HSP}_{\alpha_1}(\mathscr{K})$.

Let $\mathfrak{A} = (X, A, \delta)$ and $\mathfrak{B} = (X, B, \delta')$ be arbitrary automata, and let ψ be a homomorphism of $\mathfrak{A}$ onto $\mathfrak{B}$. Take a cycle $b_1, \dots, b_m$ in $\mathfrak{B}$ together with the input signals $x_1, \dots, x_m \in X$, for which $\delta'(b_i, x_i) = b_{i+1 \,(\mathrm{mod}\, m)}$ $(i \in [m])$. Set $p = x_1 \dots x_m$, and let $a \in A$ be an arbitrary counter image of b_1 under ψ. Obviously, there are integers k and l with $0 \leqq k < l$ satisfying $\delta(a, p^k) = \delta(a, p^l)$. Consequently, we have a cycle $a_1, \dots, a_n$ in $\mathfrak{A}$ such that, for every $i \in [n]$, $\psi(a_i) = b_{i\,(\mathrm{mod}\, m)}$. Thus, $m \mid n$. Therefore, since $\mathbf{HSP}_g(\mathscr{K})$ obviously does not satisfy Letičevskiĭ's criterion, to prove $\mathbf{HSP}_g(\mathscr{K}) \subseteq \mathscr{K}'$, it is enough to show that if a sequence $\mathbf{a}_0, \dots, \mathbf{a}_n$ $(\mathbf{a}_0 = \mathbf{a}_n)$ is a cycle in an automaton

$$\bar{\mathfrak{A}} = (X, \bar{A}, \bar{\delta}) = \prod_{i=1}^{m} \mathfrak{A}_i[X, \varphi] \quad (\mathfrak{A}_i = (X_i, A_i, \delta_i) \in \mathscr{K}, i = 1, \dots, m),$$

then n is the least common multiple of certain numbers in M. Let $\mathbf{a}_i = (a_{i1}, \dots, a_{im})$ $(i = 0, \dots, n,\ a_{ij} \in A_j,\ j = 1, \dots, m)$. Since $\mathbf{a}_0 = \mathbf{a}_n$, for every $j \in [m]$ there exists a least integer $n_j \in [n]$ with $a_{0j} = a_{n_j j}$. As $\mathscr{K}$ does not satisfy Letičevskiĭ's criterion, for every j $(1 \leqq j \leqq m)$, $a_{0j}, \dots, a_{n_j j}$ is a cycle in $\mathfrak{A}_j$ with length n_j. In the opposite case there are integers j_1 and j_2 such that $0 < j_1 < j_2 < n_j$ and $a_{j_1 j} = a_{j_2 j}$. If j_2 is the largest for all such pairs (j_1, j_2) then $a_{j_1+1 j} \neq a_{j_2+1 j}$, i.e., $\mathscr{K}$ would satisfy Letičevskiĭ's criterion under $\mathfrak{A}_j$. It is also easy to show that $a_{t_1 j} = a_{t_2 j}$ if $t_1 \equiv t_2 \pmod{n_j}$ $(0 \leqq t_1, t_2 \leqq n)$. In the opposite case, taking the least t_2 for which there exists a t_1 with $t_1 < t_2$, $t_1 \equiv t_2 \pmod{n_j}$ and $a_{t_1 j} \neq a_{t_2 j}$, we would have that $\mathscr{K}$ satisfies Letičevskiĭ's criterion with $\mathfrak{A}_j$. Thus, for every $j \in [m]$, $n_j \mid n$. Therefore, $n = \operatorname{lcm}[n_1, \dots, n_m]$, implying $\mathbf{HSP}_g(\mathscr{K}) \subseteq \mathscr{K}'$.

We next prove that $\mathscr{K}' \subseteq \mathbf{HSP}_{\alpha_1}(\mathscr{K})$. For this, some special automata are needed. For every $n \in N$, define $\mathfrak{A}_n = (\{x, y\}, \{0, \dots, n\}, \delta_n)$ by

$$\delta_n(0, z) = \begin{cases} 0 \text{ if } z = x, \\ 1 \text{ if } z = y \end{cases}$$

and $\delta_n(i, x) = \delta_n(i, y) = i + 1 \pmod{n}$ $(i \in [n])$. This $\mathfrak{A}_n$ is illustrated in Fig. 14. We show that $\mathfrak{A}_n \in \mathbf{HSP}_{\alpha_1}(\mathscr{K})$.

It is obvious that for every $n \in N$, $\mathbf{HSP}_f\mathbf{P}_{1\alpha_1}(\mathscr{K}) \subseteq \mathbf{HSP}_{\alpha_1}(\mathscr{K})$ contains all counters with n states. We next show that the inclusion $\mathfrak{A}_1 \in \mathbf{HSP}_f\mathbf{P}_{1\alpha_1}(\mathscr{K})$ holds,

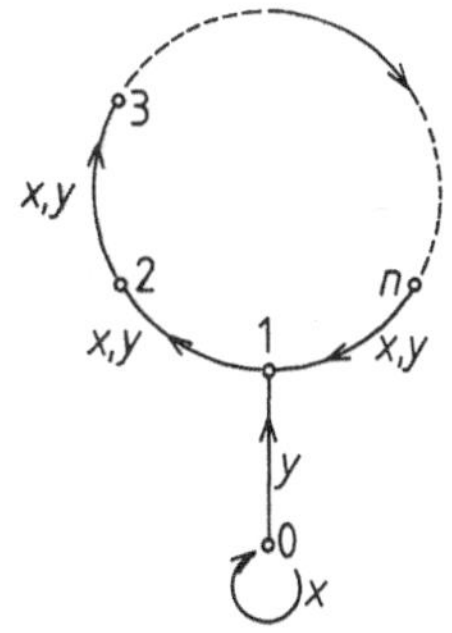

Fig. 14. Automaton $\mathfrak{A}_n$

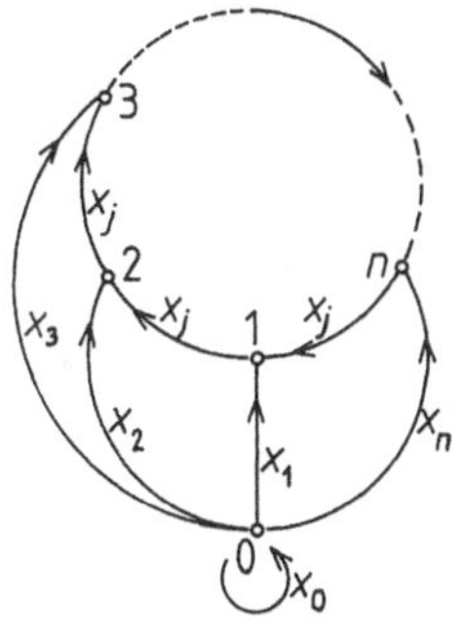

Fig. 15. Automaton $\mathfrak{B}_n$

too. By our assumptions, $\mathbf{P}_{1\alpha_1}(\mathscr{K})$ contains an automaton $\bar{\mathfrak{A}} = (\{x, y\}, \bar{A}, \bar{\delta})$ with the following properties:

(i) $\bar{A} = \{a_1, \ldots, a_n, b_1, \ldots, b_m\}$ $(n, m \geqq 1)$.
(ii) $\bar{\delta}(a_i, x) = a_{i+1 \,(\mathrm{mod}\, n)}$.
(iii) $\bar{\delta}(a_1, y) = b_1$ and, for every $i \in \{2, \ldots, n\}$, $\bar{\delta}(a_i, y) = a_{i+1\,(\mathrm{mod}\, n)}$.
(iv) For each $i \in [m]$, $\bar{\delta}(b_i, x), \bar{\delta}(b_i, y) \in \{b_1, \ldots, b_m\}$.

Denote by $\mathfrak{A}' = (\{x, y\}, A', \delta')$ the subautomaton of the direct power $\bar{\mathfrak{A}}^n$ generated by the element $(a_1, \ldots, a_n)$. Then the mapping $\psi: A' \to \{0, 1\}$ given by

$$\psi((c_1, \ldots, c_n)) = \begin{cases} 0 \text{ if } \{c_1, \ldots, c_n\} = \{a_1, \ldots, a_n\}, \\ 1 \text{ otherwise} \end{cases}$$

$((c_1, \ldots, c_n) \in A')$ is obviously a homomorphism of $\mathfrak{A}'$ onto $\mathfrak{A}_1$.

Next, let $\mathfrak{C} = (\{x\}, [n], \delta_{\mathfrak{C}})$ be a counter with $n \in N$. Take the α_0-product $\mathfrak{B} = (\{x, y\}, B, \delta_{\mathfrak{B}}) = (\mathfrak{C} \times \mathfrak{A}_1 \times \ldots \times \mathfrak{A}_1)\,[\{x, y\}, \varphi]$ with $n + 1$ factors, where φ is given as follows: $\varphi_1(x) = \varphi_1(y) = x$ and, for arbitrary $t, i \in [n]$ and $i_1, \ldots, i_{t-1} \in \{0, 1\}$, $\varphi_{1+t}(i, i_1, \ldots, i_{t-1}, x) = x$ and

$$\varphi_{1+t}(i, i_1, \ldots, i_{t-1}, y) = \begin{cases} y \text{ if } t \leqq i \text{ and } i_1 = \ldots = i_{t-1} = 0, \\ x \text{ otherwise.} \end{cases}$$

Consider a state $\mathbf{b} = (i, 0, \ldots, 0)$ of $\mathfrak{B}$. Then $\delta_{\mathfrak{B}}(\mathbf{b}, x) = (i', 0, \ldots, 0)$, where $i' = i + 1$ (mod n). Moreover,

$$\delta_{\mathfrak{B}}(\mathbf{b}, y) = (i', \underbrace{1, \ldots, 1}_{i \text{ times}}, 0, \ldots, 0),$$

where i' is the same as in the previous case. From this moment, under any input signal the contents of the last n components are unchanged. Thus, they are used to store the value of the counter at the moment when the first y arrives at $\mathfrak{B}$.

Set $B' = \{(i, i_1, \dots, i_n) \in B \mid \exists t\ (0 \leqq t \leqq n)\ (i_1 = \dots = i_t = 1, i_{t+1} = \dots = i_n = 0)\}$. It is routine computation to show that $\mathfrak{B}' = (\{x, y\}, B', \delta'_{\mathfrak{B}})$ with $\delta'_{\mathfrak{B}} = \delta_{\mathfrak{B}} \mid B' \times \{x, y\}$ is a subautomaton of $\mathfrak{B}$. Take the mapping $\psi : B' \to \{0, \dots, n\}$ given by $\psi((i, i_1, \dots, i_n)) = j$ if and only if $i_1 = \dots = i_n = j = 0$ or $j \geqq 1$ and there exists a $t \in [n]$ such that $i_1 = \dots = i_t = 1$, $i_{t+1} = \dots = i_n = 0$ and $i - t \equiv j \pmod n$, where $(i, i_1, \dots, i_n) \in B'$ and $j \in [n]$. It is obvious that ψ is a homomorphism of $\mathfrak{B}'$ onto $\mathfrak{A}_n$. Thus, we have that $\mathfrak{A}_n \in \mathbf{HSP}_{\alpha_0}\mathbf{HSP}_{\alpha_0}\mathbf{P}_{1\alpha_1}(\mathscr{K}) \subseteq \mathbf{HSP}_{\alpha_1}(\mathscr{K})$.

Again, let $n \in N$ be arbitrary, and define the automaton $\mathfrak{B}_n = (\{x_0, \dots, x_n\}, \{0, \dots, n\}, \delta_{\mathfrak{B}_n})$ in the following way: $\delta_{\mathfrak{B}_n}(0, x_0) = 0$, $\delta_{\mathfrak{B}_n}(0, x_i) = i$ $(1 \leqq i \leqq n)$ and $\delta_{\mathfrak{B}_n}(i, x_j) = i + 1 \pmod n$ $(1 \leqq i \leqq n, 0 \leqq j \leqq n)$. Fig. 15 shows $\mathfrak{B}_n$.

We shall prove that $\mathfrak{B}_n \in \mathbf{HSP}_{\alpha_1}(\mathscr{K})$. For this, form the α_0-power

$$\mathfrak{C} = (\{x_0, \dots, x_n\}, C, \delta_{\mathfrak{C}}) = (\underbrace{\mathfrak{A}_n \times \dots \times \mathfrak{A}_n}_{n \text{ times}}) [\{x_0, \dots, x_n\}, \varphi'],$$

where, for arbitrary j, t $(1 \leqq j, t \leqq n)$ and $i_1, \dots, i_n \in \{0, \dots, n\}$, $\varphi'_t(i_1, \dots, i_{t-1}, x_0) = x$ and

$$\varphi'_t(i_1, \dots, i_{t-1}, x_j) = \begin{cases} y \text{ if } t \leqq j \text{ and } i_1 = \dots = i_{t-1} = 0, \\ x \text{ otherwise.} \end{cases}$$

Assume that $\mathfrak{C}$ is in state $\mathbf{c} = (0, \dots, 0)$. Under x_0, $\mathfrak{C}$ remains in $\mathbf{c}$. Obtaining an x_j $(j \neq 0)$, it passes into

$$\delta_{\mathfrak{C}}(\mathbf{c}, x_j) = (\underbrace{1, \dots, 1}_{j \text{ times}}, 0, \dots, 0).$$

Corresponding $j \neq 0$ (as a state of $\mathfrak{B}_n$) to $\delta_{\mathfrak{C}}(\mathbf{c}, x_j)$, we have an isomorphism between the subautomaton of $\mathfrak{C}$ generated by $\delta_{\mathfrak{C}}(\mathbf{c}, x_j)$ and the subautomaton of $\mathfrak{B}_n$ generated by j.

Set

$$C' = \{(i_1, \dots, i_n) \in C \mid \exists t, i\ (0 \leqq t \leqq n; 1 \leqq i \leqq n)$$
$$(i_1 = \dots = i_t = i, i_{t+1} = \dots = i_n = 0)\}.$$

It can easily be shown that $\mathfrak{C}' = (\{x_0, \dots, x_n\}, C', \delta'_{\mathfrak{C}})$ with $\delta'_{\mathfrak{C}} = \delta_{\mathfrak{C}} \mid C' \times \{x_0, \dots, x_n\}$ is a subautomaton of $\mathfrak{C}$. Consider the mapping $\psi' : C' \to \{0, \dots, n\}$ given by $\psi'((i_1, \dots, i_n)) = j$ if and only if $i_1 = \dots = i_n = j = 0$, or $j \geqq 1$ and, for some $t, i \in [n]$, $i_1 = \dots = i_t = i$, $i_{t+1} = \dots = i_n = 0$ and $i + t - 1 \equiv j \pmod n$, where $(i_1, \dots, i_n) \in C'$ and $j \in [n]$. Taking into account our above remark, it is clear that ψ' is a homomorphism of $\mathfrak{C}'$ onto $\mathfrak{B}_n$. Thus, we have that $\mathfrak{B}_n \in \mathbf{HSP}_{\alpha_0}\mathbf{HSP}_{\alpha_1}(\mathscr{K}) \subseteq \mathbf{HSP}_{\alpha_1}(\mathscr{K})$.

Finally, using these automata $\mathfrak{B}_n$, we shall prove that $\mathscr{K}' \subseteq \mathbf{HSP}_{\alpha_1}(\mathscr{K})$. Take an arbitrary automaton $\mathfrak{D} = (X_{\mathfrak{D}}, D, \delta_{\mathfrak{D}})$ from $\mathscr{K}'$. We proceed by induction on $|D|$. If $|D| = 1$, then $\mathfrak{D} \in \mathbf{HSP}_{\alpha_1}(\mathscr{K})$ obviously holds. Thus, suppose that $|D| > 1$. Then $\mathfrak{D}$ has a subautomaton which is isomorphic to a generalized counter. Indeed, all the minimal subautomata $\bar{\mathfrak{D}} = (X_{\mathfrak{D}}, \bar{D}, \bar{\delta}_{\mathfrak{D}})$ are isomorphic to generalized counters. In the opposite case take a cycle $d_1, \dots, d_n$ in $\bar{\mathfrak{D}}$. Then, as $\mathcal{K}'$ does not satisfy Letičevskiĭ's criterion, there are an i $(1 \leqq i \leqq n)$, a $d_i' \in \bar{D}$, and an $x \in X_{\mathfrak{D}}$ such that $\bar{\delta}_{\mathfrak{D}}(d_i, x) = d_i'$, $d_i' \notin \{d_1, \dots, d_n\}$ and d_i' generates a proper subautomaton of $\bar{\mathfrak{D}}$. But this is a contradiction. Therefore, $\mathfrak{D}$ has a subautomaton $\mathfrak{D}_1$ which is isomorphic to a generalized counter. For the sake of simplicity, we suppose that $\mathfrak{D}_1$ itself is a generalized counter with n states. From the definition of $\mathcal{K}'$, $n \in N$. If $\mathfrak{D}_1 = \mathfrak{D}$, then, as already mentioned, $\mathfrak{D} \in \mathbf{HSP}_{\alpha_1}(\mathcal{K})$. Otherwise, let $D_2 = D - [n]$, and take the automaton $\mathfrak{D}_2 = (X_{\mathfrak{D}}, D_2, \delta_{\mathfrak{D}_2})$, where $\delta_{\mathfrak{D}_2}$ is given as follows:

(a) $\delta_{\mathfrak{D}_2}(d, x) = \delta_{\mathfrak{D}}(d, x)$ if $\delta_{\mathfrak{D}}(d, x) \in D_2$ $(d \in D_2, x \in X_{\mathfrak{D}})$.

(b) If for some $d \in D_2$ and $x \in X_{\mathfrak{D}}$, $\delta_{\mathfrak{D}}(d, x) \notin D_2$ and there exists a $y \in X_{\mathfrak{D}}$ with $\delta_{\mathfrak{D}}(d, y) \in D_2$, then $\delta_{\mathfrak{D}_2}(d, x) = \delta_{\mathfrak{D}}(d, y)$ under such a fixed y.

(c) $\delta_{\mathfrak{D}_2}(d, x) = d$ $(d \in D_2)$ if $\delta_{\mathfrak{D}}(d, y) \notin D_2$ for every $y \in X$.

It can easily by shown that $\mathfrak{D}_2 \in \mathcal{K}'$. All cycles in $\mathfrak{D}_2$, possibly excepting cycles of length 1, also occur in $\mathfrak{D}$. Now suppose that there are two cycles $d_1, d_2, \dots, d_k$ and $d_1', d_2', \dots, d_l'$ in $\mathfrak{D}_2$ such that $d_1 = d_1'$ and $d_2 \neq d_2'$. Then, (exactly) one of them, say the first one, has length 1, for in the opposite case both of them are cycles in $\mathfrak{D}$, and $\mathfrak{D}$ would therefore satisfy Letičevskiĭ's criterion. But again, by our assumptions about $\mathcal{K}'$, this implies that there is no $x \in X_{\mathfrak{D}}$ with $\delta_{\mathfrak{D}}(d_1, x) = d_2'$, which is a contradiction. Therefore, $\mathfrak{D}_2$ is in $\mathcal{K}'$, and thus, by the induction hypothesis, $\mathfrak{D}_2 \in \mathbf{HSP}_{\alpha_1}(\mathcal{K})$.

Finally, consider the α_0-product

$$\bar{\mathfrak{D}} = (X_{\mathfrak{D}}, \bar{D}, \bar{\delta}_{\mathfrak{D}}) = (\mathfrak{D}_2 \times \mathfrak{B}_n)[X_{\mathfrak{D}}, \bar{\varphi}],$$

where $\bar{\varphi}_1$ is the identity mapping on $X_{\mathfrak{D}}$, and for arbitrary $d \in D_2$ and $x \in X_{\mathfrak{D}}$,

$$\bar{\varphi}_2(d, x) = \begin{cases} x_i \text{ if } \delta_{\mathfrak{D}}(d, x) = i \text{ for an } i \in [n], \\ x_0 \text{ otherwise.} \end{cases}$$

Let the mapping $\bar{\psi} : \bar{D} \to D$ be given in the following way. For arbitrary $d \in D_2$ and $i \in [n]$, $\bar{\psi}((d, 0)) = d$ and $\bar{\psi}((d, i)) = i$. It is routine computation to show that $\bar{\psi}$ is a homomorphism of $\bar{\mathfrak{D}}$ onto $\mathfrak{D}$. It has been proved that $\mathfrak{D}_2, \mathfrak{B}_n \in \mathbf{HSP}_{\alpha_1}(\mathcal{K})$. By this latest result, the inclusion $\mathfrak{D} \in \mathbf{HSP}_{\alpha_1}(\mathcal{K})$ also holds.

Case 3. In this remaining case, $\mathcal{K}$ consists of automata $\mathfrak{A} = (X, A, \delta)$ with the following property: whenever $\delta(a, xp) = a$ is satisfied by some $a \in A$, $x \in X$ and $p \in X^*$, then $\delta(a, x) = \delta(a, y)$ for every $y \in X$. We shall show that $\mathbf{HSP}_g(\mathcal{K}) = \mathbf{HSP}_{\alpha_0}(\mathcal{K})$. Since $\mathbf{HSP}_g(\mathcal{K}) = \cup\,(\mathbf{HSP}_g(\bar{\mathcal{K}}) \mid \bar{\mathcal{K}} \subseteq \mathcal{K}, \bar{\mathcal{K}}$ is finite), and similarly, $\mathbf{HSP}_{\alpha_0}(\mathcal{K}) = \cup\,(\mathbf{HSP}_{\alpha_0}(\bar{\mathcal{K}}) \mid \bar{\mathcal{K}} \subseteq \mathcal{K}, \bar{\mathcal{K}}$ is finite), it is enough to show that $\mathbf{HSP}_g(\bar{\mathcal{K}}) = \mathbf{HSP}_{\alpha_0}(\bar{\mathcal{K}})$ for every finite subset $\bar{\mathcal{K}}$ of $\mathcal{K}$. Thus, we may suppose that $\mathcal{K}$ itself is finite.

It is obvious that $\mathbf{HSP}_{\alpha_0}(\mathcal{K}) \subseteq \mathbf{HSP}_g(\mathcal{K})$. To prove $\mathbf{HSP}_g(\mathcal{K}) \subseteq \mathbf{HSP}_{\alpha_0}(\mathcal{K})$, let us observe that, if none of the states of automata from $\mathcal{K}$ is ambiguous, then every product of automata in $\mathcal{K}$ is isomorphic to a quasi-direct product of the same automata. In the opposite case there exists a maximal k for which there are an $\mathfrak{A} = (X_{\mathfrak{A}}, A, \delta_{\mathfrak{A}}) \in \mathcal{K}$, an $a \in A$ and a $p \in X_{\mathfrak{A}}^*$ with $|p| = k$ such that $\delta_{\mathfrak{A}}(a, p)$ is ambiguous. Let

$$\mathfrak{B} = (X, B, \delta) = \prod_{i=1}^{m} \mathfrak{B}_i[X, \varphi] \qquad (\mathfrak{B}_i = (X_i, B_i, \delta_i) \in \mathscr{K}, i = 1, \ldots, m),$$

be an arbitrary product. Moreover, let $\{\mathbf{b}^{(1)}, \ldots, \mathbf{b}^{(n)}\}$ be a generating set of $\mathfrak{B}$. Using Lemma 5.3, by the above remark we have that, for an automaton $\mathfrak{C} = (X, C, \delta_{\mathfrak{C}}) \in \mathbf{P}_{\alpha_0}(\mathscr{K})$ and a vector $\mathbf{c} = (\mathbf{c}_1, \ldots, \mathbf{c}_n) (\in C^n)$, the system $(\mathfrak{C}, \mathbf{c})$ is k-free. Next, form the α_0-product

$$\mathfrak{D} = (X, D, \delta_{\mathfrak{D}}) = (\mathfrak{C} \times \mathfrak{B}_1 \times \ldots \times \mathfrak{B}_m)[X, \varphi'],$$

where φ_1' is the identity mapping on X. Moreover, for arbitrary t $(1 \leqq t \leqq m)$, j $(1 \leqq j \leqq n)$, $p \in X^{(k)}$, $x \in X$, and $b_i \in B_i$ $(i = 1, \ldots, t-1)$ let $\varphi'_{1+t}(\delta_{\mathfrak{C}}(c_j, p), b_1, \ldots, b_{t-1}, x) = \varphi_t(\delta(\mathbf{b}^{(j)}, p), x)$. In all other cases, φ' is given arbitrarily in accordance with the definition of the α_0-product. Since the system $(\mathfrak{C}, \mathbf{c})$ is k-free, $\mathfrak{D}$ is well defined. Moreover, by the choice of k, for all $i \in [m]$, $b \in B_i$ and $q \in X_i^*$ with $|q| > k$, we have $\delta_i(b, qx) = \delta_i(b, qy)$ $(x, y \in X_i)$. Thus, for arbitrary j $(1 \leqq j \leqq n)$, $\mathbf{b}^{(j)} = (b_1^{(j)}, \ldots, b_m^{(j)})$ and $q \in X^*$, the equality

$$\delta_{\mathfrak{D}}((\mathbf{c}_j, b_1^{(j)}, \ldots, b_m^{(j)}), q) = (\delta_{\mathfrak{C}}(\mathbf{c}_j, q), \delta_1(b_1^{(j)}, \varphi_1(\mathbf{b}^{(j)}, q)), \ldots, \delta_m(b_m^{(j)}, \varphi_m(\mathbf{b}^{(j)}, q)))$$

holds. Denote by $\mathfrak{D}' = (X, D', \delta'_{\mathfrak{D}})$ the subautomaton of $\mathfrak{D}$ generated by $\{(\mathbf{c}_1, b_1^{(1)}, \ldots, b_m^{(1)}), \ldots, (\mathbf{c}_n, b_1^{(n)}, \ldots, b_m^{(n)})\}$. Moreover, take the mapping $\psi: D' \to B$ given by $\psi((\mathbf{c}, b_1, \ldots, b_m)) = (b_1, \ldots, b_m)$ $((\mathbf{c}, b_1, \ldots, b_m) \in D')$. Since $\{\mathbf{b}^{(1)}, \ldots, \mathbf{b}^{(n)}\}$ generates $\mathfrak{B}$, the mapping ψ is a homomorphism of $\mathfrak{D}'$ onto $\mathfrak{B}$. Therefore, $\mathbf{HSP}_g(\mathscr{K}) = \mathbf{HSP}_{\alpha_0}(\mathscr{K})$. □

We end this section by showing that, for $i = 0, 1, 2$, the hierarchy is proper.

Theorem 5.5. *For $i = 0, 1$, the α_{i+1}-product is homomorphically more general than the α_i-product.*

Proof. Take the automaton $\mathfrak{A} = (\{x, y\}, \{1, 2, 3\}, \delta)$ where δ is given by the transition table below.

δ	1	2	3
x	2	2	3
y	1	3	1

It is routine work to show that every such subautomaton of arbitrary α_0-power of $\mathfrak{A}$ which is isomorphic to a counter has one state. Therefore, none of the counters with 3 states is $\mathbf{HSP}_{\alpha_0}(\{\mathfrak{A}\})$. It is also clear that all three-state counters are in $\mathbf{IP}_{1\alpha_1}(\{\mathfrak{A}\})$. Thus, the α_1-product is homomorphically more general than the α_0-product. Taking the cycle representation of permutations, it is seen immediately that none of the characteristic groups of counters with a prime number p of states is a homomorphic image of a permutation group of degree n if $n < p$. Moreover, these characteristic groups are obviously simple. Therefore, by Theorems 3.2 and 3.4, none of the counters with prime numbers of states can be represented homomorphically by α_1-products of smaller automata. Since $\mathfrak{A}$ satisfies Letičevskiĭ's criterion, by Theorem 4.10, it forms a homomorphically complete system with respect to the α_2-product. Thus, we have that the α_2-product is homomorphically more general than the α_1-product.

2.6 Homomorphically α_i-Simple Automata

In the next chapter we shall see that, if $i = 0, 1$, then for every α_i-product there exists an isomorphically complete class consisting of isomorphically α_i-simple automata, where the latter term means that, whenever the automaton in question can be represented isomorphically by an α_i-product of certain automata, then it has an isomorphic representation by a single-factor α_i-power of one of these automata. Moreover, it will also turn out that a class $\mathscr{K}$ is isomorphically complete with respect to the α_i-product ($i = 0, 1$) if and only if every isomorphically α_i-simple automaton can be represented isomorphically by an α_i-product of automata from $\mathscr{K}$. In this section we show that there exists no similar characterization for homomorphic completeness.

Definition 6.1. An automaton $\mathfrak{A}$ is *homomorphically α_i-simple* ($i = 0, 1, \ldots$) if for every class $\mathscr{K}$ of automata, whenever $\mathfrak{A}$ can be represented homomorphically by an α_i-product of automata from $\mathscr{K}$, then there is a $\mathfrak{B} \in \mathscr{K}$ such that a single-factor α_i-power of $\mathfrak{B}$ homomorphically represents $\mathfrak{A}$.

We shall prove that for each i ($= 0, 1, \ldots$) exactly the two-state nilpotent automata are homomorphically α_i-simple. For this, some preparations are needed.

Lemma 6.2. *Let $\mathfrak{A} = (X, A, \delta)$ be an arbitrary n-state automaton. If $n > 2$, then $\mathfrak{A}$ is not homomorphically α_i-simple for any of the α_i-products.*

Proof. Let $n > 2$. By Theorem 4.10, $\mathfrak{A}$ can be represented homomorphically by an α_i-power of a two-state automaton if $i > 1$. Therefore, for $i > 1$, $\mathfrak{A}$ is not homomorphically α_i-simple.

Assume that $\mathfrak{A}$ is homomorphically α_0- or α_1-simple. By Theorem 1.5, $\mathfrak{A}$ can be represented homomorphically by an α_0-product of two-state reset automata and n-state standard automata. Therefore, $\mathfrak{A}$ is isomorphic to an α_0- or α_1-power of an n-state standard automaton with a single factor. This implies that there exists an ordering $a_1, \ldots, a_n$ of elements of $\mathfrak{A}$ such that, for every m ($1 \leqq m \leqq n$) and $x \in X$,

$$\delta(a_m, x) \in \begin{cases} \{a_1, a_2\} \text{ if } m = 1\,, \\ \{a_1, a_2, a_3\} \text{ if } m = 2\,, \\ \{a_m, a_{m+1}\} \text{ if } 2 < m < n\,, \\ \{a_1, a_n\} \text{ if } m = n\,. \end{cases}$$

We first show that $\delta(a_n, x) = a_n$ does not hold for any $x \in X$. Suppose that our claim is not valid. Take the cover $\Gamma = \{A_1, A_2\}$ with $A_1 = A_2 = A$. Let $\mathfrak{B}$ and $\mathfrak{C}$ be the automata determined to this cover through Lemma 3.7. Let $\psi_1(a_i) = i$ $(i = 1, \dots, n)$ and

$$\psi_2(a_i) = \begin{cases} n \text{ if } i = 1\,, \\ 1 \text{ if } i = n\,, \\ i \text{ otherwise}\,. \end{cases}$$

The transition function δ' of $\mathfrak{B}$ is given as follows. For every $x \in X$,

$$\delta'(A_1, x) = \begin{cases} A_2 \text{ if } \delta(a_n, x) = a_n\,, \\ A_1 \text{ if } \delta(a_n, x) = a_1\,, \end{cases}$$

and

$$\delta'(A_2, x) = \begin{cases} A_1 \text{ if } \delta(a_n, x) = a_n\,, \\ A_2 \text{ if } \delta(a_n, x) = a_1 \end{cases}$$

if there exists no $z \in X$ with $\delta(a_1, z) = a_1$, and $\delta'(A_2, x) = A_1$ in the opposite case. By Lemma 3.7, $\mathfrak{A}$ can be represented homomorphically by an α_0-product of $\mathfrak{B}$ and $\mathfrak{C}$. Since $\mathfrak{A}$ is α_0- or α_1-simple, it is isomorphic to a single-factor α_0- or α_1-power of $\mathfrak{C}$. We show that this is impossible. Let $A' = \{a \in A \mid \delta(a, x) = a \text{ for some } x \in X\}$ and $C' = \{c \in C \mid \delta''(c, z) = c \text{ for some } z \in B \times X\}$. One can then easily show that there exists no $z \in B \times X$ with $\delta''(n, z) = n$ and, for every $i \in [n-1]$, if $\delta''(i, z) = i$ under some $z \in B \times X$, then there is an $x \in X$ such that $\delta(a_i, x) = a_i$, i.e., $|C'| < |A'|$. Therefore, there is no $x \in X$ with $\delta(a_n, x) = a_n$.

Assume that none of the input signals induces a permutation of $\mathfrak{A}$. Then, through Theorems 1.2.15 and 1.2.17, from Theorem 3.2 we have that $\mathfrak{A}$ can be represented homomorphically by an α_0-product of smaller automata. Therefore, $\mathfrak{A}$ has at least one input signal inducing a permutation of the state set, and by our above computations for every such input signal $x \in X$, we have $\delta(a_m, x) = a_{m+1 (\text{mod } n)}$ $(m = 1, \dots, n)$.

Again, take the above cover Γ, automata $\mathfrak{B}$ and $\mathfrak{C}$, mapping ψ_1, and now let

$$\psi_2(a_i) = \begin{cases} i \text{ if } i = 1, \dots, n-2\,, \\ n \text{ if } i = n-1\,, \\ n-1 \text{ if } i = n\,. \end{cases}$$

Moreover, for every $x \in X$,

$$\delta'(A_1, x) = \begin{cases} A_1 \text{ if } \delta(a_{n-1}, x) = a_{n-1}\,, \\ A_2 \text{ otherwise} \end{cases}$$

and

$$\delta'(A_2, x) = \begin{cases} A_2 & \text{if } \delta(a_{n-1}, x) = a_{n-1}, \\ A_1 & \text{otherwise}. \end{cases}$$

It can be verified in a trivial way that, for every $z \in B \times X$, $\delta''(n-1, z) \neq n-1$ implies $\delta''(n-1, z) = 1$, and $\delta''(n, z) = 1$ if $\delta''(n, z) \neq n$. Therefore, there is no arrangement $c_1, \dots, c_n$ of elements of C and input signals $z_1, \dots, z_n \in B \times X$ for which $\delta''(c_m, z_m) = c_{m+1 (\mathrm{mod}\ n)}$ $(m = 1, \dots, n)$. Thus, $\mathfrak{A}$ is not isomorphic to any of the single-factor α_1-powers of $\mathfrak{C}$, which contradicts the assumption that $\mathfrak{A}$ is homomorphically α_0- or α_1-simple. □

We now turn to two-state automata.

Lemma 6.3. *Let $i \geqq 0$, and take a two-state homomorphically α_i-simple automaton $\mathfrak{A} = (X, \{a_1, a_2\}, \delta)$. Then there exists an $a \in \{a_1, a_2\}$ such that $\delta(a, x) \neq a$ for every $x \in X$.*

Proof. For arbitrary s, t $(1 \leqq s, t \leqq 2)$, let X_{st} denote the set of all $x_{st} \in X$ such that

$$\delta(a_k, x_{st})) = \begin{cases} a_s & \text{if } k = 1, \\ a_t & \text{if } k = 2. \end{cases}$$

Construct the automata $\mathfrak{A}_1 = (X, [3], \delta_1)$ and $\mathfrak{A}_2 = ([3] \times X, [3], \delta_2)$ in the following way. For arbitrary states $s, t \in [3]$ and input signal $x \in X$, let

$$\delta_1(s, x) = \begin{cases} 1 & \text{if } s \neq 1, \\ 2 & \text{if } s = 1 \text{ and } x \in X_{11} \cup X_{12}, \\ 3 & \text{if } s = 1 \text{ and } x \in X_{21} \cup X_{22} \end{cases}$$

and

$$\delta_2(t, (s, x)) = \begin{cases} 2 & \text{if } t = 1 \text{ and } (s, x) \in \{2, 3\} \times X_{11} \\ & \quad \cup \{1, 2\} \times X_{12} \cup \{1, 3\} \times X_{21}, \\ 3 & \text{if } t = 2 \text{ and } (s, x) \in \{2, 3\} \times X_{11} \\ & \quad \cup \{3\} \times X_{12} \cup \{2\} \times X_{21}, \\ 1 & \text{otherwise}. \end{cases}$$

Form the α_0-product $\mathfrak{C} = (\mathfrak{A}_1 \times \mathfrak{A}_2)[X, \varphi]$, where, for all $x \in X$ and $s \in [3]$, $\varphi_1(x) = x$ and $\varphi_2(s, x) = (s, x)$. It can be checked in a trivial way that the subset $C' = \{(1, 2), (1, 3), (2, 1), (3, 2), (1, 1), (2, 2), (3, 1)\}$ is a subautomaton of $\mathfrak{C}$ which can be mapped homomorphically onto $\mathfrak{A}$ under the mapping $\psi : C' \to \{a_1, a_2\}$ given by

$$\psi((s, t)) = \begin{cases} a_1 & \text{if } (s, t) \in \{(1, 2), (1, 3), (2, 1), (3, 2)\}, \\ a_2 & \text{if } (s, t) \in \{(1, 1), (2, 2), (3, 1)\}. \end{cases}$$

It is also routine work to show that, whenever there are $x, y \in X$ with $\delta(a_1, x) = a_1$ and $\delta(a_2, y) = a_2$, then $\mathfrak{A}$ cannot be represented homomorphically by any of the single-factor α_1-powers of $\mathfrak{A}_1$ or $\mathfrak{A}_2$. □

Lemma 6.4. *Let $i \geqq 0$, and take a two-state homomorphically α_i-simple automaton $\mathfrak{A} = (X, \{a_1, a_2\}, \delta)$. Then, for arbitrary $a \in \{a_1, a_2\}$ and $x, y \in X$, the equality $\delta(a, x) = \delta(a, y)$ holds.*

Proof. For arbitrary $s, t \in [2]$, let X_{st} have the same meaning as in the proof of the previous lemma. By Lemma 6.3, we may suppose that $X_{12} = X_{22} = \emptyset$. Again, take two automata $\mathfrak{A}_1 = (X, [3], \delta_1)$ and $\mathfrak{A}_2 = ([3] \times X, [3], \delta_2)$, where for arbitrary $s, t \in [3]$ and $x \in X$,

$$\delta_1(s, x) = \begin{cases} 1 \text{ if } s \neq 1, \\ 2 \text{ if } s = 1 \text{ and } x \in X_{11}, \\ 3 \text{ if } s = 1 \text{ and } x \in X_{21} \end{cases}$$

and

$$\delta_2(t, (s, x)) = \begin{cases} 1 \text{ if } t = 3, \quad \text{or} \\ \quad t = 1 \text{ and } (s, x) \notin \{2\} \times X_{21}, \\ 2 \text{ if } t = 1 \text{ and } (s, x) \in \{2\} \times X_{21}, \quad \text{or} \\ \quad t = 2 \text{ and } (s, x) \notin \{2, 3\} \times X_{11}, \\ 3 \text{ if } t = 2 \text{ and } (s, x) \in \{2, 3\} \times X_{11}. \end{cases}$$

Consider the α_0-product $\mathfrak{C} = (\mathfrak{A}_1 \times \mathfrak{A}_2)[X, \varphi]$ with $\varphi_1(x) = x$ and $\varphi_2(s, x) = (s, x)$ $(x \in X, s \in [3])$. It can be shown in a trivial way that the mapping $\psi: [3] \times [3] \to \{a_1, a_2\}$ given by

$$\psi((s, t)) = \begin{cases} a_1 \text{ if } (s, t) \in \{(1, 1), (1, 3), (2, 1), (2, 2), (3, 2)\}, \\ a_2 \text{ if } (s, t) \in \{(1, 2), (2, 3), (3, 1), (3, 3)\} \end{cases}$$

is a homomorphism of $\mathfrak{C}$ onto $\mathfrak{A}$. Moreover, if there are $x, y \in X$ with $\delta(a_1, x) \neq \delta(a_1, y)$, then none of the single-factor α_1-powers of $\mathfrak{A}_1$ or $\mathfrak{A}_2$ represents $\mathfrak{A}$ homomorphically. □

The next result determines the class of homomorphically α_i-simple automata.

Theorem 6.5. *Let $i \geqq 0$ be an arbitrary integer. An automaton is homomorphically α_i-simple if and only if it is a two-state nilpotent automaton.*

Proof. By Lemmas 6.2, 6.3 and 6.4, every homomorphically α_i-simple automaton is a two-state nilpotent automaton or it is isomorphic to a two-state generalized counter. We show that none of the two-state generalized counters is homomorphically α_i-simple.

Let us start with $i = 0$. Let $\mathfrak{A} = (X, [2], \delta)$ be a generalized counter. Take the three-state generalized counter $\mathfrak{B} = (X, [3], \delta')$, and consider the automaton $\mathfrak{C} = ([3] \times X,\ [3] \times [2] \cup \{(0, 0)\}, \delta'')$, where, for arbitrary $(u, v) \in [3] \times [2]$ and $(k, x) \in [3] \times X$,

$$\delta''((u, v), (k, x)) = \begin{cases} (u + 1 \ (\mathrm{mod}\ 3), v + 1 \ (\mathrm{mod}\ 2)) \text{ if } u = k\,, \\ (0, 0) \text{ otherwise}\,, \end{cases}$$

and $\delta''((0, 0), (k, x)) = (0, 0)$. Form the α_0-product $(\mathfrak{B} \times \mathfrak{C})[X, \varphi]$, where $\varphi(k, (u, v), x) = (x, (k, x))$ for all $k \in [3]$, $(u, v) \in [3] \times [2] \cup \{(0, 0)\}$ and $x \in X$. Take the set $D = \{(k, (k, v)) \mid k \in [3],\ v \in [2]\}$. It is easy to show that D forms a subautomaton of $(\mathfrak{B} \times \mathfrak{C})\ [X, \varphi]$, and the mapping ψ given by $\psi((k, (k, v))) = v\ ((k, (k, v)) \in D)$ is a homomorphism of this subautomaton onto $\mathfrak{A}$. It is clear that none of the single-factor α_0-products of $\mathfrak{B}$ represents $\mathfrak{A}$ homomorphically. We arrive at the same result concerning $\mathfrak{C}$ by taking into consideration that, under the application of an input word having two consecutive occurrences of an input signal, $\mathfrak{C}$ passes into $(0, 0)$, and $\{(0, 0)\}$ forms a one-state subautomaton of $\mathfrak{C}$.

Again, let $\mathfrak{A}$ be the two-state generalized counter above. Take the automaton $\mathfrak{B} = (\{x_1, x_2\}, [3], \delta')$, where $\delta'(k, x_1) = k + 1 \ (\mathrm{mod}\ 3)$ and $\delta'(k, x_2) = k$ for arbitrary $k \in [3]$. Consider the α_1-power $\mathfrak{C} = (\mathfrak{B} \times \mathfrak{B})[X, \varphi]$ with $\varphi_1(x) = x_1$, $\varphi_2(1, 1, x) = \varphi_2(2, 1, x) = \varphi_2(2, 3, x) = x_2$, and $\varphi_2(3, 1, x) = \varphi_2(1, 2, x) = \varphi_2(3, 3, x) = x_1$. It is routine work to show that $C' = \{(1, 1), (2, 1), (2, 3), (3, 1), (1, 2), (3, 3)\}$ forms a subautomaton of $\mathfrak{C}$ and is isomorphic to a six-state generalized counter. On the other hand, it is clear that none of the single-factor α_1-powers of $\mathfrak{B}$ represents $\mathfrak{A}$ homomorphically. Therefore, $\mathfrak{A}$ is not homomorphically α_1-simple, and thus it is not homomorphically α_i-simple for any $i > 1$.

To prove the converse, take an arbitrary two-state nilpotent automaton $\mathfrak{A} = (X, A, \delta)$, and assume that $\mathfrak{A}$ can be represented homomorphically by an α_0-product of automata from a class $\mathscr{K}$. Since the α_0-products, subautomata, and homomorphic images of permutation automata are obviously permutation automata and $\mathfrak{A}$ is not a permutation automaton, $\mathscr{K}$ contains a non-permutation automaton $\mathfrak{B} = (Y, B, \delta')$ such that there are pairwise distinct states $b_0, b_1, \ldots, b_n \in B$ $(n > 0)$ and an input signal $y \in Y$ with $\delta(b_0, y) = b_1$ and, for every $t \in [n]$, $\delta(b_t, y) = b_{t+1 (\mathrm{mod}\ n)}$. Take the single factor α_0-power $\mathfrak{B}' = (X, B, \delta'') = (\mathfrak{B})[X, \varphi]$, where $\varphi_1(x) = y$ for every $x \in X$. Obviously, $\{b_0, b_1, \ldots, b_n\}$ is a subautomaton of $\mathfrak{B}'$ which can be mapped homomorphically onto $\mathfrak{A}$.

Assume next that for the above $\mathfrak{A}$ we have $\mathfrak{A} \in \mathbf{HSP}_{\alpha_1}(\mathscr{K})$. Then, by Lemma 3.3, $\mathfrak{A} \in \mathbf{HSP}_{\alpha_0}\mathbf{P}_{1\alpha_1}(\mathscr{K})$. Repeating the above arguments for $\mathbf{P}_{1\alpha_1}(\mathscr{K})$ instead of $\mathscr{K}$, we have $\mathfrak{A} \in \mathbf{P}_{1\alpha_1}(\mathscr{K})$.

Finally assume that $\mathfrak{A} \in \mathbf{HSP}_{\alpha_i}(\mathscr{K})$ and $i > 1$. If $\mathscr{K}$ satisfies Letičevskiĭ's criterion, then $\mathfrak{A} \in \mathbf{HSP}_{1\alpha_1}(\mathscr{K})$ obviously holds. In the opposite case, according to Cases 2 and 3 in the proof of Theorem 5.4 we have $\mathfrak{A} \in \mathbf{HSP}_{\alpha_1}(\mathscr{K})$ or $\mathfrak{A} \in \mathbf{HSP}_{\alpha_0}(\mathscr{K})$. As shown in both of these cases, the inclusion $\mathfrak{A} \in \mathbf{HSP}_{1\alpha_1}(\mathscr{K})$ holds. □

From our earlier results, it is clear that the class of all homomorphically α_i-simple automata is not homomorphically complete for any of the α_i-products.

2.7 A Decidability Result

Although there are finite homomorphically complete systems with respect to the general product, it is reasonable to deal with the problem of whether a given automaton can be represented homomorphically by products of automata from a fixed finite class.

Theorem 7.1. *Let* $\mathfrak{A}$ *be an automaton and* $\mathscr{K}$ *a finite class of automata. It is decidable whether* $\mathfrak{A} \in \mathbf{HSP}_g(\mathscr{K})$.

Proof. We proceed according to Cases 1–3 of the proof of Theorem 5.4.

If $\mathscr{K}$ satisfies Letičevskiĭ's criterion, then $\mathbf{HSP}_g(\mathscr{K})$ is the class of all automata.

The proof of Case 2 of Theorem 5.4 yields an algorithm to decide the inclusion $\mathfrak{A} \in \mathbf{HSP}_g(\mathscr{K})$ if $\mathscr{K}$ does not satisfy Letičevskiĭ's criterion and there is a $\mathfrak{B} = (X, B, \delta) \in \mathscr{K}$ such that $\delta(b_0, x_1) \neq \delta(b_0, y_1)$ and $\delta(b_0, y_1 p) = b_0$ for certain $b_0 \in B$, $x_1, y_1 \in X$ and $p \in X^*$.

To end the proof of Theorem 7.1, we may assume that there exists a $k \geqq 0$ such that, for arbitrary $\mathfrak{C} = (X_{\mathfrak{C}}, C, \delta_{\mathfrak{C}}) \in \mathscr{K}$, $c \in C$, $p \in X_{\mathfrak{C}}^*$ with $|p| \geqq k$ and $x_1, x_2 \in X_{\mathfrak{C}}$, $\delta_{\mathfrak{C}}(c, px_1) = \delta_{\mathfrak{C}}(c, px_2)$.

Take an automaton $\mathfrak{A} = (X, A, \delta)$ and a general product $\mathfrak{B} = (X, B, \delta') = \prod_{s=1}^{l} \mathfrak{A}_s[X, \varphi]$ with $|X| = m$ and $\mathfrak{A}_s = (X_s, A_s, \delta_s) \in \mathscr{K}$ $(s = 1, \ldots, l)$. Let $\{a_1, \ldots, a_n\}$ be a generating set of $\mathfrak{A}$. Suppose that a subautomaton of $\mathfrak{B}$ can be mapped homomorphically onto $\mathfrak{A}$, and let $\mathbf{b}_i$ be a counter image of a_i $(i = 1, \ldots, n)$ under this homomorphism. Denote by $\mathfrak{B}' = (X, B', \delta'')$ the subautomaton of $\mathfrak{B}$ generated by $\{\mathbf{b}_1, \ldots, \mathbf{b}_n\}$. Moreover, set $u = \max\{|\mathfrak{A}| \mid \mathfrak{A} \in \mathscr{K}\}$ and $v = |\mathscr{K}|$. We shall show the existence of a general product $\bar{\mathfrak{B}} = (X, \bar{B}, \bar{\delta})$ of automata from $\{\mathfrak{A}_s \mid s = 1, \ldots, l\} \subseteq \mathscr{K}$ with a number of factors not exceeding vu^{nt}, where $t = \dfrac{m^{k+1} - 1}{m - 1}$ if $m > 1$, and $t = k + 1$ for $m = 1$, such that a subautomaton $\bar{\mathfrak{B}}' = (X, \bar{B}, \bar{\delta}')$ of $\bar{\mathfrak{B}}$ is isomorphic to $\mathfrak{B}'$. This will obviously complete the proof of Theorem 7.1.

Thus, assume that $l > vu^{nt}$. Since the number of words in $X^{(k)}$ is t, there are indices i, j $(1 \leqq i < j \leqq l)$ such that $\mathfrak{A}_i = \mathfrak{A}_j$ and $\delta_i(pr_i(\mathbf{b}_r), \varphi_i(\mathbf{b}_r, p)) = \delta_j(pr_j(\mathbf{b}_r, \varphi_j(\mathbf{b}_r, p))$ hold for arbitrary r $(1 \leqq r \leqq n)$ and $p \in X^{(k)}$. By the choice of k, $\delta_i(pr_i(\mathbf{b}_r), \varphi_i(\mathbf{b}_r, q)) = \delta_j(pr_j(\mathbf{b}_r), \varphi_j(\mathbf{b}_r, q))$ is valid for any r $(1 \leqq r \leqq n)$ and $q \in X^*$.

Take the product $\mathfrak{D} = (X, D, \delta_{\mathfrak{D}}) = \prod_{s=1}^{l-1} \mathfrak{B}_s[X, \varphi']$, where $\mathfrak{B}_s = \mathfrak{A}_s$ if $s < j$, and $\mathfrak{B}_s = \mathfrak{A}_{s+1}$ otherwise. Moreover, let $\mathbf{d}_i$ $(i = 1, \ldots, n)$ be the states of $\mathfrak{D}$ for which $\mathrm{pr}_s(\mathbf{d}_i) = \mathrm{pr}_s(\mathbf{b}_i)$ if $s < j$, and $\mathrm{pr}_s(\mathbf{d}_i) = \mathrm{pr}_{s+1}(\mathbf{b}_i)$ in all other cases. Finally, for arbitrary $\mathbf{d}_i$ $(1 \leqq i \leqq n)$, $p \in X^*$ and $x \in X$ let $\varphi'_s(\delta_{\mathfrak{D}}(\mathbf{d}_i, p), x) = \varphi_s(\delta'(\mathbf{b}_i, p), x)$ if $s < j$, and $\varphi'_s(\delta_{\mathfrak{D}}(\mathbf{d}_i, p), x) = \varphi_{s+1}(\delta'(\mathbf{b}_i, p), x)$ otherwise. In all other cases, φ' is given arbitrarily. It is obvious that φ' is well defined. Denote by $\mathfrak{D}' = (X, D', \delta'_{\mathfrak{D}})$ the subautomaton of $\mathfrak{D}$ generated by $\{\mathbf{d}_1, \ldots, \mathbf{d}_n\}$. Moreover, consider the mapping $\psi : B' \to D'$ given by $\psi(\delta''(\mathbf{b}_i, p)) = \delta'_{\mathfrak{D}}(\mathbf{b}_i, p)$ $(p \in X^*, i \in [n])$. Clearly, ψ is an isomorphism of $\mathfrak{B}'$ onto $\mathfrak{D}'$.

If $l - 1 > vu^{nt}$, then apply the above process to $\mathfrak{D}$. Finally, we shall obtain a product $\bar{\mathfrak{B}}$ with the required properties. □

3. Isomorphic Representations

We now use a representation stronger than that studied in the previous chapter: we shall deal with isomorphic representations. It will be seen that there is no finite isomorphically complete system with respect to any of the α_i-products. Moreover, as regards isomorphic representation the α_i-products form a proper hierarchy, and from $i = 1$ they are equivalent to each other with respect to isomorphic completeness.

3.1 Embedding into α_i-Products of Automata with Fewer States Than a Given Integer

In this preparatory section we give necessary and sufficient conditions under which an automaton can be represented isomorphically by α_i-products of automata with fewer states than a fixed positive integer. These conditions will be used to compare the isomorphic representation capacities of α_i-products.

Definition 1.1. Let A be a set. A system $\pi_0, \pi_1, \dots, \pi_n$ of partitions of A is *regular* if the following conditions are satisfied:

(i) π_0 has one block only,
(ii) π_n has one-element blocks only, and
(iii) $\pi_0 \geqq \pi_1 \geqq \dots \geqq \pi_n$.

Consider the above set A and regular system $\pi_0, \pi_1, \dots, \pi_n$ of partitions. For each $a \in A$, denote by $\pi(a)$ the block of π containing a. Moreover, set $M_{j,a} = \{\pi_{j+1}(b) \mid b \in \pi_j(a)\}$, where $a \in A$ and $j \in \{0, \dots, n-1\}$. Finally, let $\pi_j/\pi_{j+1} = \max\{|M_{j,a}| \mid a \in A\}$ ($j = 0, \dots, n-1$).

We first deal with the representability by α_0-products of automata having fewer states than l. Since the case $l \leqq 2$ is trivial, we shall consider $l > 2$ only.

Theorem 1.2. *Let $l > 2$ be an arbitrary integer. An automaton $\mathfrak{A} = (X, A, \delta)$ can be represented isomorphically by an α_0-product of automata with fewer states than l if and only if there are an integer n and a regular system $\pi_0, \pi_1, \dots, \pi_n$ of compatible partitions of $\mathfrak{A}$ such that $\pi_j/\pi_{j+1} < l$ for every $j \in \{0, \dots, n-1\}$.*

Proof. To show the necessity, assume that $\mathfrak{A}$ can be embedded into an α_0-product

$$\mathfrak{B} = (X, B, \bar{\delta}) = \prod_{i=1}^{n} \mathfrak{B}_i[X, \varphi] \qquad (\mathfrak{B}_i = (X_i, B_i, \delta_i),\ |B_i| < l,\ i = 1, \dots, n)$$

under a mapping ψ. Let $\mathfrak{B}' = (X, B', \delta')$ be the subautomaton of $\mathfrak{B}$ determined by $B' = \psi(A)$. Define the relations ϱ_i $(i = 1, \dots, n)$ on B' in the following way: for arbitrary two states $\mathbf{b} = (b_1, \dots, b_n), \mathbf{b}' = (b_1', \dots, b_n') \in B'$,

$$\mathbf{b} \equiv \mathbf{b}'(\varrho_i) \Leftrightarrow b_j = b_j' \text{ for every } j = 1, \dots, i\,.$$

Since $\mathfrak{B}$ is an α_0-product, $\mathbf{b} \equiv \mathbf{b}'(\varrho_i)$ implies $\varphi_j(\mathbf{b}, x) = \varphi_j(\mathbf{b}', x)$ for all $x \in X$ and $j = 1, \dots, i$. Therefore, if $\delta'(\mathbf{b}, x) = (\bar{b}_1, \dots, \bar{b}_n)$ and $\delta'(\mathbf{b}', x) = (\bar{b}_1', \dots, \bar{b}_n')$, then $\bar{b}_j = \bar{b}_j'$ for every $j \in [i]$, i.e. each ϱ_i $(i = 1, \dots, n)$ is a congruence relation of $\mathfrak{B}'$. For every $i = 1, \dots, n$, denote by π_i' the partition belonging to ϱ_i, and let $\pi_0' = \{B'\}$. By the definition of ϱ_i $(1 \leqq i \leqq n)$, for every $j \in \{0, \dots, n-1\}$, $\pi_j'/\pi_{j+1}' \leqq |B_j| < l$. Finally, the partitions π_i $(i = 0, \dots, n)$ defined by $\pi_i(\psi^{-1}(\mathbf{b})) = \psi^{-1}(\pi_i'(\mathbf{b}))$ $(\mathbf{b} \in B')$ obviously satisfy the conclusions of Theorem 1.2. This ends the proof of the necessity.

Conversely, assume that $\mathfrak{A}$ and the system $\pi_0, \dots, \pi_n$ of partitions satisfy the conditions of Theorem 1.2. We construct automata $\mathfrak{B}_i = (X_i, B_i, \delta_i)$ $(i = 1, \dots, n)$ such that $|B_i| < l$ and $\mathfrak{A}$ is isomorphic to a subautomaton of an α_0-product of these automata $\mathfrak{B}_i$.

Let $B_1 = \pi_1, X_1 = X$, and for arbitrary $a \in A$ and $x \in X$, $\delta_1(\pi_1(a), x) = \pi_1(\delta(a, x))$. Moreover, for every $j \in \{2, \dots, n\}$, let B_j be an arbitrary abstract set with $|B_j| = \pi_{j-1}/\pi_j$. Further, let $X_j = B_1 \times \dots \times B_{j-1} \times X$. For every $j \in \{2, \dots, n\}$, let $\varkappa_j$ be a mapping of π_j onto B_j such that the restriction of $\varkappa_j$ to arbitrary $M_{j-1,a}$ $(a \in A)$ is one-to-one. Define the transition function δ_j $(2 \leqq j \leqq n)$ by the following rules.

(i) For arbitrary $b_j \in B_j$ and $(b_1, \dots, b_{j-1}, x) \in X_j$, if there exists an $a \in A$ such that $b_1 = \pi_1(a)$ and $b_t = \varkappa_t(\pi_t(a))$ $(t = 2, \dots, j)$, then $\delta_j(b_j, (b_1, \dots, b_{j-1}, x)) = \varkappa_j(\pi_j(\delta(a, x)))$.
(ii) In all other cases δ_j is given arbitrarily.

We show that each δ_j is well defined. For this, take a $b \in A$ satisfying the conditions of (i). We prove by induction on t that $\pi_t(a) = \pi_t(b)$ for every $t \in [j]$. This is obvious if $t = 1$. Assume that our statement has been proved for $t-1$ $(1 \leqq t \leqq j)$, i.e. $\pi_{t-1}(a) = \pi_{t-1}(b)$. Since $\varkappa_t$ is one-to-one on $M_{t-1,a}$ and $\varkappa_t(\pi_t(a)) = \varkappa_t(\pi_t(b))$ $(= b_t)$, the equality $\pi_t(a) = \pi_t(b)$ holds. In particular, $\pi_j(a) = \pi_j(b)$ which, on the assumption that π_j is compatible, implies $\pi_j(\delta_j(a, x)) = \pi_j(\delta_j(b, x))$.

Next, form the α_0-product

$$\mathfrak{B} = (X, B, \bar{\delta}) = \prod_{i=1}^{n} \mathfrak{B}_i[X, \varphi]$$

where φ_1 is the identity mapping, and for arbitrary $j \in \{2, \dots, n\}$, $x \in X$ and $b_t \in B_t$ $(t = 1, \dots, j-1)$, $\varphi_t(b_1, \dots, b_{t-1}, x) = (b_1, \dots, b_{t-1}, x)$.

Define the mapping $\psi: A \to B$ by

$$\psi(a) = (\pi_1(a), \varkappa_2(\pi_2(a)), \dots, \varkappa_n(\pi_n(a)))$$

for every $a \in A$. We show that ψ is an isomorphism of $\mathfrak{A}$ into $\mathfrak{B}$. It can be shown by an obvious induction that ψ is one-to-one. Next, take an arbitrary input signal $x \in X$.

Then

$$\bar{\delta}(\psi(a), x) = (\delta_1(\pi_1(a), x), \delta_2(\varkappa_2(\pi_2(a)), (\pi_1(a), x)),$$
$$\dots, \delta_n(\varkappa_n(\pi_n(a)), (\pi_1(a), \varkappa_2(\pi_2(a)), \dots, \varkappa_{n-1}(\pi_{n-1}(a)), x)))$$
$$= (\pi_1(\delta(a, x)), \varkappa_2(\pi_2(\delta(a, x))), \dots, \varkappa_n(\pi_n(\delta(a, x)))) = \psi(\delta(a, x)) .$$

Therefore, ψ is an isomorphism. □

We now turn to α_i-products with $i \geqq 1$.

Theorem 1.3. *Let $l > 2$ be an arbitrary integer and $i \geqq 1$. An automaton $\mathfrak{A} = (X, A, \delta)$ can be represented isomorphically by an α_i-product of automata with fewer states than l if and only if there are an integer n and a regular system $\pi_0, \dots, \pi_n$ of partitions of A such that the following conditions are satisfied.*

(i) *For every $j \in \{0, \dots, n-1\}$, $\pi_j/\pi_{j+1} < l$.*
(ii) *For arbitrary j with $i - 1 \leqq j \leqq n$, $x \in X$ and $a, b \in A$, $\pi_j(a) = \pi_j(b)$ implies $\pi_{j-i+1}(\delta(a, x)) = \pi_{j-i+1}(\delta(b, x))$.*

Proof. The proof is a natural generalization of that of Theorem 1.2. We therefore restrict ourselves to constructions only.

Assume that $\mathfrak{A}$ can be embedded into an α_i-product

$$\mathfrak{B} = (X, B, \bar{\delta}) = \prod_{j=1}^{n} \mathfrak{B}_j[X, \varphi] \qquad (\mathfrak{B}_j = (X_j, B_j, \delta_j), |B_j| < l, j = 1, \dots, n)$$

under an isomorphism ψ. Take the subautomaton $\mathfrak{B}' = (X, B', \delta')$ determined by $B = \psi(A)$. Define the relations ϱ_j $(j = 1, \dots, n)$ on B' in the same way as in the proof of Theorem 1.2: for two arbitrary states $\mathbf{b} = (b_1, \dots, b_n)$, $\mathbf{b}' = (b_1', \dots, b_n') \in B'$.

$$\mathbf{b} \equiv \mathbf{b}'(\varrho_j) \Leftrightarrow b_t = b_t' \text{ for every } t \in [j] .$$

Moreover, for every $j \in [n]$, let π_j' be the partition belonging to ϱ_j, and let π_j be the partition of A determined by $\pi_j(\psi^{-1}(\mathbf{b})) = \psi^{-1}(\pi_j'(\mathbf{b}))$ $(\mathbf{b} \in B')$. It is easy to show that the system $\pi_0, \dots, \pi_n$ satisfies the conclusions of Theorem 1.3.

Conservely, assume that $\mathfrak{A}$ and $\pi_0, \dots, \pi_n$ satisfy the conditions of Theorem 1.3. We construct automata $\mathfrak{B}_j = (X_j, B_j, \delta_j)$ $(j = 1, \dots, n)$ such that $\mathfrak{A}$ can be embedded into an α_i-product of these $\mathfrak{B}_j$.

For every $j \in [n]$, let B_j be a set with $|B_j| = \pi_{j-1}/\pi_j$. Moreover, $X_j = B_1 \times \dots \times B_{j+i-1} \times X$ if $j + i - 1 \leqq n$, and $X_j = B_1 \times \dots \times B_n \times X$ otherwise. To define δ_j, take a mapping $\varkappa_j$ of π_j onto B_j such that the restriction of $\varkappa_j$ to each $M_{j-1,a}$ $(a \in A)$ is one-to-one. Then δ_j is given as follows:

(i) $j \leqq n - i + 1$. For arbitrary $a_j \in B_j$ and $(b_1, \dots, b_{j+i-1}, x) \in X_j$, if $b_j = a_j$ and there exists an a such that $\varkappa_t(\pi_t(a)) = b_t$ $(t = 1, \dots, j + i - 1)$, then $\delta_j(a_j, (b_1, \dots, b_{j+i-1}, x)) = \varkappa_j(\pi_j(\delta(a, x)))$.

(ii) $j > n - i + 1$. For arbitrary $a_j \in B_j$ and $(b_1, \ldots, b_n, x) \in X_j$, if $b_j = a_j$ and there exists an a satisfying $\varkappa_t(\pi_t(a)) = b_t$ $(t = 1, \ldots, n)$, then $\delta_j(a_j, (b_1, \ldots, b_n, x)) = \varkappa_j(\pi_j(\delta(a, x)))$.

(iii) In all other cases δ_j is given arbitrarily.

Again, it can easily be shown that δ_j is well defined.

Let us form the product

$$\mathfrak{B} = (X, B, \bar{\delta}) = \prod_{j=1}^{n} \mathfrak{B}_j[X, \varphi]$$

where, for arbitrary $j \in [n]$, $x \in X$ and $b_t \in B_t$ $(t = 1, \ldots, n)$,

$$\varphi_j(b_1, \ldots, b_n, x) = \begin{cases} (b_1, \ldots, b_{j+i-1}, x) & \text{if } j \leqq n - i + 1 , \\ (b_1, \ldots, b_n, x) & \text{otherwise} . \end{cases}$$

Clearly, $\mathfrak{B}$ is an α_i-product.

Finally, define the mapping $\psi : A \to B$ similarly as in the proof of Theorem 1.2: for arbitrary $a \in A$,

$$\psi(a) = (\varkappa_1(\pi_1(a)), \ldots, \varkappa_n(\pi_n(a))) .$$

Again, routine computation shows that ψ is an isomorphism of $\mathfrak{A}$ into $\mathfrak{B}$. □

Comparing Theorem 1.2 with the case $i = 1$ in Theorem 1.3, we have

Corollary 1.4. *Let $\mathfrak{A}$ be an automaton and $j > 2$ an integer. Then $\mathfrak{A}$ can be represented isomorphically by an α_0-product of automata with fewer states than l if and only if $\mathfrak{A}$ can be represented isomorphically by an α_1-product of automata with fewer states than l.* □

Take an automaton $\mathfrak{A} = (X, A, \delta)$ with at least three states. Let π_1 be a proper partition of A, $\pi_2 = \{\{a\} \mid a \in A\}$ and $\pi_0 = \{A\}$. Then π_0, π_1, π_2 is a regular system which, under $l = |A|$, obviously satisfies the conclusions of Theorem 1.3 for every $i > 1$. Therefore, we have

Corollary 1.5. *Let $\mathfrak{A}$ be an automaton with at least three states. Then, for every $i > 1$, $\mathfrak{A}$ can be represented isomorphically by an α_i-product of smaller automata.* □

We end this section with

Example 1.6. Let $\mathfrak{A} = (\{x\}, [5], \delta)$ be a five-state counter. Moreover, let $l = 3$. As has been shown in the proof of Theorem 2.5.5, $\mathfrak{A}$ cannot be represented homomorphically by any of the α_0- or α_1-products of smaller automata. It therefore cannot be represented isomorphically by α_0- or α_1-products of automata with fewer states than l.

Consider the following partitions π_j ($j = 1, 2, 3, 4$) of A:

$$\pi_1 = \{\{1, 2, 3, 4\}, \{5\}\}, \qquad \pi_2 = \{\{1, 2, 3\}, \{4\}, \{5\}\},$$
$$\pi_3 = \{\{1, 2\}, \{3\}, \{4\}, \{5\}\}, \qquad \pi_4 = \{\{1\}, \{2\}, \{3\}, \{4\}, \{5\}\}.$$

Moreover, set $\pi_0 = \{[5]\}$. The system $\pi_0, \pi_1, \pi_2, \pi_3, \pi_4$ is then regular and, under $i = 2$, it satisfies the conclusions of Theorem 1.3. Further, $\pi_j/\pi_{j+1} = 2$ ($j = 0, 1, 2, 3$). To give the automata $\mathfrak{B}_j = (X_j, B_j, \delta_j)$ ($j = 1, 2, 3, 4$), let $B_j = \{b_j^{(1)}, b_j^{(2)}\}$ ($j \in [4]$) and

$$X_1 = B_1 \times B_2 \times \{x\}, \quad \varkappa_1(\{1, 2, 3, 4\}) = b_1^{(1)} \text{ and } \varkappa_2(\{5\}) = b_1^{(2)},$$

$$X_2 = B_1 \times B_2 \times B_3 \times \{x\}, \quad \varkappa_2(\{1, 2, 3\}) = b_2^{(1)} \text{ and } \varkappa_2(\{t\}) = b_2^{(2)}\ (t = 4, 5),$$

$$X_3 = B_1 \times B_2 \times B_3 \times B_4 \times \{x\}, \quad \varkappa_3(\{1, 2\}) = b_3^{(1)} \text{ and } \varkappa_2(\{t\}) = b_3^{(2)}\ (t = 3, 4, 5),$$

$$X_4 = B_1 \times B_2 \times B_3 \times B_4 \times \{x\}, \quad \varkappa_4(\{1\}) = b_4^{(1)} \text{ and } \varkappa_4(\{t\}) = b_4^{(2)}\ (t = 2, 3, 4, 5).$$

The transition functions δ_j ($j = 1, 2, 3, 4$) are given by the tables below. (In these tables we indicate only those transitions which are not chosen arbitrarily. Moreover, beside each input signal we put one of the states which determine the given transition by (i) or (ii) in the proof of Theorem 1.3.)

	δ_1	$b_1^{(1)}$	$b_1^{(2)}$
3	$(b_1^{(1)}, b_2^{(1)}, x)$	$b_1^{(1)}$	–
4	$(b_1^{(1)}, b_2^{(2)}, x)$	$b_1^{(2)}$	–
5	$(b_1^{(2)}, b_2^{(2)}, x)$	–	$b_1^{(1)}$

	δ_2	$b_2^{(1)}$	$b_2^{(2)}$
2	$(b_1^{(1)}, b_2^{(1)}, b_3^{(1)}, x)$	$b_2^{(1)}$	–
3	$(b_1^{(1)}, b_2^{(1)}, b_3^{(2)}, x)$	$b_2^{(2)}$	–
4	$(b_1^{(1)}, b_2^{(2)}, b_3^{(2)}, x)$	–	$b_2^{(2)}$
5	$(b_1^{(2)}, b_2^{(2)}, b_3^{(2)}, x)$	–	$b_2^{(1)}$

	δ_3	$b_3^{(1)}$	$b_3^{(2)}$
1	$(b_1^{(1)}, b_2^{(1)}, b_3^{(1)}, b_4^{(1)}, x)$	$b_3^{(1)}$	–
2	$(b_1^{(1)}, b_2^{(1)}, b_3^{(1)}, b_4^{(2)}, x)$	$b_3^{(2)}$	–
3	$(b_1^{(1)}, b_2^{(1)}, b_3^{(2)}, b_4^{(2)}, x)$	–	$b_3^{(2)}$
4	$(b_1^{(1)}, b_2^{(2)}, b_3^{(2)}, b_4^{(2)}, x)$	–	$b_3^{(2)}$
5	$(b_1^{(2)}, b_2^{(2)}, b_3^{(2)}, b_4^{(2)}, x)$	–	$b_3^{(1)}$

	δ_4	$b_4^{(1)}$	$b_4^{(2)}$
1	$(b_1^{(1)}, b_2^{(1)}, b_3^{(1)}, b_4^{(1)}, x)$	$b_4^{(2)}$	–
2	$(b_1^{(1)}, b_2^{(1)}, b_3^{(1)}, b_4^{(2)}, x)$	–	$b_4^{(2)}$
3	$(b_1^{(1)}, b_2^{(1)}, b_3^{(2)}, b_4^{(2)}, x)$	–	$b_4^{(2)}$
4	$(b_1^{(1)}, b_2^{(2)}, b_3^{(2)}, b_4^{(2)}, x)$	–	$b_4^{(2)}$
5	$(b_1^{(2)}, b_2^{(2)}, b_3^{(2)}, b_4^{(2)}, x)$	–	$b_4^{(1)}$

Finally, the subautomaton $\mathfrak{B}' = (\{x\}, B', \delta')$ of the α_2-product

$$\mathfrak{B} = (\{x\}, B, \bar{\delta}) = \prod_{j=1}^{4} \mathfrak{B}_j[\{x\}, \varphi]$$

together with the isomorphism $\psi : \mathfrak{A} \to \mathfrak{B}'$, is given by the table below:

δ'	$\mathbf{a}(=\psi(1))$	$\mathbf{b}(=\psi(2))$	$\mathbf{c}(=\psi(3))$	$\mathbf{d}(=\psi(4))$	$\mathbf{e}(=\psi(5))$
x	**b**	**c**	**d**	**e**	**a**

where $\mathbf{a} = (b_1^{(1)}, b_2^{(1)}, b_3^{(1)}, b_4^{(1)})$, $\mathbf{b} = (b_1^{(1)}, b_2^{(1)}, b_3^{(1)}, b_4^{(2)})$, $\mathbf{c} = (b_1^{(1)}, b_2^{(1)}, b_3^{(2)}, b_4^{(2)})$, $\mathbf{d} = (b_1^{(1)}, b_2^{(2)}, b_3^{(2)}, b_4^{(2)})$ and $\mathbf{e} = (b_1^{(2)}, b_2^{(2)}, b_3^{(2)}, b_4^{(2)})$. □

3.2 Isomorphically Complete Systems for the α_0-Product

For every natural number n, let $\mathfrak{T}_n = (T_n, [n], \delta_n)$ denote the automaton, where T_n is the set of all mappings of $[n]$ into itself (all transformations on $[n]$), and $\delta_n(j, t) = t(j)$ $(j \in [n], t \in T_n)$.

The following theorem gives necessary and sufficient conditions for a class of automata to be isomorphically complete with respect to the α_0-product.

Theorem 2.1. *A class $\mathscr{K}$ of automata is isomorphically complete with respect to the α_0-product if and only if, for every natural number n, there exists an automaton $\mathfrak{A} \in \mathscr{K}$ such that $\mathfrak{T}_n$ can be embedded into an α_0-power of $\mathfrak{A}$ with a single factor.*

Proof. Assume that $\mathscr{K}$ is isomorphically complete with respect to the α_0-product. Then, for every integer $n \geqq 1$, $\mathfrak{T}_n$ can be embedded into an α_0-product

$$\mathfrak{B} = (T_n, B, \delta) = \prod_{i=1}^{m} \mathfrak{B}_i[T_n, \varphi] \qquad (\mathfrak{B}_i = (X_i, B_i, \delta_i) \in \mathscr{K}, i = 1, \dots, m)$$

under an isomorphism ψ. We shall show that $\mathfrak{T}_n$ is isomorphic to a subautomaton of an α_0-power of some $\mathfrak{B}_i$ $(1 \leqq i \leqq m)$ with a single factor. If $n = 1$, then for every $i \in [m]$ there are a $b_i \in B_i$ and an $x_i \in X_i$ such that $\delta_i(b_i, x_i) = b_i$. Therefore, $\mathfrak{T}_1$ can be embedded into an α_0-power of any of the automata $\mathfrak{B}_i$ $(i = 1, \dots, m)$ with a single factor. For $m = 1$, $\mathfrak{B}$ itself satisfies the conclusion of the theorem. Thus, we may assume that $n, m > 1$.

Let $\mathfrak{B}' = (T_n, B', \delta')$ be the subautomaton of $\mathfrak{B}$ determined by $B' = \psi([n])$. Define the relations ϱ_i $(i = 1, \dots, m)$ on B' in exactly the same way as in the proof of Theorem 1.2. Each ϱ_i is a congruence relation of $\mathfrak{B}'$. Since $\mathfrak{T}_n$ has only the two trivial congruence relations, every ϱ_i is equal to $\iota_{B'}$ or $\omega_{B'}$. Let r be the least integer for which $\varrho_r \neq \omega_{B'}$. As $n > 1$, there exists such an r. We show that $\mathfrak{T}_n$ can be embedded into an α_0-power of $\mathfrak{B}_r$ with a single factor. For this, let $\psi(j) = (b_{j1}, \dots, b_{jm})$ $(j = 1, \dots, n)$. Then, by the choice of r, $b_{ks} = b_{ls}$ for all $k, l \in [n]$ and $s \in [r-1]$. Take the α_0-power $(\mathfrak{B}_r)[T_n, \varphi']$ of $\mathfrak{B}_r$ where $\varphi'(t) = \varphi_r(b_{11}, \dots, b_{1r-1}, t)$ $(t \in T_n)$. As $\varrho_r = \iota_{\mathfrak{B}'}$, the mapping ψ' given by $\psi'(j) = b_{jr}$ $(j = 1, \dots, n)$ is an isomorphism of $\mathfrak{T}_n$ into $(\mathfrak{B}_r)[T_n, \varphi']$.

Conversely, let $\mathfrak{A} = (X, A, \delta)$ be an automaton with n states. Moreover, let ψ be a one-to-one mapping of A onto $[n]$. Define the α_0-power $\mathfrak{B} = (\mathfrak{T}_n)\,[X, \varphi]$, with a single factor, such that $\psi(\delta(a, x)) = \delta_n(\psi(a), \varphi(x))$ for arbitrary $a \in A$ and $x \in X$. Obviously, φ can be chosen in such a way, and ψ is an isomorphism of $\mathfrak{A}$ into $\mathfrak{B}$. From our assumptions, $\mathcal{K}$ contains a $\mathfrak{C}$ such that $\mathfrak{T}_n$ is a subautomaton of an α_0-power of $\mathfrak{C}$ with a single factor. Therefore, $\mathfrak{A}$ can be represented isomorphically by an α_0-power of $\mathfrak{C}$. □

Let $\mathcal{K}$ be a class of automata which is isomorphically complete with respect to the α_i-product ($i \in \mathbb{N}$). We say that $\mathcal{K}$ is *minimal* if, for every $\mathfrak{A} \in \mathcal{K}$, the class $\mathcal{K} - \{\mathfrak{A}\}$ is not isomorphically complete with respect to the α_i-product.

From Theorem 2.1 we easily obtain

Corollary 2.2. *There exists no class of automata which is isomorphically complete with respect to the α_0-product and minimal.*

Proof. Let $\mathcal{K}$ be an arbitrary class of automata which is isomorphically complete with respect to the α_0-product. Take an $\mathfrak{A} \in \mathcal{K}$ with m states. Then, for every n ($\geqq m$), $\mathfrak{A}$ can be represented isomorphically by an α_0-power of $\mathfrak{T}_n$. Taking an n with $n > m$, by Theorem 2.1, there exists a $\mathfrak{B} \in \mathcal{K}$ with at least n states such that $\mathfrak{T}_n$ can be represented isomorphically by an α_0-power of $\mathfrak{B}$. Therefore, an α_0-power of $\mathfrak{B}$ represents $\mathfrak{A}$ isomorphically. Thus, $\mathcal{K} - \{\mathfrak{A}\}$ is also isomorphically complete with respect to the α_0-product. □

3.3 Isomorphically Complete Systems for α_i-Products with $i \geqq 1$

In our study of isomorphically complete systems with respect to α_i-products with $i \geqq 1$, the following class of automata will play a fundamental role.

Let $n \geqq 1$ be an arbitrary integer. We shall denote by $\mathfrak{D}_n$ the automaton $(X_n, [n], \delta_n)$ where $X_n = \{x_{uv} \mid 1 \leqq u, v \leqq n\}$ and, for every $m \in [n]$ and $x_{uv} \in X_n$,

$$\delta_n(m, x_{uv}) = \begin{cases} v \text{ if } u = m, \\ m \text{ otherwise.} \end{cases}$$

Figure 16 shows $\mathfrak{D}_n$ for $n = 3$.

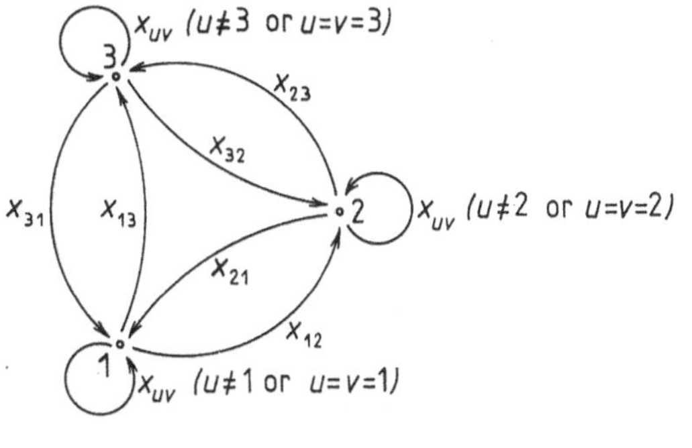

Fig. 16. Automaton $\mathfrak{D}_3$

Theorem 3.1. *A class $\mathscr{K}$ of automata is isomorphically complete with respect to the α_i-product ($i \geqq 1$) if and only if, for every integer $n \geqq 1$, there exists an $\mathfrak{A} \in \mathscr{K}$ such that $\mathfrak{D}_n$ can be embedded into an α_1-power of $\mathfrak{A}$ with a single factor.*

Proof. We first show that, whenever $\mathfrak{D}_n$ can be represented isomorphically by an α_i-product of automata from $\mathscr{K}$, then $\mathfrak{D}_n$ can be embedded into an α_i-product of automata in $\mathscr{K}$ with at most i factors. As the case $n = 1$ is trivial, we suppose that $n > 1$.

Consider an α_i-product

$$\mathfrak{B} = (X_n, B, \delta) = \prod_{t=1}^{m} \mathfrak{B}_t[X_n, \varphi] \qquad (\mathfrak{B}_t = (X'_t, B_t, \delta'_t) \in \mathscr{K}, t = 1, \dots, m).$$

Assume that $\mathfrak{D}_n$ is isomorphic to a subautomaton $\mathfrak{B}' = (X_n, B', \delta')$ of $\mathfrak{B}$, and $\psi : [n] \to B'$ is an isomorphism of $\mathfrak{D}_n$ onto $\mathfrak{B}'$. For every $k \in [n]$, let $\psi(k) = (b_{k1}, \dots, b_{km})$. We may suppose that there are integers r and s ($1 \leqq r, s \leqq n$) such that $b_{r1} \neq b_{s1}$. (Otherwise we would take a suitable α_i-product of $\mathfrak{B}_2, \dots, \mathfrak{B}_m$ with $m - 1$ factors.) If $m \leqq i$, then $\mathfrak{B}$ itself satisfies our claim. We therefore assume that $m > i$.

We show that the vectors $(b_{k1}, \dots, b_{ki})$ ($k = 1, \dots, n$) are pairwise distinct. Suppose that, for two different integers u and v ($1 \leqq u, v \leqq n$), the equality $(b_{u1}, \dots, b_{ui}) = (b_{v1}, \dots, b_{vi})$ holds. Consequently, for every $x \in X_n$, $\varphi_1(b_{u1}, \dots, b_{ui}, x) = \varphi_1(b_{v1}, \dots, b_{vi}, x)$. Since ψ is an isomorphism, under $x = x_{ur}$ we get $\delta'_1(b_{u1}, \varphi_1(b_{u1}, \dots, b_{ui}, x)) = b_{r1}$ and $\delta'_1(b_{v1}, \varphi_1(b_{v1}, \dots, b_{vi}, x)) = b_{v1}$. Thus, $b_{r1} = b_{v1}$. Choosing $x = x_{vs}$, we obtain $b_{s1} = b_{u1}$. These equalities, by $b_{u1} = b_{v1}$, imply $b_{r1} = b_{s1}$, which is a contradiction.

Denote by ψ' the mapping of $[n]$ onto $\{(b_{k1}, \dots, b_{ki}) = \mathbf{b}_k \mid k = 1, \dots, n\}$ for which $\psi'(k) = \mathbf{b}_k$ ($k = 1, \dots, n$). By the computation above, ψ is one-to-one. Moreover, for an arbitrary pair (u, v) of integers with $1 \leqq u, v \leqq n$, there exists a vector $\mathbf{y}_{uv} = (y^{(1)}_{uv}, \dots, y^{(i)}_{uv}) \in X'_1 \times \dots \times X'_i$ such that $\delta'_t(b_{ut}, y^{(t)}_{uv}) = b_{vt}$ ($t = 1, \dots, i$). Take the α_i-product

$$\mathfrak{C} = (X_n, C, \bar{\delta}) = \prod_{t=1}^{i} \mathfrak{B}_t[X_n, \varphi']$$

for which, under arbitrary integers t, u and v ($1 \leqq t, u, v \leqq n$),

$$\varphi'(b_{t1}, \dots, b_{ti}, x_{uv}) = \begin{cases} \mathbf{y}_{uv} & \text{if } t = u, \\ \mathbf{y}_{tt} & \text{otherwise.} \end{cases}$$

Obviously, ψ' is an isomorphism of $\mathfrak{D}_n$ into $\mathfrak{C}$.

We next show that, if a $\mathfrak{D}_n$ can be embedded into an α_i-product of automata from $\mathscr{K}$ with at most i factors, then $\mathfrak{D}_{[\sqrt[i]{n}]}$ is isomorphic to a subautomaton of an α_1-power of some $\mathfrak{A} \in \mathscr{K}$ with a single factor. (Here $[\sqrt[i]{n}]$ denotes the greatest integer less than or equal to $\sqrt[i]{n}$.)

Take the above α_i-product $\mathfrak{B}$ together with the isomorphism ψ of $\mathfrak{D}_n$ into $\mathfrak{B}$, and assume that $m \leqq i$. Again, for every $k \in [n]$, let $\psi(k) = (b_{k1}, \dots, b_{km})$. From our assumptions, there exists at least one j ($1 \leqq j \leqq m$) such that the number l of different elements among $b_{1j}, \dots, b_{nj}$ is at least $[\sqrt[i]{n}]$. We may assume that $b_{1j}, \dots, b_{lj}$ are pairwise distinct. Let $[\sqrt[i]{n}] = t$, and take the mapping $\psi' : [t] \to \{b_{1j}, \dots, b_{tj}\}$ given by $\psi'(k) = b_{kj}$ $(k = 1, \dots, t)$. As ψ is an isomorphism, for arbitrary integers u and v $(1 \leqq u, v \leqq t)$, there is an input signal $x_{uv}^{(j)} \in X'_j$ such that $\delta'_j(b_{uj}, x_{uv}^{(j)}) = b_{vj}$. Now consider the α_1-power $(\mathfrak{B}_j)[X_t, \varphi']$, where, for arbitrary integers k, u and v $(1 \leqq k, u, v \leqq t)$,

$$\varphi'(b_{kj}, x_{uv}) = \begin{cases} x_{uv}^{(j)} \text{ if } k = u, \\ x_{kk}^{(j)} \text{ otherwise.} \end{cases}$$

It is again clear that ψ' is an isomorphism of $\mathfrak{D}_t$ into $(\mathfrak{B}_j)[X_t, \varphi']$. Thus, taking $\mathfrak{D}_{n^i}$, we obtain that $\mathfrak{D}_n$ can be embedded into an α_1-power of some $\mathfrak{A} \in \mathscr{K}$ with a single factor.

Conversely, it is clear that every automaton with n states can be represented isomorphically by an α_1-power of $\mathfrak{D}_n$ with a single factor. Therefore, if $\mathscr{K}$ satisfies the conditions of the theorem, then it is isomorphically complete with respect to the α_1-product. □

From the above theorem, we have

Corollary 3.2. *A class of automata is isomorphically complete with respect to the α_1-product if and only if it is isomorphically complete with respect to any of the α_i-products with $i \geqq 1$.* □

It is obvious that, for arbitrary integers $m \leqq n$, $\mathfrak{D}_m$ is isomorphic to an X-subautomaton of $\mathfrak{D}_n$. We therefore have

Corollary 3.3. *There exists no system of automata which is isomorphically complete with respect to any of the α_i-products and minimal, where $i \geqq 1$.* □

It can easily be shown that, if $m \geqq 2$. then $\mathfrak{T}_m$ cannot be embedded isomorphically into α_0-powers of any of $\mathfrak{D}_n$ with a single factor. On the other hand, by Theorem 3.1, $\mathscr{K} = \{\mathfrak{D}_n \mid n = 1, 2, \dots\}$ is isomorphically complete with respect to every α_i-product with $i \geqq 1$. Thus, using Theorem 2.1, we obtain

Theorem 3.4. *There exists a class $\mathscr{K}$ of automata having the following properties:*

(1) *$\mathscr{K}$ is not isomorphically complete with respect to the α_0-product, and*
(2) *$\mathscr{K}$ is isomorphically complete with respect to every α_i-product with $i \geqq 1$.* □

3.4 Comparison of the Isomorphic Representation Powers of α_i-Products

In the previous section it was proved that, as regards isomorphic completeness, from $i = 1$ all the α_i-products have the same power. We show here that they form a proper hierarchy as concerns isomorphic representations.

Let $\mathfrak{A}_2 = (\{x, y\}, \{0, 1\}, \bar{\delta}_2)$ denote the automaton given by $\bar{\delta}_2(0, x) = \bar{\delta}_2(1, y) = 1$ and $\bar{\delta}_2(1, x) = \bar{\delta}_2(0, y) = 0$. We use this automaton to compare the isomorphic representation capacities of different α_i-products.

We first prove

Theorem 4.1. *The automaton $\mathfrak{D}_n$ can be represented isomorphically by an α_i-power of $\mathfrak{A}_2$ $(i \geqq 1)$ if and only if $1 \leqq n \leqq 2^i$.*

Proof. Assume that $\mathfrak{D}_n$ can be represented isomorphically by an α_i-power of $\mathfrak{A}_2$ with $i \geqq 1$. Then, by the proof of Theorem 3.1, $\mathfrak{D}_n$ can be represented isomorphically by an α_i-power of $\mathfrak{A}_2$ with at most i factors. Therefore, the inequality $n \leqq 2^i$ holds.

To prove the sufficiency, let $i \geqq 1$ and let n be a natural number with $1 \leqq n \leqq 2^i$. Take a one-to-one mapping ψ of $[n]$ into $\{0, 1\}^i$. For every $j \in [n]$, let $\psi(j) = (j_1, \dots, j_i)$. It is clear that, for arbitrary $u, v \in [n]$, there is a $\mathbf{y}_{uv} = (y_{uv}^{(1)}, \dots, y_{uv}^{(i)}) \in \{x, y\}^i$ such that $\bar{\delta}_2(u_t, y_{uv}^{(t)}) = v_t$ $(t = 1, \dots, i)$. Consider the α_i-power

$$\mathfrak{A} = (\underbrace{\mathfrak{A}_2 \times \dots \times \mathfrak{A}_2}_{i\,\text{times}})\,[X_n, \varphi]$$

where, for arbitrary integers t, u and v with $1 \leqq t, u, v \leqq n$,

$$\varphi(t_1, \dots, t_i, x_{uv}) = \begin{cases} \mathbf{y}_{uv} & \text{if } t = u, \\ \mathbf{y}_{tt} & \text{otherwise.} \end{cases}$$

Obviously, ψ is an isomorphism of $\mathfrak{D}_n$ into $\mathfrak{A}$. □

By Theorem 1.4.8, $\{\mathfrak{A}_2\}$ is isomorphically complete with respect to the general product. Thus, from Theorem 4.1 we obtain

Theorem 4.2. *There exists a class $\mathcal{K}$ of automata such that*

(1) *$\mathcal{K}$ is isomorphically complete with respect to the general product, and*
(2) *$\mathcal{K}$ is not isomorphically complete with respect to any of the α_i-products.* □

We end this section with

Theorem 4.3. *The general product is isomorphically more general than any of the α_i-products. Moreover, for every i $(\geqq 0)$, the α_{i+1}-product is isomorphically more general than the α_i-product.*

Proof. By Theorem 4.2, the general product is isomorphically more general than any of the α_i-products. Theorem 4.1 shows that, for every i $(\geqq 1)$, the α_{i+1}-product is isomorphically more general than the α_i-product. Finally, it follows from Theorem 3.4 that the α_1-product is isomorphically more general than the α_0-product. □

3.5 Isomorphically Complete Classes for Nilpotent Automata

In Sections 3.2 and 3.3 it was proved that there is no finite system of automata which is isomorphically complete with respect to any of the α_i-products. The non-existence of such systems is true for most of the well-known special classes of automata. We show here that the class of all nilpotent automata is an exception, and for every $i \geqq 0$ we give a full description of those systems which are isomorphically complete with respect to the α_i-product for the class of all nilpotent automata.

For every integer $n > 1$, let $\mathfrak{N}_n$ be the automaton $\mathfrak{N}_n = (\{x_1, \dots, x_{n-1}\}, [n], \delta_n)$ with $\delta_n(t, x_s) = \min\{t + s, n\}$ $(t \in [n], 1 \leqq s \leqq n - 1)$. $\mathfrak{N}_3$ is illustrated in Fig. 17.

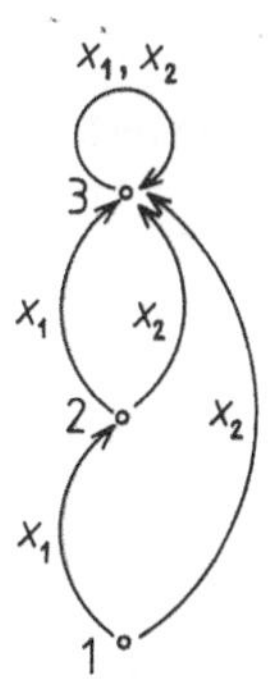

Fig. 17. Automaton $\mathfrak{N}_3$

Clearly, every $\mathfrak{N}_n$ is a nilpotent automaton.

We first deal with the α_0-product.

Theorem 5.1. *A class $\mathscr{K}$ of automata is isomorphically complete with respect to the α_0-product for the class of all nilpotent automata if and only if at least one of the following four conditions is satisfied:*

(1) *There is an automaton $\mathfrak{B} = (Y, B, \delta') \in \mathscr{K}$ having three pairwise different states b, c, d and four (not necessarily different) input signals y, z, v, w such that $\delta'(b, y) = b$, $\delta'(b, z) = c$ and $\delta'(c, v) = \delta'(d, v) = \delta'(b, w) = d$.*

(2) *$\mathscr{K}$ contains an automaton $\mathfrak{B} = (Y, B, \delta')$ which has two different states b, c and two input signals y, z such that $\delta'(b, y) = \delta'(c, y) = c$ and $\delta'(c, z) = b$.*

(3) *$\mathscr{K}$ contains an automaton $\mathfrak{B} = (Y, B, \delta')$ having two different states b, c and two input signals y, z with $\delta'(b, y) = b$ and $\delta'(b, z) = \delta'(c, z) = c$.*

(4) *For every natural number $n \geqq 3$, there is an automaton $\mathfrak{B}_n = (Y_n, B_n, \delta'_n) \in \mathscr{K}$ which has n pairwise distinct states b_t $(t = 1, \dots, n)$ and not necessarily different input signals y_{tk} $(t = 1, \dots, n - 1; k = 1, \dots, n - t)$ such that $\delta'_n(b_t, y_{tk}) = b_{t+k}$ if $t \leqq n - 1$, and $\delta'_n(b_n, y_{n-11}) = b_n$.*

Proof. To prove the necessity of the above conditions, assume that $\mathscr{K}$ is isomorphically complete with respect to the α_0-product for the class of the nilpotent automata. Then, for an arbitrary $n \geqq 3$, $\mathfrak{N}_n$ can be embedded into an α_0-product

$$\mathfrak{A} = (\{x_1, \dots, x_{n-1}\}, A, \delta) = \prod_{i=1}^{k} \mathfrak{A}_i[\{x_1, \dots, x_{n-1}\}, \varphi]$$

where $\mathfrak{A}_i = (X_i, A_i, \delta_i) \in \mathscr{K}$ $(i = 1, \ldots, k)$. Let $\psi : [n] \to A$ be an embedding of $\mathfrak{R}_n$ into $\mathfrak{A}$. For every $t \in [n]$, let $\psi(t) = (a_{t1}, \ldots, a_{tk})$ $(a_{tj} \in A_j, j = 1, \ldots, k)$. Denote by m the least j for which $a_{nj} \neq a_{n-1j}$ $(1 \leqq j \leqq k)$. Let us distinguish the following four cases.

Case 1. There is a t $(1 \leqq t \leqq n-2)$ with $a_{tm} = a_{nm}$. Then (2) is satisfied by $\mathfrak{A}_m$.
Case 2. There is a t $(1 \leqq t \leqq n-2)$ with $a_{tm} = a_{n-1m}$. Then (3) holds under $\mathfrak{B} = \mathfrak{A}_m$.
Case 3. None of a_{tm} $(1 \leqq t \leqq n-2)$ equals a_{n-1m} or a_{nm}, but there are two integers i and j $(1 \leqq i < j \leqq n-2)$ such that $a_{im} = a_{jm}$. In this case $\mathfrak{A}_m$ fulfils the requirements of (1).
Case 4. All the components a_{tm} $(t = 1, \ldots, n)$ are pairwise different. Then $\mathfrak{A}_m$ has every property required of $\mathfrak{B}_n$ by (4).

Conversely, assume that a class $\mathscr{K}$ of automata has one of the properties (1)–(4). Take a nilpotent automaton $\mathfrak{A} = (X, A, \delta)$. The case $|A| = 1$ being trivial, in the rest of the proof we suppose that $|A| \geqq 2$. First of all, observe that the relation $\leqq$ on A defined by

$$a \leqq b \Leftrightarrow ((\exists p \in X^*)\,(\delta(a, p) = b))\ (a, b \in A)$$

is a partial ordering. Let C_1 consist of all the minimal elements of A under $\leqq$. Assume that C_j has been defined for every $j \leqq t$, where $t \geqq 1$ is a fixed integer. Let $C'_t = A \setminus \cup\,(C_j \mid j = 1, \ldots, t)$ and $\leqq_t$ the restriction of $\leqq$ to C'_t. Then C_{t+1} is the set of all the minimal elements of C'_t under $\leqq_t$. Suppose that we have m such sets $C_1, \ldots, C_m$. Obviously, $\cup\,(C_j \mid j = 1, \ldots, m) = A$, $C_i \cap C_j = \emptyset$ if $i \neq j$, and C_m is a singleton set consisting of the absorbent state a_0 of $\mathfrak{A}$.

We now proceed according to cases (1)–(4) in Theorem 5.1. The proof corresponding to (i) $(i = 1, \ldots, 4)$ will be denoted by i'.

1′. If $|A| = 2$, then take the single-factor α_0-power $\bar{\mathfrak{B}} = (X, \bar{B}, \bar{\delta}) = (\mathfrak{B})\,[X, \varphi]$ given by $\varphi_1(x) = v$ for every $x \in X$. In this case, $\mathfrak{A}$ is isomorphic to the subautomaton $\{c, d\}$ of $\bar{\mathfrak{B}}$.

In the opposite case, i.e., if $|A| > 2$, take a fixed element a_1 from C_{m-1}, and define the following relation σ on A: for two elements a, b, let $a \equiv b(\sigma)$ if and only if $a = b$ or $\{a, b\} = \{a_0, a_1\}$. Clearly, σ is a congruence relation of $\mathfrak{A}$. Form the α_0-product $\bar{\mathfrak{B}} = (X, \bar{B}, \bar{\delta}) = (\mathfrak{A}/\sigma \times \mathfrak{B})\,[X, \varphi]$, where $\varphi_1(x) = x$ for every $x \in X$. Moreover, for all $a \in A$ and $x \in X$,

$$\varphi_2(\sigma(a), x) = \begin{cases} y \text{ if } a, \delta(a, x) \in C_1 \cup \ldots \cup C_{m-2}, \\ z \text{ if } a \in C_1 \cup \ldots \cup C_{m-2} \text{ and } \delta(a, x) \in C_{m-1}, \\ w \text{ if } a \in C_1 \cup \ldots \cup C_{m-2} \text{ and } \delta(a, x) = a_0, \\ v \text{ in all other cases.} \end{cases}$$

Take the subset $\bar{B}'$ of B given in the following way: an element $(\sigma(a), b')$ $(a \in A, b' \in B)$ belongs to B' if and only if the next three conditions are satisfied:

(i) if $a \in C_1 \cup \ldots \cup C_{m-2}$, then $b' = b$,
(ii) if $a \in C_{m-1}$ and $a \neq a_1$, then $b' = c$,
(iii) if $a \in \{a_0, a_1\}$, then $b' = c$ or $b' = d$.

It can be verified in a trivial way that $\bar{B}'$ is a subautomaton of $\bar{\mathfrak{B}}$ isomorphic to $\mathfrak{A}$. A suitable isomorphism ψ can be given by

$$\psi((\sigma(a), b')) = \begin{cases} a \text{ if } a \notin \{a_0, a_1\}, \\ a_1 \text{ if } a \in \{a_0, a_1\} \text{ and } b' = c, \\ a_0 \text{ if } a \in \{a_0, a_1\} \text{ and } b' = d, \end{cases}$$

where $(\sigma(a), b') \in \bar{B}'$. Assuming that our assertion is valid for nilpotent automata having fewer states than $|A|$, the proof is completed.

2'. Again if $|A| = 2$, then $\mathfrak{A}$ can obviously be represented isomorphically by a single-factor α_0-power of $\mathfrak{B}$. Thus, let $|A| > 2$, and consider the relation σ defined in 1'. Form the α_0-product $\bar{\mathfrak{B}} = (X, \bar{B}, \bar{\delta}) = (\mathfrak{A}/\sigma \times \mathfrak{B})\,[X, \varphi]$, where $\varphi_1(x) = x$ for every $x \in X$. Moreover, for all $a \in A$ and $x \in X$, let

$$\varphi_2(\sigma(a), x) = \begin{cases} z \text{ if } \delta(a, x) = a_1, \\ y \text{ otherwise.} \end{cases}$$

Consider the subset $\bar{B}'$ of $\bar{B}$ given in the following way. For every $(\sigma(a), b')$ $(a \in A,$ $b' \in B)$, $(\sigma(a), b') \in \bar{B}'$ provided that the next two conditions are fulfilled:

(i) if $a \notin \{a_0, a_1\}$, then $b' = c$,
(ii) if $a \in \{a_0, a_1\}$, then $b' = b$ or $b' = c$.

Moreover, take the mapping ψ for which

$$\psi((\sigma(a), b')) = \begin{cases} a \text{ if } a \notin \{a_0, a_1\}, \\ a_1 \text{ if } a \in \{a_0, a_1\} \text{ and } b' = b, \\ a_0 \text{ if } a \in \{a_0, a_1\} \text{ and } b' = c, \end{cases}$$

where $(\sigma(a), b') \in \bar{B}'$. Then $\bar{B}'$ is a subautomaton of $\bar{\mathfrak{B}}$ which can be mapped isomorphically onto $\mathfrak{A}$ under ψ.

3. The case $|A| = 2$ is again trivial. If $|A| > 2$, take the relation σ, and form the α_0-product $\bar{\mathfrak{B}} = (X, \bar{B}, \bar{\delta}) = (\mathfrak{A}/\sigma \times \mathfrak{B})\,[X, \varphi]$, where $\varphi_1(x) = x$ $(x \in X)$. Moreover, for arbitrary $a \in A$, $\varphi_2(\sigma(a), x) = y$ if $a \notin \{a_0, a_1\}$ and $\delta(a, x) \neq a_0$, and $\varphi_2(\sigma(a), x) = z$ otherwise. Now let $\bar{B}'$ consist of $(\sigma(a_0), b)$, $(\sigma(a_0), c)$ and all $(\sigma(a), b)$ $(a \in A \setminus \{a_0, a_1\})$. Further, take the mapping ψ given by

$$\psi((\sigma(a), b')) = \begin{cases} a \text{ if } a \notin \{a_0, a_1\}, \\ a_1 \text{ if } a \in \{a_0, a_1\} \text{ and } b' = b, \\ a_0 \text{ if } a \in \{a_0, a_1\} \text{ and } b' = c, \end{cases}$$

where $(\sigma(a), b') \in \bar{B}'$. Again, $\bar{B}'$ is a subautomaton of $\bar{\mathfrak{B}}$ which by ψ can be mapped isomorphically onto $\mathfrak{A}$.

4'. The case $|A| = 2$ being obvious, we suppose that $|A| > 2$. Take the σ above and the α_0-product $\bar{\mathfrak{B}} = (X, \bar{B}, \bar{\delta}) = (\mathfrak{A}/\sigma \times \mathfrak{B}_m)\,[X, \varphi]$. We want to define φ in such a way that the subset $\bar{B}'$ of $\bar{B}$ given below is a subautomaton of $\bar{\mathfrak{B}}$ isomorphic to $\mathfrak{A}$. Let $\bar{B}'$ consist of all $(\sigma(a), b')$ $(a \in A, b' \in B_m)$ satisfying the following conditions.

(i) if $a \notin \{a_0, a_1\}$ and $a \in C_j$ $(1 \leqq j \leqq m - 1)$, then $b' = b_j$,
(ii) if $a \in \{a_0, a_1\}$, then $b' = b_{m-1}$ or $b' = b_m$.

Moreover, we want to represent a_0 by $(\sigma(a_0), b_m)$, a_1 by $(\sigma(a_1), b_{m-1})$, and $a(\notin \{a_0, a_1\})$ by $(\sigma(a), b_j)$ if $a \in C_j$. To achieve these requirements, let $\varphi_1(x) = x$ for every $x \in X$. Moreover, for arbitrary $a \in A$ and $x \in X$, let

$$\varphi_2(\sigma(a), x) = \begin{cases} y_{tj-t} & \text{if } a \notin \{a_0, a_1\},\ a \in C_t \text{ and } \delta(a, x) \in C_j, \\ y_{m-11} & \text{otherwise.} \end{cases}$$

This ends the proof of Theorem 5.1. □

For α_i-products with $i > 0$, we have the following characterization.

Theorem 5.2. *A class $\mathscr{K}$ of automata is isomorphically complete with respect to the α_i-product $(i \geqq 1)$ for the class of all nilpotent automata if and only if at least one of the following three conditions is fulfilled by $\mathscr{K}$.*
(1) There is an automaton $\mathfrak{B} = (Y, B, \delta') \in \mathscr{K}$ having two different states b, c and three (not necessarily distinct) input signals y, z, v such that $\delta'(b, y) = \delta'(c, z) = c$ and $\delta'(c, v) = b$.
(2) $\mathscr{K}$ contains an automaton $\mathfrak{B} = (Y, B, \delta')$ which has two distinct states b, c and three (not necessarily distinct) input signals y, z, v such that $\delta'(b, y) = b$ and $\delta'(b, z) = \delta'(c, v) = c$.
(3) For every natural number $n \geqq 3$, there exists an automaton $\mathfrak{B}_n = (Y_n, B_n, \delta'_n) \in \mathscr{K}$ having n pairwise different states b_t $(t = 1, \dots, n)$ and input signals y_{tk} $(t = 1, \dots, n-1;$ $k = 1, \dots, n - t)$ and y such that $\delta'_n(b_t, y_{tk}) = b_{t+k}$ and $\delta'_n(b_n, y) = b_n$.

Proof. The necessity can be shown similarly as in the proof of Theorem 5.1.

For the sufficiency, let us note that for every i $(= 1, 2, 3)$ there exists a single-factor α_1-power of each automaton satisfying (i) in Theorem 5.2 which fulfils $(i + 1)$ in Theorem 5.1. Moreover, every α_0-product of α_1-products of automata is isomorphic to an α_1-product of the same automata. This, by Theorem 5.1, completes the proof of Theorem 5.2. □

4. Generalized Products and Simulations

In this chapter we allow feedback functions to take their values from the set of input words of the factors. Moreover, the homomorphic and isomorphic representations will be extended in such a way that input words are permitted as counter images of input signals.

4.1 Basic Concepts

We start with the definition of the generalized product.

Definition 1.1. Let $\mathfrak{A}_t = (X_t, A_t, \delta_t)$ $(t = 1, \dots, n;\ n > 0)$ be a system of automata. Moreover, let X be an alphabet and φ a mapping of $A_1 \times \dots \times A_n \times X$ into $X_1^* \times \dots \times X_n^*$. We say that the automaton $\mathfrak{A} = (X, A, \delta)$ with $A = A_1 \times \dots \times A_n$ and

$$\delta((a_1, \dots, a_n), x) = (\delta_1(a_1, p_1), \dots, \delta_n(a_n, p_n)) ,$$

where $(p_1, \dots, p_n) = \varphi(a_1, \dots, a_n, x)$ $(a_t \in A_t, t = 1, \dots, n, x \in X)$, is a *generalized product* of $\mathfrak{A}_t$ $(t = 1, \dots, n)$ with respect to X and φ. For this product, we use the notation $\mathfrak{A} = \prod_{t=1}^{n} \mathfrak{A}_t[X, \varphi]$ or $\mathfrak{A} = (\mathfrak{A}_1 \times \dots \times \mathfrak{A}_n)[X, \varphi]$. If $\mathfrak{A}_t = \mathfrak{B}$ for every $t\ (= 1, \dots, n)$, then $\mathfrak{A}$ is called a *generalized power* of $\mathfrak{B}$.

As with products, we frequently write the *feedback function* φ of the above generalized product in the form

$$\varphi(\mathbf{a}, x) = (\varphi_1(\mathbf{a}, x), \dots, \varphi_n(\mathbf{a}, x)) ,$$

where $\mathbf{a} \in A$ and $x \in X$.

A generalized product $\mathfrak{A} = \prod_{t=1}^{n} \mathfrak{A}_t[X, \varphi]$ is a *generalized* α_i*-product* $(i = 0, 1, \dots)$ if each *component feedback function* φ_t $(1 \leqq t \leqq n)$ is independent of its jth component $(1 \leqq j \leqq n)$, whenever $j \geqq t + i$. In the sequel in φ_t we shall generally indicate only those variables on which it may depend. Moreover, the concept of *generalized* α_i*-power* will be used in an obvious sense.

If, in the generalized product (generalized α_i-product) above, φ is of the form $\varphi : A_1 \times \dots \times A_n \times X \to X_1 \times \dots \times X_n$, then it is a product ($\alpha_i$-product).

Definition 1.2. An automaton $\mathfrak{A} = (X, A, \delta)$ *homomorphically simulates* $\mathfrak{B} = (X', B, \delta')$ if there exist a mapping τ_1 of X' into X^* and a mapping τ_2 of a subset A' of A onto B such that

$$\tau_2(\delta(a, \tau_1(x))) = \delta'(\tau_2(a), x)$$

for arbitrary $a \in A'$ and $x \in X'$. If, in addition, τ_2 is one-to-one, then we speak of an *isomorphic simulation.*

It should be observed that in Definition 1.2 the subset A' does not necessarily form a subautomaton of $\mathfrak{A}$.

The following result is obvious.

Lemma 1.3. *If $\mathfrak{A}$ homomorphically simulates $\mathfrak{B}$ and $\mathfrak{B}$ homomorphically simulates $\mathfrak{C}$, then $\mathfrak{C}$ can be simulated homomorphically by $\mathfrak{A}$. A similar statement is valid for isomorphic simulation.* □

Definition 1.4. A class $\mathscr{K}$ of automata is *homomorphically* S-*complete* with respect to the generalized product (generalized α_i-product) if every automaton can be simulated homomorphically by a generalized product (generalized α_i-product) of automata from $\mathscr{K}$.

If, in Definition 1.4, 'homomorphic simulation' is replaced by "isomorphic simulation", then we have the concept of *isomorphic* S-*completeness.*

The terms *homomorphic* and *isomorphic representation* by the generalized product (generalized α_i-products), as well as *homomorphic* and *isomorphic completeness* with respect to the generalized product (generalized α_i-products), will be used in theire obvious sense. Later, we shall see that the homomorphic representation is equivalent to the homomorphic simulation for any of the generalized α_i-products, as well as for the generalized product.

For every automaton $\mathfrak{A} = (X, A, \delta)$ denote by $\mathfrak{A}^* = (X^*/\varrho_{\mathfrak{A}}, A, \delta^*)$ the automaton the transition function of which is given by $\delta^*(a, p/\varrho_{\mathfrak{A}}) = \delta(a, p)$ $(a \in A, p \in X^*)$. For an arbitrary class $\mathscr{K}$ of automata, let $\mathscr{K}^{(*)} = \{\mathfrak{A}^* \mid \mathfrak{A} \in \mathscr{K}\}$.

Take a class $\mathscr{K}$ of automata. We put

$\mathbf{P}_g^*(\mathscr{K})$: generalized products of automata from $\mathscr{K}$;

$\mathbf{P}_{\alpha_i}^*(\mathscr{K})$: generalized α_i-products of automata from $\mathscr{K}$.

It is easy to prove

Lemma 1.5. *For arbitrary class $\mathscr{K}$ of automata, the equalities $\mathbf{IP}_g^*(\mathscr{K}) = \mathbf{IP}_g(\mathscr{K}^{(*)})$ and $\mathbf{IP}_{\alpha_i}^*(\mathscr{K}) = \mathbf{IP}_{\alpha_i}(\mathscr{K}^{(*)})$ $(i \in \mathbf{N})$ hold.*

In more detail, for every generalized product (generalized α_i-product) $\mathfrak{A} = \prod_{t=1}^{n} \mathfrak{A}_t[X, \varphi]$, there is a product ($\alpha_i$-product) $\mathfrak{A}' = \prod_{t=1}^{n} \mathfrak{A}_t^*[X, \varphi^*]$, such that $\mathfrak{A}'$ is isomorphic to $\mathfrak{A}$.

Conversely, for every product (α_i-product) $\mathfrak{A}' = \prod_{t=1}^{n} \mathfrak{A}_t^*[X, \varphi^*]$ there exists a generalized product (generalized α_i-product) $\mathfrak{A} = \prod_{t=1}^{n} \mathfrak{A}_t[X, \varphi]$ isomorphic to $\mathfrak{A}'$. □

4.2 Simulations by Generalized α_0-Products

We first show that for generalized α_0-products we can confine ourselves to homomorphic and isomorphic representation instead of homomorphic and isomorphic simulation.

Theorem 2.1. *Let $\mathscr{K}$ be a class of automata. If an automaton $\mathfrak{A}$ can be simulated homomorphically [isomorphically] by a generalized α_0-product $\mathfrak{B}$ of automata from $\mathscr{K}$, then $\mathfrak{A} \in \mathbf{HSP}^*_{\alpha_0}(\mathscr{K})$ [$\mathfrak{A} \in \mathbf{ISP}^*_{\alpha_0}(\mathscr{K})$].*

Proof. Assume that a generalized α_0-product $\mathfrak{B} = (Y, B, \delta') = \prod_{i=1}^{k} \mathfrak{B}_i[Y, \varphi]$ ($\mathfrak{B}_i \in \mathscr{K}$, $i = 1, \ldots, k$) homomorphically [isomorphically] simulates $\mathfrak{A} = (X, A, \delta)$ under a subset $B' \subseteq B$ and two mappings $\tau_1 : X \to Y^*$ and $\tau_2 : B' \to A$. Using Lemma 1.5, it is easy to show that an α_0-product $\mathfrak{C} = \prod_{i=1}^{k} \mathfrak{B}_i^*[Y, \varphi^*]$ homomorphically [isomorphically] simulates $\mathfrak{A}$ under the same mappings τ_1 and τ_2. Consider the product $\bar{\mathfrak{C}} = (X, \bar{C}, \bar{\delta}) = \prod_{i=1}^{k} \mathfrak{B}_i^*[X, \bar{\varphi}]$, where, for arbitrary $\mathbf{c} \in \bar{C}, x \in X$ and $i \in [k]$, $\bar{\varphi}_i(\mathbf{c}, x) = \varphi_i^*(\mathbf{c}, \tau_1(x))$. Obviously, $\bar{\mathfrak{C}}$ is an α_0-product of $\mathfrak{B}_1^*, \ldots, \mathfrak{B}_k^*$, B' forms a subautomaton of $\bar{\mathfrak{C}}$ and τ_2 is a homomorphism [isomorphism] of this subautomaton onto $\mathfrak{A}$. Thus, by Lemma 1.5, $\mathfrak{A}$ can be represented homomorphically [isomorphically] by a generalized α_0-product of $\mathfrak{B}_1, \ldots, \mathfrak{B}_k$. □

Observe that, by the proof of Theorem 2.1, if an automaton $\mathfrak{A}$ homomorphically [isomorphically] simulates an automaton $\mathfrak{B}$, then $\mathfrak{B}$ can be represented homomorphically [isomorphically] by a generalized α_0-power of $\mathfrak{A}$ with a single factor. Onviously, the converse of this statement also holds.

We next give necessary and sufficient conditions under which a class of automata is isomorphically S-complete regarding the generalized α_0-product.

Theorem 2.2. *A class $\mathscr{K}$ of automata is isomorphically* S*-complete with respect to the generalized α_0-product if and only if, for every natural number n, there exists an $\mathfrak{A} \in \mathscr{K}$ such that $\mathfrak{T}_n$ can be represented isomorphically by a generalized α_0-power of $\mathfrak{A}$ with a single factor.*

Proof. Theorem 2.2 follows from Theorem 3.2.1 by Theorem 2.1 and Lemma 1.5. □

Minimal isomorphically and homomorphically S-complete systems with respect to an arbitrary generalized α_i-product are defined in an abvious way.

From Theorem 2.2, we immediately have

Corollary 2.3. *There exists no system of automata which is isomorphically* S*-complete with respect to the generalized α_0-product and minimal.* □

We next characterize homomorphically S-complete systems as regards generalized α_0-products.

Theorem 2.4. *A class $\mathcal{K}$ of automata is homomorphically* S-*complete with respect to the generalized α_0-product if and only if the following conditions are satisfied*:

(i) *For every simple group G, there exists an $\mathfrak{A} \in \mathcal{K}$ such that G is a homomorphic image of a subgroup of $\mathcal{S}(\mathfrak{A})$.*
(ii) *There exists a $\mathfrak{B} \in \mathcal{K}$ such that the characteristic semigroup of any two-state full reset automaton is isomorphic to a subsemigroup of $\mathcal{S}(\mathfrak{B})$.*

Proof. Since $\mathcal{S}(\mathfrak{A}) \cong \mathcal{S}(\mathfrak{A}^*)$ holds for arbitrary automaton $\mathfrak{A}$, through Theorem 2.1 and Lemma 1.5 the necessity of these conditions follows from Theorem 1.4.13.

To prove the sufficiency, by Theorem 1.4.13, taking into consideration Theorem 1.4.23 and Lemma 1.5, it is enough to show that every group-like automaton $\mathfrak{G} = (G, G, \delta_{\mathfrak{G}})$ with a simple group G ($|G| > 1$) and every two-state full reset automaton can be represented homomorphically by a generalized α_0-product of automata from $\mathcal{K}$. The proof of the group-like automata case is similar to that of Theorem 1.3.2.

Take a group-like automaton $\mathfrak{G} = (G, G, \delta_{\mathfrak{G}})$, where G is a simple group with $|G| > 1$. By (i), there exists an $\mathfrak{A} = (X, A, \delta) \in \mathcal{K}$ such that G is a homomorphic image of a subgroup $\bar{G}$ of $\mathcal{S}(\mathfrak{A})$, under a homomorphism $\psi: \bar{G} \to G$. Form the α_0-power $\mathfrak{A}' = (\mathfrak{A}^*)[G, \varphi]$, where φ is a one-to-one mapping of G into $\bar{G}$ such that $\psi(\varphi(g)) = g$ for every $g \in G$. Take an arbitrary equation $up = vq$, where u, v are variables and $p, q \in G^*$. Assume that this equation holds in $\mathfrak{A}'$. Since $\mathcal{S}(\mathfrak{A}')$ is a group (isomorphic to a subgroup of $\bar{G}$), by Theorem 1.2.15, all the equations holding in $\mathfrak{A}'$ have the form $up = uq$. Moreover, $\varphi(p) = \varphi(q)$ in $\bar{G}$ if $up = uq$ holds in $\mathfrak{A}'$. Thus, by the choice of $\varphi, p = \psi(\varphi(p)) = \psi(\varphi(q)) = q$ in G, i.e., $up = uq$ holds in $\mathfrak{G}$. Therefore, by Theorem 1.2.13, $\mathfrak{G}$ is contained in the equational class generated by $\mathfrak{A}'$. Thus, taking into consideration our remark concerning finitely generated algebras in equational classes generated by finitely many finite algebras, $\mathfrak{G}$ can be represented homomorphically by a finite direct power of $\mathfrak{A}'$. From this, using Lemma 1.5, we get that $\mathfrak{G}$ can be represented homomorphically by a generalized α_0-power of $\mathfrak{A}$.

Finally, assume that (ii) holds under $\mathfrak{B} = (X, B, \delta)$. Then $\mathcal{S}(\mathfrak{B})$ contains three different elements $p_0/\varrho_{\mathfrak{B}}$, $p_1/\varrho_{\mathfrak{B}}$ and $p_2/\varrho_{\mathfrak{B}}$ satisfying the multiplication table below:

	$p_0/\varrho_{\mathfrak{B}}$	$p_1/\varrho_{\mathfrak{B}}$	$p_2/\varrho_{\mathfrak{B}}$
$p_0/\varrho_{\mathfrak{B}}$	$p_0/\varrho_{\mathfrak{B}}$	$p_1/\varrho_{\mathfrak{B}}$	$p_2/\varrho_{\mathfrak{B}}$
$p_1/\varrho_{\mathfrak{B}}$	$p_1/\varrho_{\mathfrak{B}}$	$p_1/\varrho_{\mathfrak{B}}$	$p_2/\varrho_{\mathfrak{B}}$
$p_2/\varrho_{\mathfrak{B}}$	$p_2/\varrho_{\mathfrak{B}}$	$p_1/\varrho_{\mathfrak{B}}$	$p_2/\varrho_{\mathfrak{B}}$

Obviously, we may suppose that $p_0 = e$. Since $p_1/\varrho_{\mathfrak{B}} \neq p_2/\varrho_{\mathfrak{B}}$, there exists a $b \in B$ such that $b_1 = \delta^*(b, p_1/\varrho_{\mathfrak{B}}) \neq \delta^*(b, p_2/\varrho_{\mathfrak{B}}) = b_2$. Therefore, $\delta^*(b_1, p_0/\varrho_{\mathfrak{B}}) = b_1$, $\delta^*(b_1, p_1/\varrho_{\mathfrak{B}}) = b_1$, $\delta^*(b_1, p_2/\varrho_{\mathfrak{B}}) = b_2$ and $\delta^*(b_2, p_0/\varrho_{\mathfrak{B}}) = b_2$, $\delta^*(b_2, p_1/\varrho_{\mathfrak{B}}) = b_1$, $\delta^*(b_2, p_2/\varrho_{\mathfrak{B}}) = b_2$. Thus, the subset $\{b_1, b_2\}$ of B, together with the input signals $p_0/\varrho_{\mathfrak{B}}$, $p_1/\varrho_{\mathfrak{B}}$ and $p_2/\varrho_{\mathfrak{B}}$, forms an X-subautomaton of $\mathfrak{B}^*$, and is a two-state full reset automaton. Consequently, every two-state reset automaton can be represented isomorphically by a generalized α_0-power of $\mathfrak{B}$ with a single factor. □

Since every simple group can be embedded as a subgroup into a larger simple group, from Theorem 2.4 we have

Corollary 2.5. *There exists no class of automata which is homomorphically* S-*complete with respect to the generalized* α_0-*product and minimal.* □

Comparing Theorems 2.2 and 2.4, we obtain

Corollary 2.6. *There exists a class* $\mathscr{K}$ *of automata such that* $\mathscr{K}$ *is homomorphically* S-*complete with respect to the generalized* α_0-*product and* $\mathscr{K}$ *is not isomorphically* S-*complete with respect to the generalized* α_0-*product.* □

4.3 Simulations by Generalized α_1-Products

We start with the analogue of Theorem 2.1.

Theorem 3.1. *Let* $\mathscr{K}$ *be a class of automata. If an automaton* $\mathfrak{A}$ *can be simulated homomorphically [isomorphically] by a generalized* α_1-*product* $\mathfrak{B}$ *of automata from* $\mathscr{K}$, *then* $\mathfrak{A} \in \mathbf{HSP}^*_{\alpha_1}(\mathscr{K})$ $[\mathfrak{A} \in \mathbf{ISP}^*_{\alpha_1}(\mathscr{K})]$.

Proof. Repeat the proof of Theorem 2.1 with 'α_1-product' instead of 'α_0-product'. □

We next give necessary and sufficient conditions under which a class of automata is homomorphically S-complete as regards the generalized α_1-product.

Theorem 3.2. *A class* $\mathscr{K}$ *of automata is homomorphically* S-*complete with respect to the generalized* α_1-*product if and only if, for an arbitrary natural number n, there exist an automaton* $\mathfrak{A} = (X, A, \delta)$ *in* $\mathscr{K}$, *pairwise distinct states* $a_1, \dots, a_n \in A$ *and (not necessarily different) input words* $p_{jl} \in X^*$ $(1 \leqq j, l \leqq n)$ *such that* $\delta(a_j, p_{jl}) = a_l$.

Proof. Assume that $\mathscr{K}$ is homomorphically S-complete with respect to the generalized α_1-product. Let n be a natural number, and let r be a prime with $r \geqq n$. Take the r-state counter $\mathfrak{C} = (\{x\}, [r], \delta_{\mathfrak{C}})$. Assume that $\mathfrak{C}$ can be simulated homomorphically by a generalized α_1-product

$$\mathfrak{B} = (X', B, \delta_{\mathfrak{B}}) = \prod_{i=1}^{k} \mathfrak{B}_i[X', \varphi] \qquad (\mathfrak{B}_i = (X_i, B_i, \delta_i) \in \mathscr{K}, i = 1, \dots, k) .$$

Thus, by Lemma 1.5 and Theorem 3.1, there exists an α_1-product

$$\bar{\mathfrak{B}} = (\{x\}, B, \bar{\delta}_{\mathfrak{B}}) = \prod_{i=1}^{k} \mathfrak{B}^*_i[\{x\}, \varphi^*]$$

which homomorphically represents $\mathfrak{C}$ under a subautomaton $\mathfrak{B}' = (\{x\}, B', \delta'_{\mathfrak{B}})$ and mapping $\tau: B' \to [r]$.

Define the relations ϱ'_j ($j = 1, \dots, k$) on B by $\mathbf{b} \equiv \mathbf{b}'(\varrho'_j)$ ($\mathbf{b}, \mathbf{b}' \in B$) if and only if $\mathrm{pr}_{[j]}(\mathbf{b}) = \mathrm{pr}_{[j]}(\mathbf{b}')$. Then each ϱ'_j is a congruence relation of $\mathfrak{B}$.

By the definition of $\mathfrak{C}$, there exists a subset $B'' = \{\mathbf{b}_1, \dots, \mathbf{b}_u\}$ ($u > 1$) of B' such that r divides u and $\delta'_{\mathfrak{B}}(\mathbf{b}_l, x) = \mathbf{b}_{l+1 \,(\mathrm{mod}\, u)}$ ($l = 1, \dots, u$). Let ϱ_j be the restriction of ϱ'_j to $B'' \times B''$ ($j = 1, \dots, k$). As in the proof of Theorem 2.2.2, for each j ($1 \leqq j \leqq k$), all the blocks $\mathbf{b}_l/\varrho_j$ ($l = 1, \dots, u$) have the same cardinality. Let $m_1 = |\{\mathbf{b}_l/\varrho_1 \mid l = 1, \dots, u\}|$. Moreover, it is easy to show that $\varrho_1 \geqq \varrho_2 \geqq \dots \geqq \varrho_k$, and each block $\mathbf{b}_l/\varrho_j$ ($\leqq l \leqq u$, $1 \leqq j < k$) contains the same number m_{j+1} of blocks from $\{\mathbf{b}_t/\varrho_{j+1} \mid t = 1, \dots, u\}$. Therefore, $u = m_1 m_2 \dots m_k$. Since r divides u and r is a prime, there exists an l ($1 \leqq l \leqq k$) such that r divides m_l, implying that the number of states of $\mathfrak{B}^*_l$ occurring as the lth components of elements from B'' is at least $m_l \geqq r$. Let us denote them by $c_1, \dots, c_s$. For two arbitrary states $\mathbf{b}', \mathbf{b}'' \in B''$, there exists an input word $q (= x^t$ for some $t)$ such that $\delta'_{\mathfrak{B}}(\mathbf{b}', q) = \mathbf{b}''$. Therefore, for any two states c_i and c_j ($1 \leqq i, j \leqq s$) there is an input signal x_{ij} of $\mathfrak{B}^*_l$ with $\delta^*_l(c_i, x_{ij}) = c_j$. Consequently, since $s \geqq n$, $\mathfrak{B}_l$ satisfies the conditions of Theorem 3.2.

Conversely, assume that the conditions of Theorem 3.2 are satisfied. Take an arbitrary automaton $\mathfrak{B} = (X', B, \delta')$ with $B = \{b_1, \dots, b_n\}$, and consider the automaton $\mathfrak{A}$ of Theorem 3.2. Form the generalized α_1-product $\bar{\mathfrak{A}} = (X', A, \bar{\delta}) = (\mathfrak{A})\,[X', \varphi]$, where, for every $x \in X'$, $\varphi(a_i, x) = p_{ij}$ if $\delta'(b_i, x) = b_j$ ($i, j = 1, \dots, n$). Clearly, $\bar{\mathfrak{A}}$ *isomorphically* represents $\mathfrak{B}$. □

From the above proof, we have the following results:

Corollary 3.3. *A class of automata is homomorphically* S-*complete with respect to the generalized* α_1-*product if and only if it is isomorphically* S-*complete with respect to the generalized* α_1-*product.* □

Corollary 3.4. *There exists no class of automata which is homomorphically or isomorphically* S-*complete with respect to the generalized* α_1-*product and minimal.* □

The next result shows that the homomorphic and isomorphic simulations regarding the generalized α_1-product do not coincide if they are taken over an arbitrary class of automata.

Theorem 3.5. *There exist a class* $\mathscr{K}$ *of automata and an automaton* $\mathfrak{A}$ *such that* $\mathfrak{A}$ *can be simulated homomorphically by a generalized* α_1-*product of automata from* $\mathscr{K}$, *but* $\mathfrak{A}$ *cannot be simulated isomorphically by any of the generalized* α_1-*products of automata from* $\mathscr{K}$.

Proof. Let $\mathfrak{A} = (X, A, \delta)$, where $X = \{x, y\}$, $A = \{a, b, c\}$, $\delta(a, x) = \delta(c, y) = b$, $\delta(b, x) = \delta(c, x) = c$ and $\delta(b, y) = \delta(a, y) = a$. Moreover, let $\mathscr{K}$ consist of all two-state automata. If $\mathfrak{A}$ can be simulated isomorphically by a generalized α_1-product of automata from $\mathscr{K}$, then, by the proof of Theorem 3.2, $\mathfrak{A}$ has a nontrivial congruence relation. But it can be easily verified that $\mathfrak{A}$ has only the two trivial congruence relations.

Take the system $\Gamma = \{\{a, b\}, \{b, c\}\}$. It can be seen in an obvious way that Γ is a cover of $\mathfrak{A}$. Thus, by Lemma 2.3.7, $\mathfrak{A}$ can be represented homomorphically by an α_0-product of two-state automata. □

4.4 Simulations by Generalized Products and Generalized α_i-Products with $i > 1$

For an automaton $\mathfrak{A} = (X, A, \delta)$, let $(X^*)_{g(\mathfrak{A})}$ denote an arbitrarily fixed generating set of $\mathscr{S}(\mathfrak{A})$.

Theorem 4.1. *Let $l > 2$ be a natural number and let $i > 1$. For an automaton $\mathfrak{A} = (X, A, \delta)$, $\mathfrak{A}^*$ is X-isomorphic to some $\mathfrak{B}^*$, where $\mathfrak{B}$ is a subautomaton of a generalized α_i-product of automata having fewer states than l, if and only if, for some $(X^*)_{g(\mathfrak{A})}$, there exists a regular system $\pi_0, \pi_1, \dots, \pi_n$ of partitions of $\mathfrak{A}$ such that*

(i) $\pi_j/\pi_{j+1} < l$ *for all* $j = 0, \dots, n-1$, *and*
(ii) $\pi_j(a) = \pi_j(b)$ *implies* $\pi_{j-i+1}(\delta^*(a, p/\varrho_{\mathfrak{A}})) = \pi_{j-i+1}(\delta^*(b, p/\varrho_{\mathfrak{A}}))$ *for all* j *with* $i-1 \leqq j \leqq n$, $p/\varrho_{\mathfrak{A}} \in (X^*)_{g(\mathfrak{A})}$ *and* $a, b \in A$.

Proof. Assume that $\mathfrak{A}^*$ is X-isomorphic to $\mathfrak{B}^*$, where $\mathfrak{B}$ is a subautomaton of a generalized α_i-product $\prod_{j=1}^{n} \mathfrak{A}_j[X, \varphi]$ of automata $\mathfrak{A}_j = (X_j, A_j, \delta_j)$ with $|A_j| < l$ $(j = 1, \dots, n)$. By Lemma 1.5, $\mathfrak{B}$ is isomorphic to a subautomaton of an α_i-product $\bar{\mathfrak{A}} = (\bar{X}, \bar{A}, \bar{\delta}) = \prod_{j=1}^{n} \mathfrak{A}_j^*[\bar{X}, \varphi^*]$. Without loss of generality, we may suppose that $\mathfrak{B}$ is a subautomaton of $\bar{\mathfrak{A}}$. Moreover, let $\psi_1: \mathscr{S}(\mathfrak{A}) \to \mathscr{S}(\mathfrak{B})$, $\psi_2: A \to B$ determine an X-isomorphism of $\mathfrak{A}^*$ onto $\mathfrak{B}^*$. Define the partitions π_j $(j = 1, \dots, n)$ of A in the following way: for arbitrary $a, b \in A$, $\pi_j(a) = \pi_j(b)$ if and only if $\mathrm{pr}_{[j]}(\psi_2(a)) = \mathrm{pr}_{[j]}(\psi_2(b))$. Moreover, let $\pi_0 = \{A\}$. It is obvious that $\pi_0, \pi_1, \dots, \pi_n$ is a regular system of partitions, and (i) is satisfied by this system.

We next show that (ii) also holds for $\pi_0, \pi_1, \dots, \pi_n$. Denote by $(X^*)_{g(\mathfrak{A})}$ the subset of $\mathscr{S}(\mathfrak{A})$ consisting of all $p/\varrho_{\mathfrak{A}}$ $(p \in X^*)$ for which $\psi_1(p/\varrho_{\mathfrak{A}})$ contains an $x \in \bar{X}$. Since $\{\psi_1(p/\varrho_{\mathfrak{A}}) \mid p/\varrho_{\mathfrak{A}} \in (X^*)_{g(\mathfrak{A})}\}$ obviously generates $\mathscr{S}(\mathfrak{B})$, $(X^*)_{g(\mathfrak{A})}$ is a generating set of $\mathscr{S}(\mathfrak{A})$.

Take a j with $i-1 \leqq j \leqq n$, and two elements $a, b \in A$ such that $\pi_j(a) = \pi_j(b)$. Let $\psi_2(a) = (a_1, \dots, a_n)$ and $\psi_2(b) = (b_1, \dots, b_n)$ $(a_t, b_t \in A_t, t = 1, \dots, n)$. Then by the definition of π_j, the equalities $a_1 = b_1, \dots, a_j = b_j$ hold. Now consider an arbitrary $p/\varrho_{\mathfrak{A}} \in (X^*)_{g(\mathfrak{A})}$, and let $x \in \bar{X}$ such that $x \in \psi_1(p/\varrho_{\mathfrak{A}})$. Moreover, let $\varphi^*(\psi_2(a), x) = (p_1, \dots, p_n)$ and $\varphi^*(\psi_2(b), x) = (q_1, \dots, q_n)$. Since $a_t = b_t$ for all $t = 1, \dots, j$, by the definition of the α_i-product, $p_1 = q_1, \dots, p_{j-i+1} = q_{j-i+1}$. Therefore, $\mathrm{pr}_t(\bar{\delta}(\psi_2(a), x)) = \mathrm{pr}_t(\bar{\delta}(\psi_2(b), x))$ holds for all $t = 1, \dots, j-i+1$, showing that $\pi_{j-i+1}(\delta^*(a, p/\varrho_{\mathfrak{A}})) = \pi_{j-i+1}(\delta^*(b, p/\varrho_{\mathfrak{A}}))$. This ends the proof of the necessity.

Conversely, suppose that, for an $\mathfrak{A} = (X, A, \delta)$ and an $(X^*)_{g(\mathfrak{A})}$, there exists a regular system $\pi_0, \pi_1, \dots, \pi_n$ of partitions satisfying (i) and (ii). Take the automaton

$\bar{\mathfrak{A}} = ((X^*)_{g(\mathfrak{A})}, A, \bar{\delta})$, where $\bar{\delta}(a, p/\varrho_{\mathfrak{A}}) = \delta(a, p)$ for all $a \in A$ and $p/\varrho_{\mathfrak{A}} \in (X^*)_{g(\mathfrak{A})}$. By Theorem 3.1.3, there exists an α_i-product of automata with fewer states than l which contains a subautomaton $\mathfrak{B} = ((X^*)_{g(\mathfrak{A})}, B, \delta')$ isomorphic to $\bar{\mathfrak{A}}$. Therefore, $\bar{\mathfrak{A}}^* \cong \mathfrak{B}^*$. On the other hand, $\mathfrak{A}^*$ is obviously X-isomorphic to $\bar{\mathfrak{A}}^*$. Thus, $\mathfrak{A}^*$ is X-isomorphic to $\mathfrak{B}^*$. □

As in Section 3.4, let $\mathfrak{A}_2 = (\{x, y\}, \{0, 1\}, \bar{\delta}_2)$ denote the automaton for which $\bar{\delta}_2(0, x) = \bar{\delta}_2(1, y) = 1$ and $\bar{\delta}_2(1, x) = \bar{\delta}_2(0, y) = 0$.

Theorem 4.2. *Every automaton can be simulated isomorphically by an α_2-power of $\mathfrak{A}_2$.*

Proof. Let $\mathfrak{A} = (X, A, \delta)$ be an arbitrary automaton. As has already been shown, every $\mathfrak{T}_n = (T_n, [n], \delta_n)$ with $n \geqq |A|$ isomorphically simulates $\mathfrak{A}$. Therefore, in order to prove Theorem 4.2, by Lemma 1.3, it is enough to show that, for every even n, $\mathfrak{T}_n$ can be simulated isomorphically by an α_2-power of $\mathfrak{A}_2$.

Take the following elements t_1, t_2 and t_3 of T_n:

$$t_1(i) = i + 1 \pmod n \text{ for all } i = 1, \dots, n,$$

$$t_2(1) = 2,\ t_2(2) = 1 \text{ and } t_2(i) = i \text{ for all } i = 3, \dots, n,$$

$$t_3(1) = t_3(2) = 1 \text{ and } t_3(i) = i \text{ for all } i = 3, \dots, n.$$

As noted in Section 1.2, $\{t_1/\varrho_{\mathfrak{T}_n}, t_2/\varrho_{\mathfrak{T}_n}, t_3/\varrho_{\mathfrak{T}_n}\}$ generates $\mathscr{S}(\mathfrak{T}_n)$.

We first prove that $\mathfrak{T}_n$ can be simulated isomorphically by a generalized α_2-product of two-state automata. By Theorem 4.1, it is sufficient to show that there exists a regular system $\pi_0, \pi_1, \dots, \pi_k$ of partitions of $[n]$ such that

(i) $\pi_j/\pi_{j+1} \leqq 2$ for all $j = 0, \dots, k-1$, and
(ii) $\pi_j(r) = \pi_j(s)$ implies $\pi_{j-1}(\delta_n^*(r, \bar{t})) = \pi_{j-1}(\delta_n^*(s, \bar{t}))$ for all $r, s \in [n]$, $\bar{t} \in \{t_1/\varrho_{\mathfrak{T}_n}, t_2/\varrho_{\mathfrak{T}_n}, t_3/\varrho_{\mathfrak{T}_n}\}$, and j with $1 \leqq j \leqq k$.

Let π_1 consist of the following two blocks: $\{1, \dots, k\}$ and $\{k+1, \dots, n\}$, where $k = n/2$. Let us assume that the partitions π_t have been defined for all $t \leqq m (< k)$, and suppose that π_m has the following blocks: $\{1, \dots, k-m+1\}, \{k-m+2\}, \dots, \{k\}$, $\{k+1, \dots, n-m+1\}$, $\{n-m+2\}, \dots, \{n\}$. Then π_{m+1} is defined to be the partition with the blocks

$$\{1, \dots, k-m\}, \{k-m+1\}, \dots, \{k\}, \{k+1, \dots, n-m\}, \{n-m+1\}, \dots, \{n\}.$$

It is obvious that the resulting system $\pi_0, \pi_1, \dots, \pi_k$ of partitions is regular and satisfies (i). It is also clear that (ii) holds for π_1 and π_k. Now take an arbitrary m with $1 \leqq m < k-1$, and two $r, s \in [n]$ such that $\pi_{m+1}(r) = \pi_{m+1}(s)$. We may suppose that $r \neq s$. Then, either $1 \leqq r, s \leqq k-m$ or $k+1 \leqq r, s \leqq n-m$. For any $\bar{t} \in \{t_1/\varrho_{\mathfrak{T}_n}, t_2/\varrho_{\mathfrak{T}_n}, t_3/\varrho_{\mathfrak{T}_n}\}$, we have $1 \leqq \delta_n^*(r, \bar{t}), \delta_n^*(s, \bar{t}) \leqq k-m+1$ in the first case, and $k+1 \leqq \delta_n^*(r, \bar{t}), \delta_n^*(s, \bar{t}) \leqq n-m+1$ in the second case, showing that (ii) holds for every π_j $(1 \leqq j \leqq k)$. Thus, we have proved that $\mathfrak{A}$ can be simulated isomorphically by a generalized α_2-product of two state automata, and hence, by

Lemma 1.5, $\mathfrak{A}$ can be simulated isomorphically by an α_2-product of two-state automata.

Finally, it can easily be shown that every two-state automaton is isomorphic to an α_1-power of $\mathfrak{A}_2$ with a single factor. Since an α_2-product of α_1-products with single factors is isomorphic to an α_2-product of the same automata, $\mathfrak{A}$ can be simulated isomorphically by an α_2-power of $\mathfrak{A}_2$. □

Corollary 4.3. *If $i > 1$, then there is a finite class of automata which is isomorphically* S*-complete with respect to the (generalized) α_i-product.* □

We next give necessary and sufficient conditions under which a class $\mathscr{K}$ is homomorphically S-complete with respect to the generalized product.

Theorem 4.4. *A class $\mathscr{K}$ of automata is homomorphically* S*-complete with respect to the generalized product if and only if $\mathscr{K}$ contains a nonmonotone automaton.*

Proof. In order to show the necessity of the condition above, it is enough to prove that the following two statements hold:

(i) The generalized products of monotone automata are monotone.
(ii) The homomorphic simulation preserves monotonity.

The first statement is obviously valid. It is also easy to show that (ii) holds. For this, assume that a monotone automaton $\mathfrak{A}$ homomorphically simulates an automaton $\mathfrak{B}$. Then, from our remark following the proof of Theorem 2.1 through Lemma 1.5 we have that an α_0-power $\mathfrak{C}$ of $\mathfrak{A}^*$ with a single factor homomorphically represents $\mathfrak{B}$. Since $\mathfrak{C}$ is obviously monotone, by the proof of Theorem 2.5.4, $\mathfrak{B}$ is also monotone. (See Case 2 in the proof of Theorem 2.5.4.)

Conversely, assume that $\mathscr{K}$ contains a nonmonotone automaton $\mathfrak{A} = (X, A, \delta)$. Then there are a state $a \in A$ and two input words $p, q \in X^*$ such that $\delta(a, p) \neq a$ and $\delta(a, pq) = a$. Form the generalized α_1-product $\mathfrak{B} = (\{x, y\}, A, \delta') = (\mathfrak{A})[\{x, y\}, \varphi]$, where $\varphi(a, x) = p$, $\varphi(\delta(a, p), x) = q$ and $\varphi(a, y) = \varphi(\delta(a, p), y) = e$. Clearly, the mapping ψ given by $\psi(0) = a$ and $\psi(1) = \delta(a, p)$ is an isomorphism of $\mathfrak{A}_2$ into $\mathfrak{B}$. Since every α_2-product of generalized α_1-powers with single factors is obviously isomorphic to a generalized α_2-product of the same automata, by Theorem 4.2, $\mathscr{K}$ is *isomorphically* S-complete with respect to the generalized α_2-product. □

From the proof of Theorem 4.4, we have

Corollary 4.5. *A class $\mathscr{K}$ of automata is homomorphically* S*-complete with respect to the generalized product if and only if, for arbitrary $i \geqq 2$, $\mathscr{K}$ is isomorphically* S*-complete with respect to the generalized α_i-product.* □

Moreover, if $\mathfrak{A}$ is a nonmonotone automaton then $\mathfrak{A}^*$ satisfies Letičevskiĭ's criterion. Thus, from Theorem 4.4 through Theorem 2.4.10 we obtain

Corollary 4.6. *A class $\mathscr{K}$ of automata is homomorphically* S*-complete with respect to the generalized α_i-product ($i > 1$) if and only if it is homomorphically complete with respect to the generalized α_2-product.* □

We shall prove that the generalized α_2-product regarding isomorphic simulation is as powerful as the generalized product with respect to homomorphic simulation.

Let $\mathfrak{E}_{(2)} = (X_{(2)}, E_{(2)}, \delta_{(2)})$ be the automaton for which $X_{(2)} = \{x, x_e\}$, $E_{(2)} = \{e_1, e_2\}$, $\delta_{(2)}(e_1, x_e) = e_1$, $\delta_{(2)}(e_2, x_e) = e_2$ and $\delta_{(2)}(e_i, x) = e_2$ $(i = 1, 2)$.

Lemma 4.7. *Let $\mathfrak{A} = (X, A, \delta)$ be an arbitrary monotone automaton. Then the inclusion $\mathfrak{A} \in \mathbf{ISP}_{\alpha_0}(\{\mathfrak{E}_{(2)}\})$ holds.*

Proof. There exists a linear ordering $\leqq$ on A such that $a \leqq \delta(a, x)$ for arbitrary $a \in A$ and $x \in X$. We may suppose that $A = \{a_1, \dots, a_n\}$ and $a_i \leqq a_j$ if $i \leqq j$ $(i, j \in [n])$.

Consider the α_0-power

$$\mathfrak{B} = (X, B, \delta') = (\underbrace{\mathfrak{E}_{(2)} \times \dots \times \mathfrak{E}_{(2)}}_{n \text{ times}})[X, \varphi]$$

where, for arbitrary $b_1, \dots, b_n \in E_{(2)}$, $i \in \{2, \dots, n\}$ and $x \in X$,

$$\varphi_1(x) = x_e,$$

and

$$\varphi_i(b_1, \dots, b_{i-1}, x) = \begin{cases} x & \text{if there is an } r \in [i-1] \\ & \text{such that } b_1 = \dots = b_r = e_2, \\ & b_{r+1} = \dots = b_{i-1} = e_1,\ \delta(a_r, x) = a_s \\ & \text{and } s \geqq i, \\ x_e & \text{otherwise}. \end{cases}$$

For every $r \in [n]$, let $\mathbf{b}_r$ denote the element of B given by

$$\mathrm{pr}_j(\mathbf{b}_r) = \begin{cases} e_2 & \text{if } j \leqq r, \\ e_1 & \text{otherwise}. \end{cases}$$

Obviously, $\{\mathbf{b}_1, \dots, \mathbf{b}_n\}$ forms a subautomaton of $\mathfrak{B}$, and the mapping $\psi: A \to B$, for which $\psi(a_r) = \mathbf{b}_r$ $(r = 1, \dots, n)$, is an isomorphism of $\mathfrak{A}$ into $\mathfrak{B}$. □

Theorem 4.8. *Let $\mathcal{K}$ be a class of automata. An automaton $\mathfrak{A}$ can be simulated homomorphically by a generalized product of automata from $\mathcal{K}$ if and only if $\mathfrak{A}$ can be simulated isomorphically by a generalized α_2-product of automata from $\mathcal{K}$.*

If $\mathcal{K}$ contains a nonmonotone automaton then, by Theorem 4.4 and Corollary 4.5, our claim is true.

Let $\mathcal{K}$ consist only of monotone automata. Take an arbitrary automaton $\mathfrak{A} = (X, A, \delta)$ which can be simulated homomorphically by a generalized product of automata from $\mathcal{K}$. Then $\mathfrak{A}$ is monotone.

Suppose that $\mathfrak{A}$ is not discrete. Then $\mathcal{K}$ contains a nondiscrete automaton $\mathfrak{B} = (Y, B, \delta')$. Therefore, there are two states $b_1, b_2 \in B$ and an input signal $y \in Y$ such that $\delta'(b_1, y) = \delta'(b_2, y) = b_2$. Therefore, $\mathfrak{E}_{(2)}$ is isomorphic to a subautomaton of a generalized α_0-power $(\mathfrak{B})[X_{(2)}, \varphi]$ for which $\varphi(x) = y$ and $\varphi(x_e) = e$ hold.

By Lemma 4.7, every monotone automaton can be represented isomorphically by an α_0-power of $\mathfrak{E}_{(2)}$. Thus, every monotone automaton can be represented isomorphically by a generalized α_0-power of $\mathfrak{B}$.

Next, assume that $\mathfrak{A}$ is discrete, but not trivial. Then there is a $\mathfrak{B} = (Y, B, \delta')$ $\in \mathscr{K}$ having at least two distinct states. Since the empty word over Y is always at our disposal, $\mathfrak{A}$ obviously can be represented isomorphically by a generalized α_0-power of $\mathfrak{B}$. If $|A| = 1$ also holds, then $\mathfrak{A}$ can be represented isomorphically by a single-factor generalized α_0-power of any automaton from $\mathscr{K}$. □

It is apparent from the proof of Theorem 4.8 that, whenever $\mathscr{K}$ consists only of monotone automata, then an automaton $\mathfrak{A}$ can be simulated homomorphically by a generalized product of automata from $\mathscr{K}$, if and only if $\mathfrak{A}$ is isomorphically representable by a generalized α_0-product of automata from $\mathscr{K}$.

Using Corollary 4.6, from the proof of Theorem 4.8 we obtain

Corollary 4.9. *Let $\mathscr{K}$ be a class of automata. An automaton $\mathfrak{A}$ can be simulated homomorphically by a generalized product of automata from $\mathscr{K}$ if and only if $\mathfrak{A}$ can be represented homomorphically by a generalized α_2-product of automata from $\mathscr{K}$.* □

By Theorems 2.1 and 3.1 and Corollary 4.9, as regards generalized α_i-products for every $i \geqq 0$, the homomorphic representation is as powerful as the homomorphic simulation, while the next example shows that, with respect to the general product and for every $i \geqq 0$ with respect to the α_i-product, the homomorphic simulation is more general than the homomorphic representation.

Example 4.10. Let $\mathfrak{A} = (\{x, y\}, [n], \delta)$ be an automaton with $n > 1$ such that $\delta(t, x) = t + 1 \pmod n$ and $\delta(t, y) = t$ for every $t \in [n]$. Take an n-state counter $\mathfrak{B} = (\{x\}, [n], \delta')$. It is obvious that $\mathfrak{A} \notin \mathbf{HSP}_g(\{\mathfrak{B}\})$, since in every power of $\mathfrak{B}$ all the input signals have the same effect. On the other hand, the mapping $\tau_1 : \{x, y\} \to \{x\}^*$ given by $\tau_1(x) = x$ and $\tau_1(y) = e$, together with the identity mapping τ_2 on $[n]$, determines an isomorphic simulation of $\mathfrak{A}$ by $\mathfrak{B}$. □

This example also shows that as regards both homomorphic and isomorphic representations, for every $i \geqq 0$, the generalized α_i-product is more powerful than the α_i-product. The same holds as concerns the generalized product and the general product. For this, take the generalized α_0-product $(\mathfrak{B})\,[\{x, y\}, \varphi] = \mathfrak{C}$ where $\varphi(x) = x$ and $\varphi(y) = e$. Then $\mathfrak{C}$ is isomorphic to $\mathfrak{A}$. It can easily be shown that we arrive at the same result by replacing "homomorphic and isomorphic representations" by "homomorphic and isomorphic simulations". (See the proof of Lemma 2.1.2.)

By virtue of Corollary 3.3.3, there exists no finite system of automata which is isomorphically complete with respect to any of the α_i-products. Therefore, by Lemma 1.5, there is no finite isomorphically complete system for any of the generalized α_i-products. Comparing this with Theorem 4.2, we see that from $i = 2$, as regards generalized α_i-products, the isomorphic representation is weaker than the isomorphic simulation. On the other hand, for the generalized product the isomorphic simulation is equivalent to the isomorphic representation.

Example 4.10 shows that with respect to the general product and, for every $i \geqq 0$, with respect to the α_i-product the isomorphic simulation is more powerful than the isomorphic representation.

Finally, observe that in Theorem 3.4.1 the automaton $\mathfrak{A}_2$ can be replaced by any two-state automaton $\mathfrak{A} = (X, A, \delta)$ such that, for an arbitrary pair (a, b) of states from A, there is an $x \in X$ with $\delta(a, x) = b$. Moreover, let $\mathscr{K}$ be the class of all counters. Then $\mathscr{K}$ is isomorphically complete with respect to the generalized α_1-product and, by Lemma 1.5 and Theorem 3.2.1, $\mathscr{K}$ is not isomorphically complete as regards the generalized α_0-product. With respect to the isomorphic representation, therefore, the generalized α_i-products form a proper hierarchy. It is obvious that, as concerns the isomorphic representation, the generalized product is more general than any of the generalized α_i-products.

4.5 Homomorphic Representations by a Restricted Form of Generalized Products

In the previous section we saw that, as regards generalized products and generalized α_i-products, the homomorphic simulation is equivalent to the homomorphic representation. Here we show that, under the homomorphic representation, in most cases we can confine ourselves to generalized products and generalized α_i-products where the values of the feedback functions are words with a length of at most one. For this, some preparations are needed.

For every automaton $\mathfrak{A} = (X, A, \delta)$, define the automaton $\mathfrak{A}^e = (X \cup \{x_e\}, A, \delta^e)$ by $\delta^e(a, x) = \delta(a, x)$, if $x \in X$, and $\delta^e(a, x_e) = a$ where $a \in A$ is arbitrary. Observe that $\mathscr{S}(\mathfrak{A}^e) = \mathscr{S}(\mathfrak{A})$.

Let $\mathscr{K}$ be an arbitrary class of automata. We put

$$\mathscr{K}^{(e)} = \{\mathfrak{A}^e \mid \mathfrak{A} \in \mathscr{K}\}.$$

Definition 5.1. Let $\mathfrak{A} = (X, A, \delta) = \prod_{1}^{k} \mathfrak{A}_t[X, \varphi]$ be a generalized product of automata $\mathfrak{A}_t$ $(t = 1, \ldots, k)$. If, for arbitrary $\mathbf{a} \in A$, $x \in X$ and $t \in [k]$, $|\varphi_t(\mathbf{a}, x)| \leqq 1$, then $\mathfrak{A}$ is called an *e-product* of $\mathfrak{A}_1, \ldots, \mathfrak{A}_k$ with respect to X and φ. Moreover, if additionally $\mathfrak{A}$ is a generalized α_i-product for an $i \in \mathbf{N}$, then we speak of an *α_i^e-product*.

The concepts of *homomorphic representations* by e-products and α_i^e-products, as well as those of *homomorphically complete classes* with respect to the e-products and α_i^e-products, will be used in their obvious sense.

Take a class $\mathscr{K}$ of automata. We put

$\mathbf{P}_g^e(\mathscr{K})$: e-products of automata from $\mathscr{K}$;
$\mathbf{P}_{\alpha_i}^e(\mathscr{K})$: α_i^e-products of automata from $\mathscr{K}$;
$\mathbf{P}_{1\alpha_1}^*(\mathscr{K})$: generalized α_1-products of automata from $\mathscr{K}$ with single factors;
$\mathbf{P}_{1\alpha_1}^e(\mathscr{K})$: α_1^e-products of automata from $\mathscr{K}$ with single factors.
Observe that, for an arbitrary class $\mathscr{K}$ of automata, the equalities

$$\mathbf{IP}_g^e(\mathscr{K}) = \mathbf{IP}_g(\mathscr{K}^{(e)}) \quad \text{and} \quad \mathbf{IP}_{\alpha_i}^{(e)}(\mathscr{K}) = \mathbf{IP}_{\alpha_i}(\mathscr{K}^{(e)}) \; (i \in \mathbf{N})$$

hold.

To study α_0^e-products, we need the following two lemmas. Lemma 5.2 can be obtained by combining the proof of Theorem 2.4 with the Krohn-Rhodes theorem.

Lemma 5.2. *Let $\mathcal{K}$ be a class of automata containing an automaton $\mathfrak{A}$ such that the characteristic semigroup of a two-state full reset automaton is isomorphic to a subsemigroup of $\mathcal{S}(\mathfrak{A})$. Then, for an arbitrary automaton $\mathfrak{B}$, we have $\mathfrak{B} \in \mathbf{HSP}^*_{\alpha_0}(\mathcal{K})$ if and only if, whenever a simple group G is a homomorphic image of a subgroup of $\mathcal{S}(\mathfrak{B})$, there is an automaton $\mathfrak{C} \in \mathcal{K}$ such that a subgroup of $\mathcal{S}(\mathfrak{C})$ can be mapped homomorphically onto G.* □

By the proof of Lemma 2.1.2, we have

Lemma 5.3. *Let $\mathcal{K}$ be a class of automata. If $\mathbf{HSP}^e_{\alpha_0}(\mathcal{K})$ contains a nontrivial counter, then in $\mathbf{HSP}^e_{\alpha_0}(\mathcal{K})$ there are infinitely many counters of different lengths.* □

We say that a class $\mathcal{K}$ of automata is *counter-free* if, whenever a counter $\mathfrak{C}$ is isomorphic to an X-subautomaton of an automaton from $\mathcal{K}$, then $\mathfrak{C}$ is trivial.

The following theorem will be of fundamental importance in our discussions.

Theorem 5.4. *Let $\mathcal{K}$ be a class of automata. Suppose that $\mathcal{K}$ is not counter-free and $\mathbf{HSP}^e_{\alpha_0}(\mathcal{K})$ contains a two-state full reset automaton. Then $\mathcal{K}^{(*)} \subseteq \mathbf{HSP}^e_{\alpha_0}(\mathcal{K})$.*

Proof. Take an automaton $\mathfrak{A} = (X, A, \delta)$ from $\mathcal{K}$. Since $\mathbf{HSP}^e_{\alpha_0}(\mathcal{K}) = \mathbf{HSP}_{\alpha_0}(\mathcal{K}^{(e)})$, it is enough to show that $\mathfrak{A}^* \in \mathbf{HSP}_{\alpha_0}(\mathcal{K}^{(e)})$. Let $\mathcal{S}(\mathfrak{A}) = \{p_1/\varrho_{\mathfrak{A}}, \dots, p_k/\varrho_{\mathfrak{A}}\} = Y$ where $p_1, \dots, p_k \in X^*$. By Lemma 5.3, we may suppose that, for an integer n (> 0), $|p_1|, \dots, |p_k| \leqq n$, and there is an n-state counter in $\mathbf{HSP}_{\alpha_0}(\mathcal{K}^{(e)})$. Since x_e induces the identity mapping of A, there exists a mapping $\tau : Y^n \to X^n$ satisfying the equation $\delta^*(a, p) = \delta^e(a, \tau(p))$ for any $a \in A$ and $p \in Y^n$. Moreover, both $\mathfrak{A}^e$ and $\mathfrak{A}^*$ have input signals inducing the identity mapping on A. Thus, $\{\delta^*(\delta^e(a, q), p) \mid a \in A, (p, q) \in R_\tau\} = A$ is valid, too. Therefore, by Lemmas 2.1.3 and 2.1.4, $\mathfrak{A}^* \in \mathbf{HSP}_{\alpha_0}(\mathcal{K}^{(e)})$. □

The next result gives sufficient conditions under which, as regards homomorphic representations, the α_0^e-product is equivalent to the generalized α_0-product over a class $\mathcal{K}$ of automata.

Theorem 5.5. *Assume that a class $\mathcal{K}$ of automata is not counter-free and $\mathbf{HSP}^e_{\alpha_0}(\mathcal{K})$ contains a two-state full reset automaton. Then, $\mathbf{HSP}^e_{\alpha_0}(\mathcal{K}) = \mathbf{HSP}^*_{\alpha_0}(\mathcal{K})$. Moreover, an automaton $\mathfrak{A}$ is in $\mathbf{HSP}^e_{\alpha_0}(\mathcal{K})$ if and only if, whenever a simple group G is a homomorphic image of a subgroup of $\mathcal{S}(\mathfrak{A})$, then, for a $\mathfrak{B} \in \mathcal{K}$, a subgroup of $\mathcal{S}(\mathfrak{B})$ can be mapped homomorphically onto G.*

Proof. The inclusion $\mathbf{HSP}^e_{\alpha_0}(\mathcal{K}) \subseteq \mathbf{HSP}^*_{\alpha_0}(\mathcal{K})$ is obviously valid. Conversely, $\mathbf{HSP}^*_{\alpha_0}(\mathcal{K}) = \mathbf{HSP}_{\alpha_0}(\mathcal{K}^{(*)}) \subseteq \mathbf{HSP}_{\alpha_0}\mathbf{HSP}^e_{\alpha_0}(\mathcal{K}) = \mathbf{HSP}^e_{\alpha_0}(\mathcal{K})$ follows from Theorem 5.4. The second statement is a consequence of the first one and of Lemma 5.2 through Theorem 1.4.13. □

Using Theorem 5.5, we prove

Theorem 5.6. *A class $\mathscr{K}$ of automata is homomorphically complete for the α_0^e-product if and only if the following conditions are satisfied:*

(i) *$\mathscr{K}$ is not counter-free,*
(ii) *$\mathbf{HSP}^e_{\alpha_0}(\mathscr{K})$ contains a two-state full reset automaton, and*
(iii) *for every simple group G, there exists an automaton $\mathfrak{A} \in \mathscr{K}$ such that G is a homomorphic image of a subgroup of $\mathscr{S}(\mathfrak{A})$.*

Proof. By Theorem 5.5, conditions (i)–(iii) are sufficient.

The necessity of condition (ii) is trivial. Condition (i) is also necessary, since only the trivial counters are in $\mathbf{HSP}^e_{\alpha_0}(\mathscr{K})$ if $\mathscr{K}$ is counter-free. Finally, the necessity of (iii) follows from Theorem 5.5. □

Since every simple group is isomorphic to a subgroup of a larger simple group, from Theorem 5.6 we have

Corollary 5.7. *There exists no class of automata which is homomorphically complete with respect to the α_0^e-product and minimal.* □

The following example shows that the generalized α_0-product is homomorphically more general than the α_0^e-product.

Example 5.8. Let $\mathfrak{A}_0$ be an arbitrary two-state full reset automaton. Moreover, for every integer $n \geqq 2$, take the automaton $\mathfrak{A}_n = (\{x_1, x_2, x_3, x_4\}, [2n] \cup \{2'\}, \delta_n)$ with transitions $\delta_n(i, x_1) = i + 1$ if i is odd, $\delta_n(i, x_2) = i + 1 \pmod{2n}$ if i is even, $\delta_n(1, x_3) = 2$, $\delta_n(2, x_4) = 3$, $\delta_n(3, x_3) = 2'$, $\delta_n(2', x_4) = 1$, and $\delta_n(i, x) = i$, $\delta_n(2', x) = 2'$ in all remaining cases. Put $\mathscr{K} = \{\mathfrak{A}_0\} \cup \{\mathfrak{A}_n \mid n \geqq 2\}$. We show that $\mathscr{K}$ is homomorphically complete with respect to the generalized α_0-product. For this, observe that, for every integer $n \geqq 2$, an n-state standard automaton $\mathfrak{B}_n$ is isomorphic to a subautomaton of a generalized α_0-power of $\mathfrak{A}_n$ with a single factor. Thus, taking into consideration that, by Theorem 2.1.5, $\{\mathfrak{A}_0\} \cup \{\mathfrak{B}_n \mid n \geqq 2\}$ is homomorphically complete with respect to the α_0-product, $\mathbf{HSP}^*_{\alpha_0}(\mathscr{K})$ is the class of all automata. On the other hand, $\mathscr{K}$ is counter-free. Therefore, by Theorem 5.6, $\mathscr{K}$ is not homomorphically complete with respect to the α_0^e-product. □

We now turn to α_1^e-products.

Lemma 5.9. *Assume that an automaton $\mathfrak{A} = (X, A, \delta)$ has a cycle with a length of at least 2. Then $\mathbf{HSP}^e_{\alpha_1}(\mathscr{K})$ contains all two-state full reset automata.*

Proof. Let $a_1, \ldots, a_n$ be a nontrivial cycle in $\mathfrak{A}$ and let $x_1, \ldots, x_n \in X$ be input signals such that $\delta(a_i, x_i) = a_{i+1 \pmod{n}}$.

Construct the α_1^e-product

$$\mathfrak{B} = (\{y_0, y_1, y_2\}, B, \delta') = (\underbrace{\mathfrak{A} \times \ldots \times \mathfrak{A}}_{n+2 \text{ times}})\,[\{y_0, y_1, y_2\}, \varphi]$$

where, for any i $(1 \leqq i \leqq n+2)$, j $(1 \leqq j \leqq n)$ and $b_1, \dots, b_{n+2} \in A$,

$$\varphi_i(b_1, \dots, b_i, y_0) = e\,,$$

$$\varphi_i(b_1, \dots, b_i, y_1) = \begin{cases} x_j \text{ if } b_i = a_j \neq a_1, \\ x_1 \text{ if } b_i = a_1 \text{ and } b_m \neq a_1 \text{ for} \\ \quad \text{every } m \in [i-1], \\ e \text{ in all other cases,} \end{cases}$$

$$\varphi_i(b_1, \dots, b_i, y_2) = \begin{cases} x_j \text{ if } b_i = a_j \neq a_1, \\ x_1 \text{ if } b_i = a_1 \text{ and } b_m = b_n = a_1 \\ \quad \text{for some } m, n \text{ with } 1 \leqq m < n < i, \\ e \text{ otherwise.} \end{cases}$$

Let C denote the set of all vectors $\mathbf{b} \in B$ such that each a_i $(i \in [n])$ is a component of $\mathbf{b}$ and a_1 occurs exactly three times in $\mathbf{b}$. Obviously, $\mathfrak{C} = (\{y_0, y_1, y_2\}, C, \delta'')$ with $\delta'' = \delta' \mid C \times \{y_0, y_1, y_2\}$ is a subautomaton of $\mathfrak{B}$. Take the subset C_1 consisting of all $\mathbf{b} = (b_1, \dots, b_{n+2}) \in C$ for which there are integers i, j and k with $1 \leqq i < j < k \leqq n+2$ such that $b_i = a_2$ and $b_j = b_k = a_1$, i.e., in $\mathbf{b}$ the occurrence of a_2 precedes at least two occurrences of a_1. Moreover, let $C_2 = C \setminus C_1$. Then $\{C_1, C_2\}$ is a compatible partition of $\mathfrak{C}$. Finally, for arbitrary $\mathbf{c} \in C$, we have $\delta''(\mathbf{c}, y_1) \in C_1$ and $\delta''(\mathbf{c}, y_2) \in C_2$. □

We next prove

Theorem 5.10. *Let $\mathscr{K}$ be a class of automata. Assume that $\mathscr{K}$ contains a nonmonotone automaton, and let $\mathfrak{A}$ be an arbitrary automaton. Then, $\mathfrak{A} \in \mathbf{HSP}^e_{\alpha_1}(\mathscr{K})$ $[\mathfrak{A} \in \mathbf{HSP}^*_{\alpha_1}(\mathscr{K})]$ if and only if, whenever a simple group G is a homomorphic image of a subgroup of $\mathscr{S}(\mathfrak{A})$, there exists a $\mathfrak{B} \in \mathbf{P}^e_{1\alpha_1}(\mathscr{K})$ $[\mathfrak{B} \in \mathbf{P}^*_{1\alpha_1}(\mathscr{K})]$ such that a subgroup of $\mathscr{S}(\mathfrak{B})$ can be mapped homomorphically onto G. Otherwise, i.e. if $\mathscr{K}$ consists only of monotone automata, the equality $\mathbf{HSP}^e_{\alpha_1}(\mathscr{K}) = \mathbf{HSP}^*_{\alpha_1}(\mathscr{K})$ holds, and three cases arise:*

(i) *If there is a nondiscrete automaton in $\mathscr{K}$, then $\mathbf{HSP}^e_{\alpha_1}(\mathscr{K})$ is the class of all monotone automata.*
(ii) *If every automaton from $\mathscr{K}$ is discrete and $\mathscr{K}$ contains a nontrivial automaton, then $\mathbf{HSP}^e_{\alpha_1}(\mathscr{K})$ is the class of all discrete automata.*
(iii) *If $\mathscr{K}$ contains only trivial automata, then $\mathbf{HSP}^e_{\alpha_1}(\mathscr{K})$ is the class of all trivial automata.*

Proof. Assume that $\mathscr{K}$ contains a nonmonotone automaton. Then, $\mathbf{P}^e_{1\alpha_1}(\mathscr{K})$ is not counter-free and, by Lemma 5.9, $\mathbf{HSP}^e_{\alpha_1}(\mathscr{K})$ contains all two-state full reset automata. Since $\mathbf{HSP}^e_{\alpha_1}(\mathscr{K}) = \mathbf{HSP}_{\alpha_0}\mathbf{P}^e_{1\alpha_1}(\mathscr{K}) = \mathbf{HSP}^e_{\alpha_0}\mathbf{P}^e_{1\alpha_1}(\mathscr{K})$, for α_1^e-products, the first statement of Theorem 5.10 follows by Theorem 5.5. As regards generalized α_1-products, the proof is similar because of the equalities $\mathbf{HSP}^*_{\alpha_1}(\mathscr{K}) = \mathbf{HSP}_{1\alpha_0}\mathbf{P}^*_{1\alpha_1}(\mathscr{K}) = \mathbf{HSP}^e_{\alpha_0}P^*_{1\alpha_1}(\mathscr{K})$.

Now suppose that $\mathscr{K}$ contains only monotone automata.

If there is a nondiscrete automaton in $\mathscr{K}$, then, by the proof of Theorem 4.8, $\mathbf{ISP}^e_{\alpha_0}(\mathscr{K}) = \mathbf{HSP}^*_g(\mathscr{K})$ is the class of all monotone automata.

The proof in the remaining two cases is trivial. □

If a class $\mathscr{K}$ of automata is homomorphically complete with respect to the generalized α_1-product, then $\mathscr{K}$ contains a nonmonotone automaton. Moreover, the subgroups of characteristic semigroups of monotone automata are trivial. Thus, from Theorem 5.10 we have

Corollary 5.11. *A class $\mathscr{K}$ of automata is homomorphically complete with respect to the α_1^e-product [generalized α_1-product] if and only if, for every simple group G, there exists an automaton $\mathfrak{A} \in \mathbf{P}^e_{1\alpha_1}(\mathscr{K})$ [$\mathfrak{A} \in \mathbf{P}^*_{1\alpha_1}(\mathscr{K})$] such that a subgroup of $\mathscr{S}(\mathfrak{A})$ can be mapped homomorphically onto G.* □

Corollary 5.11 implies

Corollary 5.12. *There is no class of automata which is homomorphically complete with respect to the α_1^e-product and minimal.* □

We close the study of α_1^e-products with an example showing the existence of a class $\mathscr{K}$ of automata such that $\mathscr{K}$ is homomorphically complete with respect to the generalized α_1-product and $\mathscr{K}$ is not homomorphically complete with respect to the α_1^e-product.

Example 5.13. Let $\mathscr{K}$ be the class of all counters $\mathfrak{C}_n = (\{x\}, [n], \delta_n)$ $(n \geqq 1)$. By Theorems 3.1 and 3.2, $\mathscr{K}$ is homomorphically complete with respect to the generalized α_1-product.

Let $\mathfrak{A} = (X, [n], \delta) \in \mathbf{P}^e_{1\alpha_1}(\{\mathfrak{C}_n\})$ be arbitrary for an $n \geqq 1$. We show that every subgroup of $\mathscr{S}(\mathfrak{A})$ is cyclic. For $n = 1$, this obviously holds. Thus, assume that $n > 1$, and take a subgroup $G = \{p_1/\varrho_{\mathfrak{A}}, \dots, p_t/\varrho_{\mathfrak{A}}\}$ $(p_1, \dots, p_t \in X^*)$ of $\mathscr{S}(\mathfrak{A})$. By the proof of Theorem 1.2.15, there is a subset $N = \{i_1, \dots, i_k\}$ $(i_1 < \dots < i_k)$ of $[n]$ such that, for arbitrary $j \in [t]$, the mapping $i_l \to \delta(i_l, p_j)$ $(l = 1, \dots, k)$ is a permutation of N, and the group G' formed by these permutations is isomorphic to G. Let $p \in \{p_1, \dots, p_t\}$ be arbitrary. Observe that, for any $i \in [n]$ and $x \in X$, we have $\delta(i, x) \in \{i, i + 1\}$ if $i < n$, and $\delta(n, x) \in \{n, 1\}$. Therefore, since p induces a permutation of N, there are integers $u_1, \dots, u_k$ with $0 \leqq u_1, \dots, u_k < k$ such that $\delta(i_j, p) = i_{j+u_j (\text{mod } k)}$ for every $j \in [k]$, and $u_r < u_s + (s - r)$ if $1 \leqq r < s \leqq k$. Taking $u = \max \{u_1, \dots, u_k\}$, we obviously have that $u = u_1 = \dots = u_k$. Consequently, G' is isomorphic to a subgroup of $\mathscr{S}(\mathfrak{C}_k)$, and thus it is cyclic. Since the homomorphic images of cyclic groups are cyclic and there are noncyclic simple groups, by Corollary 5.11, $\mathscr{K}$ is not homomorphically çomplete with respect to the α_1^e-product. □

We next show that as regards homomorphic representations from $i = 2$, the α_i^e-product is as powerful as the generalized product.

Theorem 5.14. *For an arbitrary class $\mathscr{K}$ of automata, the equality $\mathbf{HSP}^e_{\alpha_2}(\mathscr{K}) = \mathbf{HSP}^*_g(\mathscr{K})$ holds. Further, four cases arise:*

(i) *If $\mathscr{K}$ contains a nonmonotone automaton, then* $\mathbf{HSP}^e_{\alpha_2}(\mathscr{K})$ *is the class of all automata.*

(ii) *If $\mathscr{K}$ consists of monotone automata, one of which is not discrete, then* $\mathbf{HSP}^e_{\alpha_2}(\mathscr{K})$ *is the class of all monotone automata.*

(iii) *If $\mathscr{K}$ consists of discrete automata and there is a non-trivial automaton in $\mathscr{K}$, then* $\mathbf{HSP}^e_{\alpha_2}(\mathscr{K})$ *is the class of all discrete automata.*

(iv) *If every automaton in $\mathscr{K}$ is trivial, then* $\mathbf{HSP}^e_{\alpha_2}(\mathscr{K})$ *is the class of all trivial automata.*

Proof. Suppose that $\mathscr{K}$ contains an automaton which is not monotone. Then, $\mathscr{K}^{(e)}$ satisfies Letičevskiĭ's criterion. Thus, by Theorem 2.4.10, $\mathbf{HSP}^e_{\alpha_2}(\mathscr{K}) = \mathbf{HSP}_{\alpha_2}(\mathscr{K}^{(e)})$ is the class of all automata. From this, by the inclusion $\mathbf{HSP}^e_{\alpha_2}(\mathscr{K}) \subseteq \mathbf{HSP}^*_g(\mathscr{K})$, we have that $\mathbf{HSP}^*_g(\mathscr{K})$ is also the class of all automata.

For the remaining cases, see the proof of Theorem 5.10. □

We close this chapter by summarizing our comparison results as regards the homomorphic representation powers of different forms of products.

Let $\mathbf{X}$ and $\mathbf{Y}$ be operators on automata. We write $\mathbf{X} = \mathbf{Y}$ if $\mathbf{X}(\mathscr{K}) = \mathbf{Y}(\mathscr{K})$ holds for an arbitrary class $\mathscr{K}$ of automata. The opposite case is expressed by $\mathbf{X} \neq \mathbf{Y}$. Moreover, $\mathbf{X} \leqq \mathbf{Y}$ means that the inclusion $\mathbf{X}(\mathscr{K}) \subseteq \mathbf{Y}(\mathscr{K})$ is valid for any class $\mathscr{K}$ of automata. If $\mathbf{X} \leqq \mathbf{Y}$ and $\mathbf{X} \neq \mathbf{Y}$, then we write $\mathbf{X} < \mathbf{Y}$, for short. Finally, if none of $\mathbf{X} \leqq \mathbf{Y}$ and $\mathbf{Y} \leqq \mathbf{X}$ holds, then it is said that $\mathbf{X}$ and $\mathbf{Y}$ are incomparable.

Figure 18 shows the relation between the operators $\mathbf{P}_{\alpha_0}$, $\mathbf{P}_{\alpha_1}$, $\mathbf{P}_{\alpha_2}$, $\mathbf{P}_g$, $\mathbf{P}^e_{\alpha_0}$, $\mathbf{P}^e_{\alpha_1}$, $\mathbf{P}^e_{\alpha_2}$, $\mathbf{P}^*_{\alpha_0}$, $\mathbf{P}^*_{\alpha_1}$ and $\mathbf{P}^*_g$. In this diagram there is a path from $\mathbf{X}$ to $\mathbf{Y}$ if and only if $\mathbf{X} < \mathbf{Y}$.

The incomparability of $\mathbf{P}^e_{\alpha_0}$ and $\mathbf{P}_{\alpha_1}$, $\mathbf{P}^e_{\alpha_0}$ and $\mathbf{P}_{\alpha_2}$, $\mathbf{P}^*_{\alpha_0}$ and $\mathbf{P}_{\alpha_1}$, $\mathbf{P}^*_{\alpha_0}$ and $\mathbf{P}_{\alpha_2}$, $\mathbf{P}^e_{\alpha_1}$ and $\mathbf{P}_{\alpha_2}$, and of $\mathbf{P}_{\alpha_1}$ and $\mathbf{P}_{\alpha_2}$ follows from the three statements below:

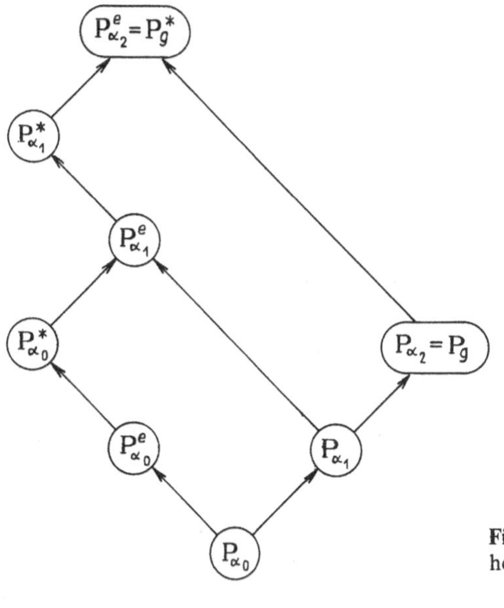

Fig. 18. Comparison of product operators under homomorphic representation

(i) From Example 4.10 through a remark following it we have that there are a class $\mathcal{K}$ of automata and an automaton $\mathfrak{A}$ such that $\mathfrak{A} \in \mathbf{IP}^e_{\alpha_0}(\mathcal{K})$ and $\mathfrak{A} \notin \mathbf{HSP}_g(\mathcal{K})$.

(ii) Let $\mathfrak{A}$ be the same automaton as in Example 4.10. Then $\mathbf{HSP}^*_{\alpha_0}(\{\mathfrak{A}\})$ contains only permutation automata, and there are nonpermutation automata in $\mathbf{P}_{\alpha_1}(\{\mathfrak{A}\})$.

(iii) By Theorem 2.4.10, there exists a finite class of automata which is homomorphically complete with respect to the α_2-product. On the other hand, from Corollary 3.4 through Theorem 3.1 we have that there is no class of automata which is homomorphically complete with respect to the generalized α_1-product and minimal.

The relation $\mathbf{P}_{\alpha_2} = \mathbf{P}_g$ is valid by Theorem 2.5.4, while $\mathbf{P}^e_{\alpha_2} = \mathbf{P}^*_g$ is stated in Theorem 5.14.

By Theorem 2.5.5, $\mathbf{P}_{\alpha_0} < \mathbf{P}_{\alpha_1} < \mathbf{P}_{\alpha_2}$. Statement (i) implies $\mathbf{P}_{\alpha_0} < \mathbf{P}^e_{\alpha_0}$, $\mathbf{P}_{\alpha_1} < \mathbf{P}^e_{\alpha_1}$ and $\mathbf{P}_{\alpha_2} < \mathbf{P}^e_{\alpha_2}$. By Examples 5.8 and 5.13, the relations $\mathbf{P}^e_{\alpha_0} < \mathbf{P}^*_{\alpha_0}$ and $\mathbf{P}^e_{\alpha_1} < \mathbf{P}^*_{\alpha_1}$ hold. The validity of $\mathbf{P}^*_{\alpha_1} < \mathbf{P}^*_g$ follows from (iii).

It remains to be shown that $\mathbf{P}^*_{\alpha_0} < \mathbf{P}^e_{\alpha_1}$. For this, take a class $\mathcal{K}$ of automata. If $\mathcal{K}$ contains a nonmonotone automaton, then, since the "only if" part of the conclusion of Lemma 5.2 is valid for an arbitrary class of automata, from Theorem 5.10 through Lemma 5.2 we have $\mathbf{HSP}^*_{\alpha_0}(\mathcal{K}) \subseteq \mathbf{HSP}^e_{\alpha_1}(\mathcal{K})$. If $\mathcal{K}$ consists only of monotone automata, then $\mathbf{HSP}^*_{\alpha_0}(\mathcal{K}) = \mathbf{HSP}^e_{\alpha_1}(\mathcal{K})$. Therefore, by (ii), $\mathbf{P}^*_{\alpha_0} < \mathbf{P}^e_{\alpha_1}$.

5. Representation of Automaton Mappings in Finite Length. Infinite Products

There is no finite system of automata which is complete with respect to the α_0-product. We show the existence of such finite systems if we restrict ourselves to representations of automaton mappings in finite but unbounded lengths. It will also be seen that in this representation the α_0-product is as powerful as the general product. This will follow from the result that, for an arbitrary class $\mathscr{K}$ of automata, the minimal equational class containing $\mathscr{K}$ and closed under the infinite α_0-product coincides with the minimal equational class containing $\mathscr{K}$ and closed under the infinite general product.

5.1 Metric Completeness

We start with some basic concepts concerning metric representations of automaton mappings.

Definition 1.1. Let $\tau: X^* \to Y^*$ be an arbitrary automaton mapping, $\mathfrak{A} = (X, A, Y, \delta, \lambda)$ a Mealy machine, and $k \geqq 0$ an integer. We say that $\mathfrak{A}$ *induces* τ *in length* k if there exists an $a \in A$ such that $\tau_{\mathfrak{A},a}(p) = \tau(p)$ for arbitrary $p \in X^{(k)}$.

For arbitrary automaton $\mathfrak{A} = (X, A, \delta)$, state $a \in A$, and integer $k \geqq 0$, set $A^{(k)}_{\mathfrak{A},a} = \{\delta(a, p) \mid p \in X^{(k)}\}$. If there is no danger of confusion, then we omit the indices $\mathfrak{A}$ and a in $A^{(k)}_{\mathfrak{A},a}$.

Definition 1.2. Take the systems $(\mathfrak{A}, a)$ and $(\mathfrak{B}, b)$, where $\mathfrak{A} = (X, A, \delta)$ and $\mathfrak{B} = (X, B, \delta')$ are automata, $a \in A$ and $b \in B$. Moreover, let $k \geqq 0$ be an arbitrary integer. We say that a mapping $\psi: A^{(k)} \to B^{(k)}$ is a *k-homomorphism* of $(\mathfrak{A}, a)$ into $(\mathfrak{B}, b)$ if the equality $\psi(\delta(a, p)) = \delta'(b, p)$ holds for every $p \in X^{(k)}$; and $(\mathfrak{B}, b)$ is a *k-homomorphic* image of $(\mathfrak{A}, a)$. If, in addition, ψ is one-to-one, then we speak of a *k-isomorphism*.

Clearly, for arbitrary automata $\mathfrak{A} = (X, A, \delta)$, $\mathfrak{B} = (X, B, \delta')$ and states $a \in A$, $b \in B$, if $(\mathfrak{A}, a)$ is k-free, then $(\mathfrak{B}, b)$ is a k-homomorphic image of $(\mathfrak{A}, a)$.

The following result is obvious.

Lemma 1.3. *Let $(\mathfrak{B}, b)$ be a k-homomorphic image of $(\mathfrak{A}, a)$, where $\mathfrak{A} = (X, A, \delta)$, $\mathfrak{B} = (X, B, \delta')$, $a \in A$, $b \in B$ and $k \geqq 0$ is an integer. Then, for every Mealy machine $\bar{\mathfrak{B}} = (X, B, Y, \delta', \lambda')$, there exists a Mealy macine $\bar{\mathfrak{A}} = (X, A, Y, \delta, \lambda)$ such that $\tau_{\bar{\mathfrak{A}},a}(p) = \tau_{\bar{\mathfrak{B}},b}(p)$ for arbitrary $p \in X^{(k)}$.* □

After defining metric completeness, we shall give two necessary and sufficient conditions for a class of automata to be metrically complete with respect to the α_i-product ($i \in \mathbf{N}$) and to the product.

Definition 1.4. class $\mathscr{K}$ of automata is said to be *metrically complete* with respect to the general product [with respect to the α_i-product ($i \in \mathbf{N}$)] if, for every automaton mapping $\tau: X^* \to Y^*$ and integer $k \geqq 0$, there is an $\mathfrak{A} = (X, A, \delta) \in \mathbf{P}_g(\mathscr{K})$ [$\mathfrak{A} = (X, A, \delta) \in \mathbf{P}_{\alpha_i}(\mathscr{K})$] such that an $\bar{\mathfrak{A}} = (X, A, Y, \delta, \lambda)$ induces τ in length k.

Theorem 1.5. *A class $\mathscr{K}$ of automata is metrically complete with respect to the general product [with respect to the α_i-product ($i \in \mathbf{N}$)] if and only if, for every alphabet X and integer $k \geqq 0$, there exist an $\mathfrak{A} \in \mathbf{P}_g(\mathscr{K})$ [$\mathfrak{A} \in \mathbf{P}_{\alpha_i}(\mathscr{K})$] with input alphabet X and a state a of $\mathfrak{A}$ such that $(\mathfrak{A}, a)$ is k-free.*

Proof. If $\mathscr{K}$ satisfies the conditions of Theorem 1.5, then, by Lemma 1.3, $\mathscr{K}$ is metrically complete with respect to the general product [with respect to the α_i-product].

Conversely, assume that, for an alphabet X and integer $k \geqq 0$, none of the systems $(\mathfrak{A}, a)$ with $\mathfrak{A} = (X, A, \delta)$, $a \in A$ and $\mathfrak{A} \in \mathbf{P}_g(\mathscr{K})$ [$\mathfrak{A} \in \mathbf{P}_{\alpha_i}(\mathscr{K})$] is k-free. (Since every system $(\mathfrak{A}, a)$ is 0-free, we may suppose that $k > 0$.) Take a $(k + 1)$-free $(\mathfrak{B}, b)$ where $\mathfrak{B} = (X, B, \delta')$ and $b \in B$. Consider the Mealy machine $\bar{\mathfrak{B}} = (X, B, B, \delta', \lambda')$ with $\lambda'(b', x) = b'$ ($b' \in B, x \in X$). Assume that $\mathscr{K}$ is metrically complete with respect to the general product [with respect to the α_i-product]. Then there exist an $\mathfrak{A} \in \mathbf{P}_g(\mathscr{K})$ [$\mathfrak{A} \in \mathbf{P}_{\alpha_i}(\mathscr{K})$] with $\mathfrak{A} = (X, A, \delta)$ and an $a \in A$ such that $\tau_{\bar{\mathfrak{B}}, b}(p) = \tau_{\bar{\mathfrak{A}}, a}(p)$ for a Mealy machine $\bar{\mathfrak{A}} = (X, A, B, \delta, \lambda)$ and for every $p \in X^{(k+1)}$, i.e., $\bar{\mathfrak{A}}$ induces $\tau_{\bar{\mathfrak{B}}, b}$ in length $k + 1$. Since, on our assumptions, $(\mathfrak{A}, a)$ is not k-free, there are two different words $p, q \in X^{(k)}$ such that $\delta(a, p) = \delta(a, q)$. Therefore, if $x \in X$ is an arbitrary input signal, then the last letters of $\lambda(a, px)$ and $\lambda(a, qx)$ coincide, which obviously does not hold for $\lambda'(b, px)$ and $\lambda'(b, qx)$. □

Using Theorem 1.5, we give another characterization of metrically complete classes.

Theorem 1.6. A *class $\mathscr{K}$ of automata is metrically complete with respect to the general product or any of the α_i-products ($i \in \mathbf{N}$) if and only if, for arbitrary integer $k \geqq 0$, there exist an automaton $\mathfrak{A} = (X, A, \delta) \in \mathscr{K}$, a state $a \in A$, and an input word $p \in X^*$ with $|p| = k$ such that $\delta(a, p)$ is ambiguous.*

Proof. If $\mathscr{K}$ satisfies the conditions of Theorem 1.6, then, using Lemma 2.5.3, from Theorem 1.5 we have that $\mathscr{K}$ is metrically complete with respect to the α_0-product. Therefore $\mathscr{K}$ is metrically complete with respect to the general product and with respect to any of the α_i-products.

Conversely, suppose that there is an integer $k \geqq 0$ such that, for arbitrary $\mathfrak{A} = (X, A, \delta) \in \mathscr{K}$, $a \in A$ and $p \in X^*$ with $|p| = k$, the state $\delta(a, p)$ is not ambiguous. This implies that, for arbitrary alphabet Y with $|Y| > 1$, general product $\mathfrak{B} = (Y, B, \delta')$ of automata from $\mathscr{K}$, state $b \in B$, input word $q \in Y^*$ with $|q| = k$, and input signals

$y_1, y_2 \in Y$, the equality $\delta'(b, qy_1) = \delta'(b, qy_2)$ holds. Therefore, for any of the general products $\mathfrak{B} = (Y, B, \delta')$ of automata from $\mathscr{K}$ and state $b \in B$, the system $(\mathfrak{B}, b)$ is not $(k + 1)$-free. Thus, by Theorem 1.5, $\mathscr{K}$ is not metrically complete with respect to the general product. □

From Theorem 1.6 we directly obtain

Corollary 1.7. *A class $\mathscr{K}$ of automata is metrically complete with respect to the general product if and only if $\mathscr{K}$ is metrically complete with respect to the α_0-product.* □

It should be noted that we can easily give an algorithm based on Theorem 1.6 to decide whether a finite class of automata is metrically complete for the general product, and thus for any of the α_i-products.

We end this section with an example showing the existence of a one-element class which is metrically complete with respect to the α_0-product.

Example 1.8. Let $\mathfrak{A} = (\{x, y\}, [2], \delta)$ be the automaton given by $\delta(1, x) = 1$, $\delta(2, x) = 2$, $\delta(1, y) = 2$ and $\delta(2, y) = 2$. Then, for arbitrary integer $k \geqq 0$, the state $\delta(1, x^k) = 1$ is ambiguous. Therefore, by Theorem 1.6, $\{\mathfrak{A}\}$ is metrically complete with respect to the α_0-product. □

5.2 Equational Classes of Automata

In this section we characterize equational classes of automata which are closed under the general product. For this, we allow an automaton to have infinitely many states, and extend the products of the automata in such a way that they may have infinitely many components.

Definition 2.1. Let $\mathfrak{A}_i = (X_i, A_i, \delta_i)$ $(i \in I)$ be a nonvoid family of automata, X an alphabet and

$$\varphi : \prod (A_i \mid i \in I) \times X \to \prod (X_i \mid i \in I)$$

a mapping. Consider the automaton $\mathfrak{A} = (X, A, \delta)$ with $A = \prod (A_i \mid i \in I)$ and $\mathrm{pr}_i(\delta(\mathbf{a}, x)) = \delta_i(\mathrm{pr}_i(\mathbf{a}), \mathrm{pr}_i(\varphi(\mathbf{a}, x)))$ for arbitrary $\mathbf{a} \in A$, $x \in X$, and $i \in I$. This $\mathfrak{A}$ is called the (general) *product* of $\mathfrak{A}_i$ $(i \in I)$ with respect to X and φ *with possibly infinitely many factors.*

For arbitrary $\mathbf{a} \in A$, $x \in X$ and $i \in I$, let $\varphi_i(\mathbf{a}, x)$ be the ith component of $\varphi(\mathbf{a}, x)$. If there exists a linear ordering $\leqq$ on I such that, for every $i \in I$, φ_i is independent of its jth component $(j \in I)$ whenever $j \geqq i$, then $\mathfrak{A}$ is an *α_0-product with possibly infinitely many factors.*

Let $\mathscr{K}$ be a class of automata. Then the operators $\mathbf{P}_{i,g}$ and $\mathbf{P}_{i,\alpha_0}$ are defined in the following way:

$\mathbf{P}_{i,g}(\mathscr{K})$ is the class of all products of automata from $\mathscr{K}$ with possibly infinitely many factors, and

$\mathbf{P}_{i,\alpha_0}(\mathscr{K})$ is the class of all α_0-products of automata from $\mathscr{K}$ with possibly infinitely many factors.

We keep the notation $\mathbf{P}_{\alpha_0}(\mathscr{K})$ for the class of all α_0-products of automata from $\mathscr{K}$ with finitely many factors, even in the case when $\mathscr{K}$ may have infinite automata. Obviously, the formation of such α_0-products is also transitive (up to isomorphism).

Finally, for every alphabet X, $\mathscr{K}_X$ will stand for the class of all automata with input alphabet X.

To characterize equational classes of automata closed under the product, we need some special equations. These equations can be given by certain patterns.

Definition 2.2. A *p-equation* is

(i) $m = n$, or
(ii) $(l, m) = (l, n)$

where m, n and l are arbitrary non-negative integers.

We next define what it means that a p-equation is satisfied by an automaton.

Definition 2.3. Let $\mathfrak{A} = (X, A, \delta)$ be an automaton. $\mathfrak{A}$ *satisfies* the p-equation (i) of Definition 2.2 if $\mathfrak{A}$ satisfies all equations $ux_1 \dots x_m = vy_1 \dots y_n$ for arbitrary $x_1, \dots, x_m, y_1, \dots, y_n \in X$. Moreover, $\mathfrak{A}$ *satisfies* (ii) in Definition 2.2 if it satisfies all equations $ux_1 \dots x_l y_1 \dots y_m = ux_1 \dots x_l z_1 \dots z_n$ for arbitrary $x_1, \dots, x_l, y_1, \dots, y_m, z_1, \dots, z_n \in X$.

We also say that (i) or (ii) *holds* in $\mathfrak{A}$.

In this chapter, for a class $\mathscr{K}$ of automata, $\mathscr{K}^*$ denotes the set of all p-equations holding in every automaton from $\mathscr{K}$. Moreover, $\mathscr{K}^{**}$ stands for the class of all automata which satisfy every p-equation in $\mathscr{K}^*$.

Theorem 2.4. *For arbitrary alphabet X and class $\mathscr{K}$ of automata,* $\mathbf{HSP}_{i,g}(\mathscr{K}) \cap \mathscr{K}_X = \mathscr{K}^{**} \cap \mathscr{K}_X = \mathbf{HSPP}_{\alpha_0}(\mathscr{K}) \cap \mathscr{K}_X = \mathbf{HSP}_{i,\alpha_0}(\mathscr{K}) \cap \mathscr{K}_X$.

Proof. First of all, let us extend Definitions 2.5.1 and 2.5.2 to automata where the finiteness of the state sets is not required. Clearly, under these concepts of ambiguity and k-freeness, Lemma 2.5.3 remains valid for automata with possibly infinitely many states. (Only the finiteness of Y is needed for the proof of Lemma 2.5.3.)

Obviously, p-equations are preserved by products with possibly infinitely many factors. Thus, $\mathscr{K}^{**} \supseteq \mathbf{HSP}_{i,g}(\mathscr{K})$. Therefore, since $\mathbf{HSP}_{i,\alpha_0}(\mathscr{K}) \supseteq \mathbf{HSPP}_{\alpha_0}(\mathscr{K})$ obviously holds, to prove Theorem 2.4 it is enough to show that $\mathbf{HSPP}_{\alpha_0}(\mathscr{K}) \cap \mathscr{K}_X \supseteq \mathscr{K}^{**} \cap \mathscr{K}_X$, which follows from statements (i) and (ii) below:

(i) Let $ux_1 \dots x_m = vy_1 \dots y_n$ $(x_1, \dots, x_m, y_1, \dots, y_n \in X)$ be an X-equation satisfied by $\mathbf{HSPP}_{\alpha_0}(\mathscr{K}) \cap \mathscr{K}_X$. Then, the p-equation $m = n$ is in $\mathscr{K}^*$.
(ii) Let $ux_1 \dots x_l y_1 \dots y_m = ux_1 \dots x_l z_1 \dots z_n$ $(x_1, \dots, x_l, y_1, \dots, y_m, z_1, \dots, z_n \in X)$ be an X-equation holding in $\mathbf{HSPP}_{\alpha_0}(\mathscr{K}) \cap \mathscr{K}_X$ such that $y_1 \neq z_1$ if $m, n > 0$. Then, the p-equation $(l, m) = (l, n)$ is in $\mathscr{K}^*$.

If $\mathscr{K}$ consists only of trivial automata, then Theorem 2.4 obviously holds. Moreover, if, for every integer $k \geqq 0$, there are an $\mathfrak{A} = (X, A, \delta) \in \mathbf{P}_{\alpha_0}(\mathscr{K}) \cap \mathscr{K}_X$

and an $\mathbf{a} \in A^2$ such that $(\mathfrak{A}, \mathbf{a})$ is k-free, then in $\mathbf{HSPP}_{\alpha_0}(\mathscr{K}) \cap \mathscr{K}_X$ only the trivial equations $(up = up\ (p \in X^*))$ hold. Therefore, $\mathbf{HSPP}_{\alpha_0}(\mathscr{K}) \supseteq \mathscr{K}_X$.

Next assume that k is the largest integer for which there exist an $\mathfrak{A} = (X, A, \delta) \in \mathbf{P}_{\alpha_0}(\mathscr{K}) \cap \mathscr{K}_X$ and an $\mathbf{a} = (a^{(1)}, a^{(2)}) \in A^2$ such that $(\mathfrak{A}, \mathbf{a})$ is k-free. Then, by Lemma 2.5.3, for an arbitrary automaton $\mathfrak{B} = (X_{\mathfrak{B}}, B, \delta_{\mathfrak{B}}) \in \mathscr{K}$, $b \in B$, $p \in X_{\mathfrak{B}}^*$ with $|p| \geqq k + 1$ and $x_{\mathfrak{B}}^{(1)}, x_{\mathfrak{B}}^{(2)} \in X_{\mathfrak{B}}$, we have $\delta_{\mathfrak{B}}(b, px_{\mathfrak{B}}^{(1)}) = \delta_{\mathfrak{B}}(b, px_{\mathfrak{B}}^{(2)})$.

Let the equation $ux_1 \dots x_m = vy_1 \dots y_n$ $(x_1, \dots, x_m, y_1, \dots, y_n \in X)$ hold in $\mathbf{HSPP}_{\alpha_0}(\mathscr{K}) \cap \mathscr{K}_X$. Assume that the p-equation $m = n$ is not in $\mathscr{K}^*$. We then find an automaton $\mathfrak{A}' = (X', A', \delta') \in \mathscr{K}$, two states $a_1', a_2' \in A'$ and input signals $x_1', \dots, x_m', y_1', \dots, y_n' \in X'$ such that $\delta'(a_1', x_1' \dots x_m') \neq \delta'(a_2', y_1' \dots y_n')$. Take the k-free system $(\mathfrak{A}, \mathbf{a})$ above, and form the α_0-product $\bar{\mathfrak{A}} = (X, A \times A', \bar{\delta})$ of $\mathfrak{A}$ and $\mathfrak{A}'$ given by the feedback function $\varphi: A \times A' \times X \to X \times X'$ such that φ_1 is the identity mapping on X. Moreover,

$$\varphi_2(\delta(a^{(1)}, x_1 \dots x_i), x_{i+1}) = x_{i+1}' \quad \text{if} \quad i \leqq \max\{k, m-1\}, \quad \text{and}$$
$$\varphi_2(\delta(a^{(2)}, y_1 \dots y_i), y_{i+1}) = y_{i+1}' \quad \text{if} \quad i \leqq \max\{k, n-1\}.$$

In $\bar{\mathfrak{A}}$ we then have

$$\begin{aligned}\bar{\delta}((a^{(1)}, a_1'), x_1 \dots x_m) &= (\delta(a^{(1)}, x_1 \dots x_m), \delta'(a_1', x_1' \dots x_m')) \\ &\neq (\delta(a^{(2)}, y_1 \dots y_n), \delta'(a_2', y_1' \dots y_n')) = \bar{\delta}((a^{(2)}, a_2'), y_1 \dots y_n),\end{aligned}$$

which is a contradiction.

Case (ii) can be treated similarly, with $(\mathfrak{A}, a^{(1)})$ instead of $(\mathfrak{A}, \mathbf{a})$. For this, let the equation $ux_1 \dots x_l y_1 \dots y_m = ux_1 \dots x_l z_1 \dots z_n$ $(x_1, \dots, x_l, y_1, \dots, y_m, z_1, \dots, z_n \in X)$ hold in $\mathbf{HSPP}_{\alpha_0}(\mathscr{K}) \cap \mathscr{K}_X$, where $y_1 \neq z_1$, if $m, n > 0$. Suppose that the p-equation $(l, m) = (l, n)$ is not in $\mathscr{K}^*$. Then there are an $\mathfrak{A}' = (X', A', \delta') \in \mathscr{K}$, an $a' \in A'$ and $x_1', \dots, x_l', y_1', \dots, y_m', z_1', \dots, z_n' \in X'$ such that

$$\delta'(a', x_1' \dots x_l' y_1' \dots y_m') \neq \delta'(a', x_1' \dots x_l' z_1' \dots z_n').$$

Consider the α_0-product $\bar{\mathfrak{A}} = (X, A \times A', \bar{\delta}) = (\mathfrak{A} \times \mathfrak{A}')[X, \varphi]$, where φ_1 is the identity mapping on X. Further,

$$\varphi_2(\delta(a^{(1)}, x_1 \dots x_i), x_{i+1}) = x_{i+1}' \quad \text{if} \quad i \leqq \max\{k, l-1\},$$
$$\varphi_2(\delta(a^{(1)}, x_1 \dots x_l y_1 \dots y_i), y_{i+1}) = y_{i+1}' \quad \text{if} \quad l + i \leqq \max\{k, l+m-1\},$$

and

$$\varphi_2(\delta(a^{(1)}, x_1 \dots x_l z_1 \dots z_i), z_{i+1}) = z_{i+1}' \quad \text{if} \quad l + i \leqq \max\{k, l+n-1\}.$$

We then have

$$\begin{aligned}&\bar{\delta}((a^{(1)}, a'), x_1 \dots x_l y_1 \dots y_m) \\ &= (\delta(a^{(1)}, x_1 \dots x_l y_1 \dots y_m), \delta'(a', x_1' \dots x_l' y_1' \dots y_m')) \\ &\neq (\delta(a^{(1)}, x_1 \dots x_l z_1 \dots z_n), \delta'(a', x_1' \dots x_l' z_1' \dots z_n')) \\ &= \bar{\delta}((a^{(1)}, a'), x_1 \dots x_l z_1 \dots z_n)\end{aligned}$$

which is again a contradiction. □

We end this section by showing that Theorem 2.7.1 remains valid for products with possibly infinitely many factors.

Theorem 2.5. *Let $\mathscr{K}$ be a finite class of finite automata and $\mathfrak{A}$ an arbitrary finite automaton. It is then decidable whether $\mathfrak{A} \in \mathbf{HSP}_{i,g}(\mathscr{K})$.*

Proof. Assume that there are a $\mathfrak{B} = (X, B, \delta)$ in $\mathscr{K}$, a $b \in B$, and a $p = xq$ ($x \in X$, $q \in X^*$) such that $\delta(b, p) = b$ and $\delta(b, x) \neq \delta(b, x')$ for some $x' \in X$. Then, by Lemma 2.5.3, for any $k \geqq 0$ and $n > 0$, there exists a k-free system $(\mathfrak{C}, \mathbf{c})$ with $\mathfrak{C} = (X', C, \delta')$ $\in \mathbf{P}_{\alpha_0}(\mathscr{K})$ and $\mathbf{c} \in C^n$. This, by the proof of Theorem 2.4, implies that $\mathbf{HSP}_{i,g}(\mathscr{K})$ is the class of all automata.

If the above assumption does not hold, then an obvious modification of the procedure given in the proof of Theorem 2.7.1 (under the same bound) shows the existence of a desired algorithm. □

5.3 Metric Equivalence of Products

In Section 5.1 it was shown that the α_0-product is equivalent to the general product from the point of view of metric completeness. We now prove that even more is true: as regards metric representations, the α_0-product is as powerful as the general product.

As in Section 5.2, an automaton may have infinitely many states.

Definition 3.1. Let i and j be non-negative integers. The α_i-product is *metrically equivalent* to the α_j-product if, for arbitrary integer $k \geqq 0$ and class $\mathscr{K}$ of finite automata, an automaton mapping $\tau : X^* \to Y^*$ can be induced in length k by a Mealy machine $\mathfrak{A} = (X, A, Y, \delta, \lambda)$ with $(X, A, \delta) \in \mathbf{P}_{\alpha_i}(\mathscr{K})$ if and only if τ can be induced in length k by a Mealy machine $\mathfrak{B} = (X, B, Y, \delta', \lambda')$ with $(X, B, \delta') \in \mathbf{P}_{\alpha_j}(\mathscr{K})$.

The metric equivalence between an α_i-product ($i \in \mathbf{N}$) and the general product is defined in a similar way.

For a class $\mathscr{K}$ of automata, $\mathbf{1}(\mathscr{K})$ will denote the subclass consisting of all connected automata in $\mathscr{K}$.

Theorem 3.2. *The α_0-product is metrically equivalent to the general product.*

Proof. From Theorem 2.4, we have the equality

$$\mathbf{1HSP}_{i,g}(\mathscr{K}) = \mathbf{1HSPP}_{\alpha_0}(\mathscr{K}) \tag{*}$$

holds for every class $\mathscr{K}$ of automata. Let $\mathscr{K}$ be a fixed class of finite automata. Take an automaton $\mathfrak{A} = (X, A, \delta)$ from $\mathbf{1SP}_g(\mathscr{K})$, and let $\mathbf{a}_0$ be a generating element of $\mathfrak{A}$. Then, by (*), there are a $\mathfrak{B} = (X, B, \delta') \in \mathbf{PP}_{\alpha_0}(\mathscr{K})$ and a $\mathbf{b}_0 \in B$ such that the subautomaton $\mathfrak{B}' = (X, B', \delta'')$ of $\mathfrak{B}$ generated by $\mathbf{b}_0$ can be mapped homomorphically onto $\mathfrak{A}$ under a homomorphism ψ for which $\psi(\mathbf{b}_0) = \mathbf{a}_0$. Let

$$\mathfrak{B} = \prod (\mathfrak{B}_i \mid i \in I) \quad (\mathfrak{B}_i = (X, B_i, \delta_i) \in \mathbf{P}_{\alpha_0}(\mathscr{K}),\ i \in I)\,.$$

Take an integer $k \geqq 0$, and consider the subset $B'' = \{\delta''(\mathbf{b}_0, p) \mid p \in X^{(k)}\}$ of B'. Denote by J a minimal subset of I such that, for two arbitrary distinct states $\mathbf{a}, \mathbf{b} \in B''$, there is a $j \in J$ with $\mathrm{pr}_j(\mathbf{a}) \neq \mathrm{pr}_j(\mathbf{b})$. Obviously, J is finite. Define $\bar{\mathbf{b}}_0 \in \prod(B_j \mid j \in J)$ by $\mathrm{pr}_J(\bar{\mathbf{b}}_0) = \mathrm{pr}_J(\mathbf{b}_0)$. Let $\bar{\mathfrak{B}} = (X, \bar{B}, \bar{\delta})$ be the subautomaton of $\prod(\mathfrak{B}_j \mid j \in J)$ generated by $\bar{\mathbf{b}}_0$. Then, $\bar{\mathfrak{B}} \in \mathbf{SP}_{\alpha_0}(\mathscr{K})$, and there exists a one-to-one mapping ψ' of $\{\bar{\delta}(\bar{\mathbf{b}}_0, p) \mid p \in X^{(k)}\}$ onto B'' such that $\psi'(\bar{\delta}(\bar{\mathbf{b}}_0, p)) = \delta''(\mathbf{b}_0, p)$ for arbitrary $p \in X^{(k)}$. Thus, $(\bar{\mathfrak{B}}, \bar{\mathbf{b}}_0)$ can be mapped k-homomorphically onto $(\mathfrak{A}, \mathbf{a}_0)$. Therefore, by Lemma 1.3, for every Mealy macine $\mathfrak{A}' = (X, A, Y, \delta, \lambda)$ there exists a Mealy macine $\bar{\mathfrak{B}}' = (X, \bar{B}, Y, \bar{\delta}, \bar{\lambda})$ inducing $\tau_{\mathfrak{A}', \mathbf{a}_0}$ in length k, ending the proof of Theorem 3.2. □

The above theorem directly implies

Corollary 3.3. *The α_i-products ($i \geqq 0$) are metrically equivalent to each other, and they are metrically equivalent to the general product.* □

Bibliographical Remarks

Chapter 1. Extensive treatments of universal algebra can be found in Cohn (1981) and Grätzer (1979). The proof of Theorem 2.17 is based on Agibalov and Evtušenko (1984). Finite automata are studied comprehensively in Salomaa (1969). An extensive algebraic treatment of finite automata is given in Eilenberg (1974, 1976). Proofs of Theorems 4.6 and 4.8 can be found in Gécseg and Peák (1972) and Gluškov (1961). The loop-free product is due to Harmanis (1962). An attractive presentation of the Krohn-Rhodes theory is given in Ginzburg (1968). The hierarchy of the α_i-products was introduced by Gécseg (1974). Finally, mention may be made of some books concerning products of automata. The monograph Hartmanis and Stearns (1966) is devoted entirely to the structure theory of automata. Parts of the volumes Dassow (1981), Eilenberg (1976) and Nelson (1968) also deal with products of automata.

Chapter 2. The standard automata of Section 2.1 were introduced by Dömösi (1984), and the results of Section 2.1 are also from his paper. Evtušenko (1979) defines a similar class of automata, but his n-state standard automata have n input signals. It should be noted that recently Ésik and Virágh (1986) have shown the existence of a class containing only automata with two input signals which is homomorphically complete with respect to the α_0-product. The minimal homomorphically complete system with respect to the α_0-product presented in Section 2.2 is from Dömösi (1976). An algorithm to decide whether an automaton can be represented homomorphically by an α_0-product of smaller automata was given first by Dömösi (1975). Our proof of Theorem 3.2 is based on Agibalov and Evtušenko (1984). Example 2.3.8 can be found in Dömösi (1975). Section 2.4 is based entirely on Ésik (1985). We note that Dömösi (1983) showed the existence of a finite system which is homomorphically complete with respect to the α_2-product. The concept of a k-free automaton was introduced in Gécseg (1966). Lemma 5.3 is a generalization of a statement in the proof of the Theorem in Gécseg (1975). The fact that the α_2-product is homomorphically equivalent to the general product was proved by Ésik and Horváth (1983). Homomorphically α_i-simple automata were studied by Dömösi (1981). The method used in Section 2.6 is a combination of those of Agibalov and Evtušenko (1979) and Dömösi (1981). Finally, we mention that Ésik (1983) studies homomorphic completeness with respect to the α_0-, the α_1-, and the general products for the class of all monotone automata.

Chapter 3. Theorem 1.2 (for loop-free products) can be found essentially in Hartmanis (1962). Theorem 1.3 is from Imreh (1978). A similar characterization with respect to generalized α_i-products is given in Gécseg (1976). The results of Sections 3.2–3.4 are contained in Imreh (1978). Isomorphically complete classes for nilpotent automata are studied in Imreh (1981). It may be noted that Imreh (1980) also studies isomorphic completeness for the class of commutative automata.

Chapter 4. A stronger form of the simulation appears in Hartmanis and Stearns (1966). Sections 4.1–4.4 are based on Gécseg (1976). The results in Section 4.5 are from Ésik and Virágh (1986).

Chapter 5. Metric completeness is studied in Gécseg (1966, 1968, 1975). Products of automata with infinitely many factors are used in Gécseg (1973) to characterize completeness. Theorem 2.4 is from Ésik and Gécseg (1983). The relation between infinite products of automata and finite representations of automaton mappings appears in Gécseg (1984).

References

Agibalov, G. P., Evtušenko, N. V. (1979): Characterization condition of existence and other problems of cascade connections of finite automata (Russian). MTA SZTAKI Tanulmányok 99 (1979), 181–197

Agibalov, G. P., Evtušenko, N. V. (1984): Algebraic characterization of permutation automata decomposable into cascade connection of smaller components (Russian). Kibernetika No. 1 (1984), 9–15

Cohn, P. M. (1981): Universal algebra. D. Reidel, Dordrecht (2nd edn. 1981)

Dassow, J. (1981): Completeness problems in the structural theory of automata. Akademie-Verlag, Berlin (1981)

Dömösi, P. (1975): On superpositions of automata. Acta Cybernetica 2 (1975), 335–343

Dömösi, P. (1976): On minimal R-complete systems of finite automata. Acta Cybernetica 3 (1976), 37–41

Dömösi, P. (1981): On homomorphically α_i-simple automata. Papers on Automata Theory III, No. DM 81-2, 93–124, Karl Marx University of Economics, Department of Mathematics, Budapest (1981)

Dömösi, P. (1983): On homomorphically α_i-complete systems of automata. Acta Cybernetica 6 (1983), 85–88

Dömösi, P. (1984): On cascade products of standard automata. Automata, languages and mathematical systems: conference proceedings, No. DM 84-2, 37–45, Salgótarján, 1984), Karl Marx University of Economics, Department of Mathematics, Budapest (1984)

Eilenberg, S. (1974): Automata, languages, and machines, vol. A. Academic Press, London New York (1974)

Eilenberg, S. (1976): Automata, languages, and machines, vol. B. Academic Press, London New York (1976)

Ésik, Z. (1983): On homomorphic realization of monotone automata. Papers on Automata Theory V, No. DM 83-3, 63–76, Karl Marx University of Economics, Department of Mathematics, Budapest (1983)

Ésik, Z. (1985): Homomorphically complete classes of automata with respect to the α_2-product. Acta Sci. Math., 48 (1985), 135–141

Ésik, Z., Gécseg, F. (1983): General products and equational classes of automata. Acta Cybernetica 6 (1983), 281–284

Ésik, Z., Horváth, Gy. (1983): The α_2-product is homomorphically general. Papers on Automata Theory V, No. DM 83-3, 49–62, Karl Marx University of Economics, Department of Methematics, Budapest (1983)

Ésik, Z., Virágh, J. (1986): On products of automata with identity. Acta Cybernetica 7 (1986), 299–311

Evtušenko, N. V. (1979): On realization of automata by cascade connection of standard automata (Russian). Avtomatika i vyčislitel'naja tehnika No. 2 (1979), 50–53

Gécseg, F. (1966): On R-products of automata, I. Studia Sci. Math. Hung. 1 (1966), 437–441

Gécseg, F. (1968): Metrically complete systems of automata (Russian). Kibernetika No. 3 (1968), 96–98

Gécseg, F. (1973): Model theoretical methods in the theory of automata. Mathematical Foundations of Computer Science: symposium proceedings, High Tatras (1973), 57–63

Gécseg, F. (1974): Composition of automata. Automata, languages and programming: 2nd Colloquium, Saarbrücken, 1974. Lecture Notes in Computer Science (Springer-Verlag, Berlin Heidelberg New York Tokyo) 14 (1974), 351–363

Gécseg, F. (1975): Representation of automaton mappings in finite length. Acta Cybernetica 2 (1975), 285–289

Gécseg, F. (1976): On products of abstract automata. Acta Sci. Math. 38 (1976), 21–43

Gécseg, F. (1984): Finite representations and infinite products. Automata, languages and mathematical systems: conference proceedings, No. DM 84-2, 55–66. Salgótarján, 1984, Karl Marx University of Economics, Department of Mathematics, Budapest (1984)

Gécseg, F., Peák, I. (1972): Algebraic theory of automata. Akadémiai Kiadó, Budapest (1972).

Ginzburg, A. (1968): Algebraic theory of automata. Academic Press, London New York (1968)

Gluškov, V. M. (1961): Abstract theory of automata (Russian). Uspehi matematičeskih nauk 16: 5 (101) (1961), 3–62. Correction: ibid., 17: 2 (104) (1962), 270

Grätzer, G. (1979): Universal algebra. Springer-Verlag, New York Berlin Heidelberg Tokyo (2nd edn. 1979)

Hartmanis, J. (1962): Loop-free structure of sequential machines. Information and Control 5 (1962), 25–43

Hartmanis, J., Stearns, R. E. (1966): Algebraic structure theory of sequential machines. Prentice-Hall, Englewood Cliffs, New Jersey (1966)

Imreh, B. (1978): On α_i-products of automata. Acta Cybernetica 3 (1978), 301–307

Imreh, B. (1980): On isomorphic representations of commutative automata with respect to α_i-products. Acta Cybernetica 5 (1980), 21–32

Imreh, B. (1981): On finite nilpotent automata. Acta Cybernetica 5 (1981), 281–293

Nelson, R. J. (1968): Introduction to automata. John Wiley & Sons, New York London Sydney (1968)

Salomaa, A. (1969): Theory of automata. Pergamon Press, Oxford (1969)

Subject Index